Spatial Knowledge Spillovers
and the Dynamics of Agglomeration
and Regional Growth

Contributions to Economics

Christoph M. Schneider
**Research and Development Management:
From the Soviet Union to Russia**
1994. ISBN 3-7908-0757-5

Lars Olof Persson/Ulf Wiberg
Microregional Fragmentation
1995. ISBN 3-7908-0855-5

Ernesto Felli/Furio C. Rosati/
Giovanni Tria (Eds.)
**The Service Sector:
Productivity and Growth**
1995. ISBN 3-7908-0875-X

Giovanni Galizzi/
Luciano Venturini (Eds.)
**Economics of Innovation:
The Case of Food Industry**
1996. ISBN 3-7908-0911-X

David T. Johnson
Poverty, Inequality and Social Welfare in Australia
1996. ISBN 3-7908-0942-X

Rongxing Guo
Border-Regional Economics
1996. ISBN 3-7908-0943-8

Oliver Fratzscher
The Political Economy of Trade Integration
1996. ISBN 3-7908-0945-4

Ulrich Landwehr
Industrial Mobility and Public Policy
1996. ISBN 3-7908-0949-7

Arnold Picot/Ekkehard Schlicht (Eds.)
Firms, Markets, and Contracts
1996. Corr. 2nd printing 1997
ISBN 3-7908-0947-0

Thorsten Wichmann
Agricultural Technical Progress and the Development of a Dual Economy
1997. ISBN 3-7908-0960-8

Ulrich Woitek
Business Cycles
1997. ISBN 3-7908-0997-7

Michael Carlberg
International Economic Growth
1997. ISBN 3-7908-0995-0

Massimo Filippini
Elements of the Swiss Market for Electricity
1997. ISBN 3-7908-0996-9

Frank Hoster/Heinz Welsch/
Christoph Böhringer
CO_2 Abatement and Economic Structural Change in the European Internal Market
1997. ISBN 3-7908-1020-7

Christian M. Hafner
Nonlinear Time Series Analysis with Applications to Foreign Exchange Rate Volatility
1997. ISBN 3-7908-1041-X

Sardar M. N. Islam
Mathematical Economics of Multi-Level Optimisation
1998. ISBN 3-7908-1050-9

Sven-Morten Mentzel
Real Exchange Rate Movements
1998. ISBN 3-7908-1081-9

Lei Delsen/Eelke de Jong (Eds.)
The German and Dutch Economies
1998. ISBN 3-7908-1064-9

Mark Weder
Business Cycle Models with Indeterminacy
1998. ISBN 3-7908-1078-9

Tor Rødseth (Ed.)
Models for Multispecies Management
1998. ISBN 3-7908-1001-0

Michael Carlberg
Intertemporal Macroeconomics
1998. ISBN 3-7908-1096-7

Sabine Spangenberg
The Institutionalised Transformation of the East German Economy
1998. ISBN 3-7908-1103-3

Hagen Bobzin
Indivisibilities
1998. ISBN 3-7908-1123-8

Helmut Wagner (Ed.)
Current Issues in Monetary Economics
1998. ISBN 3-7908-1127-0

Max Keilbach

Spatial Knowledge Spillovers and the Dynamics of Agglomeration and Regional Growth

With 43 Figures
and 21 Tables

Physica-Verlag
A Springer-Verlag Company

Series Editors
Werner A. Müller
Martina Bihn

Author
Dr. Max Keilbach
Zentrum für Europäische Wirtschaftsforschung (ZEW)
Forschungsbereich Industrieökonomik
und Internationale Unternehmensführung
L 7,1
68161 Mannheim
Germany

ISSN 1431-1933
ISBN 3-7908-1321-4 Physica-Verlag Heidelberg New York

Die Deutsche Bibliothek – CIP-Einheitsaufnahme
Keilbach, Max: Spatial knowledge spillovers and the dynamics of agglomeration and regional growth: with 21 tables / Max Keilbach. – Heidelberg; New York: Physica-Verl., 2000
(Contributions to economics)
ISBN 3-7908-1321-4

This work is subject to copyright. All rights are reserved, whether the whole or part of the material is concerned, specifically the rights of translation, reprinting, reuse of illustrations, recitation, broadcasting, reproduction on microfilm or in any other way, and storage in data banks. Duplication of this publication or parts thereof is permitted only under the provisions of the German Copyright Law of September 9, 1965, in its current version, and permission for use must always be obtained from Physica-Verlag. Violations are liable for prosecution under the German Copyright Law.

Physica-Verlag Heidelberg
a member of BertelsmannSpringer Science+Business Media GmbH

© Physica-Verlag Heidelberg 2000
Printed in Germany

The use of general descriptive names, registered names, trademarks, etc. in this publication does not imply, even in the absence of a specific statement, that such names are exempt from the relevant protective laws and regulations and therefore free for general use.

Typeset by the Author
Softcover-Design: Erich Kirchner, Heidelberg

SPIN 10773265   88/2202-5 4 3 2 1 0 – Printed on acid-free paper

Acknowledgements

This thesis has been written during my employment at the chair of econometrics at the Technical University of Berlin. Parts have been written at the International Institute for Applied Systems Analysis (IIASA), Laxenburg and others at the Centre for European Economic Research (ZEW), Mannheim.

During the period of preparation I received help and support in a high variety of ways from a large number of persons. First of all, it is a great pleasure to express my thanks to Prof. Dieter Friedrich, who holds the chair of econometrics at the TU Berlin. During my stay there, I did not only experience very stimulating discussions but also a very open-minded atmosphere that did not limit my research ambitions in any way. Thank you very much for five very stimulating years! It is also a big pleasure to thank Prof. Helmut Seitz who holds the chair of macroeconomics at the Viadrina University in Frankfurt/Oder. At several opportunities he gave me strong support in the direction of my research and in something much more down to earth but not less important: data. Thank you also very much!

My stays at IIASA were very productive and this is especially due to two persons: Prof. Giovanni Dosi and Dr. Yuri Kaniovski. They both contributed critical comments to my work and Yuri Kaniovski, with never decreasing motivation, went through my papers again and again. This made my months at IIASA very important ones. Thank you very much!

It is also a great pleasure to thank Prof. Michael Burda from the Humboldt University Berlin for his critical comments on my model, Dr. Werner Bönte, Dipl. Volksw. Anja Kettner, Dr. Ulrich Lehmann-Grube and Prof. Wilhelm Pfähler from the University of Hamburg for their invitation to a very productive seminar, Prof. Alan Kirman, Aix-en-Provence, for his comments on the self-organizing approach, Prof. Manfred Fischer, Vienna, and Dr. Herbert Buscher, Mannheim, for valuable comments, Prof. Dominique Foray, Paris, for putting me on the right track when this was necessary and my former colleagues Dr. Stefan Marx and Dipl. Volksw. Jens Oelker for their mental support. Special thanks go to Dipl. Volksw. Jürgen Egeln and to Dr. Georg Licht, both ZEW, for sharing their data with me during the preparation of this thesis. Last but definitely not least I am grateful to my wife and my daughters, Bettina, Clara and Amelia for their patience.

Contents

1 **Introduction and Motivation** 1
   1.1 Background of the Analysis 1
   1.2 Contribution of the Book 2

2 **Why and How Does Economic Activity Grow?**
   An Overview of the Literature 5
   2.1 Introduction 5
   2.2 A Summary of Growth Theory in the Neoclassical Tradition 5
      2.2.1 The Model of Solow 5
      2.2.2 The Theory of Endogenous Growth 8
          2.2.2.1 The Concept of Learning by Doing 9
          2.2.2.2 Technological Change as an Intentional Process 10
   2.3 Implications of Neoclassical and Endogenous Growth Theories for
      Regional Growth 13
      2.3.1 Factor Migration 13
          2.3.1.1 Implications of the Solowian Growth Model 14
          2.3.1.2 Implications of the Endogenous Growth Model 15
      2.3.2 The Convergence Debate 16
          2.3.2.1 The Hypotheses of Convergence 16
          2.3.2.2 Critics of the Convergence Hypotheses 20
   2.4 Summary and Conclusion 25

3 **Why and How Does Economic Activity Concentrate in Space?**
   Another Overview of the Literature 29
   3.1 Introduction 29
   3.2 The Role of Transportation Costs 31
      3.2.1 Thünen's Rings 31
      3.2.2 Central Place Theory 33
      3.2.3 Krugman's Core-Periphery Model 36
      3.2.4 A Heuristic Approach: The Idea of Economic Potential 40

3.3	The Role of Spatial Externalities in Production		41
	3.3.1	The Godfathers: Externalities in the Works of Alfred Marshall and Jane Jacobs	42
	3.3.2	Models that Refer to Increasing Returns in Production	46
	3.3.3	Models that Refer to Spatial Density	50
	3.3.4	Models that Refer to Distance	56
3.4	Summary and Conclusion		59

4 Spatial Knowledge Spillovers and the Dynamics of Agglomeration and Regional Growth   61

4.1	Introduction		61
4.2	Positive External Effects in Production. Properties and Implementation		64
	4.2.1	Externalities: General Definition and Properties	64
	4.2.2	Functional Implementation of Externalities	66
4.3	The Model		68
	4.3.1	The Incidence of Spillovers Between Firms of One Region	68
	4.3.2	The Incidence of Spillovers Between Regions	71
		4.3.2.1 Dynamics of Factor Allocation if the Coefficient of Spillover $\Delta = 0$	72
		4.3.2.2 Dynamics of Factor Allocation if the Coefficient of Spillover $\Delta > 0$	74
4.4	Marshallian Externalities and the Convergence of Regions		75
	4.4.1	Convergence Properties of Firms	77
	4.4.2	Convergence Properties of the Regional Aggregate of Firms	78
	4.4.3	Convergence Properties of an Aggregate of Regions	79
4.5	Summary and Conclusion		81

5 Marshallian Externalities, Spatial Self-Organization and Regional Growth – an Agent Based Approach   83

5.1	Introduction		83
5.2	Who Organizes the Economy?		84
5.3	Cellular Automata as a Tool for Modelling Local Economic Interaction		87
5.4	Local Interaction and the Dynamics of Agglomeration		91
	5.4.1	A Hybrid Model	91
	5.4.2	The Rules of the Automaton	91
5.5	Simulation Results		94
	5.5.1	Results When Labour is Immobile	95
		5.5.1.1 Evolution of the Automaton Under Decreasing Returns in the R&D-Sector	95
		5.5.1.2 Evolution of the Automaton Under Constant Returns in the R&D-Sector	96

| | 5.5.1.3 | Evolution of the Automaton Under Increasing Returns in the R&D-Sector . . . . 97 |
| | 5.5.1.4 | Consequences for the Convergence of Regional Growth Rates . . . . 97 |

5.5.2 Results When Labour Migrates 99
    5.5.2.1 Evolution of the Automaton 99
    5.5.2.2 Consequences for the Convergence of Regional Growth Rates 101

5.6 Summary and Conclusion 101

6 Spatial Processes in the Economy – an Empirical Investigation   103

6.1 Introduction 103
6.2 Data: Sources and Construction 104
6.3 Spatial Spillovers of Knowledge – First Evidence from the Data 108
    6.3.1 How Do Spillovers Appear in the Data? 108
    6.3.2 A Useful Matrix – the Spatial Weight Matrix 115
        6.3.2.1 The Simplest Case – the Binary Contiguity Matrix . 115
        6.3.2.2 Generalized Spatial Weight Matrices 117
    6.3.3 Spatial Correlation of Variables 118
6.4 Spatial Econometrics – an Overview 120
    6.4.1 Why *Spatial* Econometrics? 120
    6.4.2 OLS–Regression Analysis with Spatial Effects in the Dataset . 122
        6.4.2.1 OLS–Estimation with Spatially Lagged External Variables 123
        6.4.2.2 OLS–Estimation in the Case of Spatial Autocorrelation in the Dependent Variable 123
        6.4.2.3 OLS–Estimation in the Presence of Spatial Residual Autocorrelation 125
    6.4.3 Different Approaches: Regression Analysis Based on ML or EGLS 125
        6.4.3.1 ML-Estimation in the Case of Spatial Autocorrelation in the Dependent Variable 126
        6.4.3.2 ML-Estimation in the Case of Spatial Residual Autocorrelation 127
    6.4.4 Test Procdedures 128
        6.4.4.1 Testing for Spatial Autocorrelation in the Dependent Variable 129
        6.4.4.2 Testing for Spatial Autocorrelation in the Error Term 129
        6.4.4.3 A General Test for Heteroscedasticity: The White Test 131
6.5 Empirical Implementation of the Model and Results 131

	6.5.1	Evidence from a Dataset of West-German Kreise	134
		6.5.1.1 The Case of R&D-Personnel	134
		6.5.1.2 The Case of Human Capital	137
		6.5.1.3 The Case of Infrastructure	139
	6.5.2	Evidence from a Dataset of National States	140
		6.5.2.1 Regressions Without Spatial Effects	140
		6.5.2.2 Regression Including Spatial Effects	141
6.6	Summary and Conclusion		143

7 Summary and Conclusion   145

Appendix   149

A Generalization of the Model Developed in Chapter 4   149
    A.1 Illustration of the Allocation Dynamics for a Region with an Arbitrary Number of Firms   149
    A.2 Proof that Firms Employ Identical Factor Ratios or Identical Factor Shares   150

B Mathematical Appendix   153
    B.1 Proof that the Bias of an OLS Estimation in the Presence of Spatial Autocorrelation is Biased   153
    B.2 Derivation of the Log-Likelihood Function of Model (6.2)   154

C Data   155

List of Symbols   169

List of Figures   179

List of Tables   181

References   183

Index   189

Chapter 1

Introduction and Motivation

> *Knowledge is our most powerful engine of*
> *production; it enables us to subdue Nature*
> *and force her to satisfy our wants.*
> ALFRED MARSHALL

1.1 Background of the Analysis

The question of why economic activity grows is amongst the oldest and most prominent ones in economic analysis. In his classic paper, Solow [1956] suggested a formal model of macroeconomic growth where this growth is driven by the accumulation of factors of production (labour and capital) and by technical change. The dynamics of technical change has not been further specified in this neoclassical growth model but has been assumed to occur *exogenously* or "autonomously". Although this assumption was strongly simplifying with regard to the process of technical change it allowed the implications of mere factor accumulation to be distinguished from the effects of technical change on the dynamics of economic growth. Hence the neoclassical growth theory allowed both phenomena to be considered as two different and isolated ones.

This approach can therefore be seen as the basis for further investigation of the phenomenon of technical change as was suggested in the literature on endogenous growth in the mid 1980s and early 1990s. One important contribution of this literature has been to assess how exactly technical change occurs and what its macroeconomic implications are. Thus, this literature investigated how technolgical change can be *endogenized* into the production function. One important result of this literature is that *knowledege* has several characteristics that make it different to privately appropriable production factors such as capital. It can be communicated – and thus appropriated by others – without loosing its useability for the one who communicates it. Thus, knowledge has the potential of *spilling over* horizontally (i.e. to firms of the same industry) and vertically (i.e. to other industries). This process has a bidirectional and reciprokal characteristic: firms create knowledge that spills over to other firms. This in turn will enable the receiving firms to use it in their own production and innovation process; this again will create new knowledge that can spill over to other firms, including the one that started the process. As an outcome of this recursive process, returns to innovation may be non-decreasing or even increasing for the economy as a whole, although they might be decreasing for one firm alone.

From this it follows that the neoclassical and the endogenous growth models have different implications with regard to the regional dynamics of growth. The neoclassical growth model implies that the higher the actual level of per capita income of a region, the slower it grows, i.e. the regional growth rates of per capita income *converge* with increasing per capita income and hence over time. This behaviour is due to the fact that the neoclassical production function specifies decreasing returns to the factors of production. On the other hand, given the above described implications of knowledge, the endogenous growth theory predicts that the difference in the growth rates of regional per capita income will stay constant or increase with the accumulation of (a broad notion of) capital. Hence, the regional growth rates of per capita income may *diverge*, i.e. the findings of the literature on neoclassical and endogenous growth contradict each other with regard to their implications on regional growth.

Convergence of per-capita incomes of regions has been found in a considerable number of empirical studies. These results have been taken as evidence against the findings of the literature on endogenous growth and thus in favour of the neoclassical growth model. But rejecting the latter implies of course that its explanation of the process of innovation is rejected as well and thus, implicitely, a return to the Solow model of the 1950s.

1.2 Contribution of the Book

With the analysis given in this book, I suggest an approach that aims at explaining growth convergence under existence of a local endogenous growth structure. The model to be suggested for that purpose in chapter 4 will be based on *spatial knowledge spillovers*. The argument is along the following lines: an important aspect of knowledge is that it has "tacit" dimensions. Marshall [1920] refers to "something in the air" when alluding to this phenomenon. This tacit aspect of knowledge makes it difficult to codify it (e.g. into a blueprint) and thus easily transfer it (e.g. through a book, through telecommunication or the internet). Agents living in a certain region can therefore more easily access that region's stock of knowlegde (as embodied in the region's inhabitants). For the same reason, agents who want to participate in that stock of knowledge will have an advantage when moving into that region. Thus, the process of knowledge spillover has a *spatial dimension*. Marshall [1920] saw this process as the origin of the formation of cities. Correspondingly, knowledge spillovers can be considered as one of the driving forces in the formation of industrial districts since the same arguments apply on the industry level. Numerous examples can be found to support this, from the semiconductor industry in California to the shoe industry in Italy.

The fact that knowledge spillovers lead to constant or increasing returns in the production function on one the hand and to an agglomeration of industries on the other hand, suggests that agglomerated areas will realise a different growth trajectory than non-agglomerated ones since knowledge spillovers can be assumed to be stronger in densely populated areas. In this context it is noticeable that the empirical literature on convergence only studies large regional aggregates, i.e. regions that include agglomerated and non-agglomerated areas. Therefore, this literature can not distinguish between different growth trajectories of different types of regions. Hence, the spatial aggregate of different regions might display converging behaviour although this is not necessarily the case for its subaggregates. In this book, I will investigate the conditions which favour the occurrence of such a behaviour. Therefore, the analysis of this book contributes to the *convergence debate*.

In this book I will suggest different models that take into account the dynamics of agglomeration and regional growth simultaneously, i.e. as the outcome of one single driving force: the accumulation of knowledge and its spillover property. These models are based on two fields, the so-called *new growth theory* and *new economic geography*. I will thus first give an overview on these fields in chapter 2 and chapter 3 respectively. In both chapters I will discuss early contributions and recent developments.

In chapter 4 I suggest a formal model that integrates these two fields. This model is able to show that indeed, regions display converging behaviour although their subaggregates may display diverging behaviour, the driving force of this process being spatial knowledge spillovers. This model takes into consideration two regions with each region hosting two firms. In chapter 5 this model is extended to an arbitrary number of regions. This is done on the basis of a tool from theoretical computer science (cellular automata) and a simulation study. The purpose of this chapter is to elaborate on the self-organizing properties of the formation of cities and give support for the results obtained in chapter 4. The use of cellular automata is still quite new in economic analysis although (as I will try to demonstrate in chapter 5) this tool may have quite some potential for economic modelling. Finally, in chapter 6, I will test for the presence of spatial knowledge spillovers on the basis of the model in chapter 4. Here I use two datasets, a newly assembled one for German counties and another one for national states. In both datasets I can find evidence in favour of spaital knowledge spillovers and thus evidence in favour of the models in chapters 4 and 5. Chapter 7 concludes this book.

Chapter 2

Why and How Does Economic Activity Grow? An Overview of the Literature

> *Überholen ohne Einzuholen!* (Overtaking without catching up!)
> Slogan of the government of GDR in the early 50's
> concerning economic growth as compared to FRG

2.1 Introduction

The question of why economic activity grows is amongst the oldest and most prominent in economic analysis. Starting with Smith[1776], growth theory has attracted a considerable number of scholars. Recently the discussion on economic growth has been revived and has entered the literature under the notion of "new growth theory". Since this thesis is on the dynamics of regional growth, I will start the theoretical exposition with an overview of the literature on growth. In particular, I will summarize the new growth theory but before, I will recapitulate its origin – the neoclassical growth theory. I will also discuss in how far the neoclassical growth theory will help to understand differences in regional growth. This discussion will consider theories of regional convergence of growth rates. Keynesian or Schumpeterian approaches to growth will not be considered. The findings of this chapter will be summarized in section 2.4.

2.2 A Summary of Growth Theory in the Neoclassical Tradition

2.2.1 The Model of Solow

In his classic paper, Solow[1956] suggested a formal model of economic growth. The paper is nowadays considered as one of the founding contributions to neoclassical growth theory. Suppose a production function of the form[1]

$$Y = A \cdot F(K, L) \qquad (2.1)$$

where K is capital and L is labour used in production of Y, the output (say GDP). A is *total factor productivity* (TFP), i.e. a technological coefficient which embodies exogenous influences on the productivity of K and L. Suppose that this production function satisfies the following 3 conditions (so called *Inada conditions*):

1. $\frac{\partial F}{\partial K}, \frac{\partial F}{\partial L} > 0$ and $\frac{\partial^2 F}{\partial K^2}, \frac{\partial^2 F}{\partial L^2} < 0$, i.e. the function is *concave*.

2. The function is homogeneous of degree 1, i.e $F(\lambda K, \lambda L) = \lambda F(K, L)$

3. $\lim_{K \to \infty} \frac{\partial F}{\partial K} = \lim_{L \to \infty} \frac{\partial F}{\partial L} = 0$ and $\lim_{K \to 0} \frac{\partial F}{\partial K} = \lim_{L \to 0} \frac{\partial F}{\partial L} = \infty$

then function (2.1) is said to be a *neoclassical* production function. Since this function is homogeneous of degree 1 it can be rewritten

$$Y = A \cdot F(K, L) = L \cdot A \cdot F(K/L, 1) = L \cdot A \cdot f(k),$$

where $k = K/L$, the per capita endowment of capital in the economy. Dividing by L we obtain the *intensive form* of the production function:

$$y = A \cdot f(k), \qquad (2.2)$$

which is concave in k. y is output per worker or *labour productivity*. The engine of growth in such a neoclassical economy is the accumulation of factors i.e. of capital and labour. Labour is assumed to grow at a constant, exogenously given rate $\dot{L}/L = n$ and the stock of capital is assumed to increase with investment and to decrease with depreciation: $\dot{K} = I - \delta_K K$, δ_K being the depreciation rate of capital. It is a basic statement in macroeconomics that investment equals savings ex post: $I = S$. Expressing savings as a part of the actual output we

---

[1] In the following presentation I will follow Barro and Sala-i-Martin [1995, pp. 16 f.]. Note that A in equation (2.1) is specified to be *Hicks-neutral*, i.e. a change in this factor leaves the ratio of marginal factor products constant.

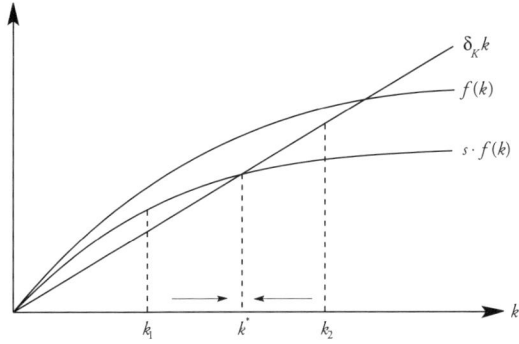

Figure 2.1: Graphical representation of the Solow Model.

obtain $S = s \cdot F(K, L)$, s being the *saving rate* of the economy. Dividing both sides by L we obtain[2]

$$\dot{K}/L = I/L - \delta_K K/L = s \cdot A \cdot f(k) - \delta_K k.$$

From the quotient rule we derive the equation $\dot{k} = \dot{K}/L - nk$. Inserting the above equation we obtain the *fundamental differential equation of the neoclassical growth model*:

$$\dot{k} = s \cdot A \cdot f(k) - (\delta_K + n)k. \qquad (2.3)$$

This equation shows that capital increases ($\dot{k} > 0$) if $s \cdot A \cdot f(k) > (\delta_K + n)k$, i.e. "effective" depreciation of capital (i.e. depreciation in terms of K/L) is inferior to investment. This situation is shown by k_1 in Figure 2.1. On the other hand, capital *decreases* ($\dot{k} < 0$) if the relation is inverse (see k_2). Thus, the economy will converge to a stable equilibrium k^*, where $s \cdot A \cdot f(k^*) = (\delta_K + n)k^*$. The fact that in this *steady state* the per capita variable $k = K/L$ remains constant implies that both, capital and labour, grow at the same rate n which is given exogenously. Thus, if A is assumed to be constant, all variables, K, L and Y will all grow at the same rate.[3] This can be shown as follows.

---

[2] Note that in the model of Solow the saving rate is exogenously given. Ramsey[1928] suggested a model where the saving rate is endogenous which allows to maximize consumers' utility subject to a budget constraint. Although this is an important part of the neoclassical growth model I will not consider it here. See e.g. Barro and Sala-i-Martin[1995, chapter 2].

[3] Note that k^* is determined by s, δ_K and the parameters that enter $f(k)$, it may therefore may differ between regions. The behaviour in the steady state is however independent of these parameters. Note that supposing constant population, the economy is in a zero-growth situation.

Interpreting the variables of equation (2.1) as a function of time t, deriving both sides with respect to t and dividing by Y we obtain

$$\frac{\dot{Y}}{Y} = \frac{\dot{A}}{A} + \left(\frac{AF_K}{Y}\right)\dot{K} + \left(\frac{AF_L}{Y}\right)\dot{L}$$

$$= \frac{\dot{A}}{A} + \left(\frac{AF_K K}{Y}\right)\frac{\dot{K}}{K} + \left(\frac{AF_L L}{Y}\right)\frac{\dot{L}}{L}$$

where F_i is the partial derivative of production function (2.1) with respect to factor i. Assuming that factor markets are competitive, the terms in brackets equal the share of wage (rent) of total income obtained by labour (capital). If we assume returns to scale to be constant, these shares will sum to unity and we can rewrite the above equation

$$g_Y = g_A + \alpha g_K + (1-\alpha)g_L, \qquad (2.4)$$

where g_i denote growth rates. This is the *growth accounting equation*[4] which makes explicit that if K and L both grow at rate n, Y will equally grow at this rate.

A second possible source of growth is of course the growth of total factor productivity A. This factor will increase through innovation and technological change and thus will increase the productivity of K and L. Solow did not offer an explanation for the evolution of A. Rather he assumed that A grows *exogenously* at a given rate of around 2% per annum. Once α is estimated, an estimate of g_A can be obtained by reorganizing equation (2.4). With this procedure however, g_A is implicitly considered as a residual, sometimes referred to in the literature as the *Solow-residual*.

2.2.2 The Theory of Endogenous Growth

Solow's growth model considerably stimulated further research, of which an important part was measuring the residual g_A. On the other hand, it provoked some criticism which focussed mainly on two points. First, it seemed to be unsatisfactory to explain economic growth simply by growth of population (or of labour force to be more precise). This explanation ignores the fact that economic agents undertake considerable research and development effort to increase factor productivity – and thus efficiency of production. However, with

---
[4] See Solow[1957] or Barro and Sala-i-Martin[1995, p. 346].

its assumption of exogenous growth of TFP, the model says nothing about the motivation of agents to engage in R&D. Thus, put plainly, the model does not give an economically relevant explanation of growth, rather it offers a technical relation.

Starting with Arrow[1962] and continuing in the mid-eighties, economists tried to fill this gap and to model the evolution of total factor productivity *endogenously*. Basically, this means to model the dynamics of A more or less explicitely. It seems useful to distinguish two different apporaches: those which model the increase of TFP as a by-product and those which consider the increase of TFP as an intentional process. Both approaches have in common that they assume *spillovers of knowledge*, i.e. that knowledge (created by whatever process) can be more or less accessed by other firms at zero cost. I will discuss these two approaches in the following subsections.

2.2.2.1 The Concept of Learning by Doing

Arrow[1962] discussed the implications of learning by doing in a production theoretic framework. His approach was extended in Romer[1986]. Romer supposed a production function of the form

$$Y_i = h(w_i, W, \mathbf{x}_i)$$

where w_i and $\mathbf{x}_i$ are firm-specific inputs (w_i is the stock of knowledge that is used by firm i), W is a stock of knowledge that can only partially be kept secret and cannot be patented, . Therefore it will (partially) spill over to all existing firms. $h(\cdot)$ is supposed to be a concave and linear homogeneous function of the firm-specific inputs (i.e. assumptions 1 and 2 on page 6 are fulfilled). The assumption of the learning-by-doing approach is that investment and the use of capital goods generates knowledge such as knowledge about how to use a machine and how to improve it. Thus, knowledge is bound to capital. A simple specification of this process is that

$$W = \sum_{i=1}^{N} w_i$$

where N is the number of firms. If all w_i are used at identical quantity, the Romer production function becomes $Y_i = h(w_i, Nw_i, \mathbf{x}_i)$, which is now *convex* in w_i (i.e. assumption 1 on page 6 is not fulfilled). Basically, this implies that a growth-accounting equation comparable to (2.4) would have the form

$$g_Y = \alpha g_{\mathbf{X}} + (1 + N)(1 - \alpha)g_w.$$

Therefore the sum of the right hand side is greater than unity and the growth of the economy will accelerate. This approach was the first to model the growth of technological knowledge endogenously. A second type of endogenous growth literature considers the role of human capital and research and development explicitely.

2.2.2.2 Technological Change as an Intentional Process

The hypothesis on which this second approach is based is that agents engage in research since they expect some kind of return from this activity. However, since R&D yields *knowledge* (or blueprints) the output is not appropriable by its very nature since agents in principal *do not rival* in "consumption" of these goods. Of course if the blueprints that result from a costly R&D process could immediately be used by other agents there would not be an incentive to invest in R&D anymore. Firms therefore have a vivid interest to *exclude* others from the use of their R&D output, which is usually done through patent law. However, it is not possible to exclude agents completely from the use of others' blueprints: they can use parts or underlying ideas for their own development. Thus, R&D-output is nonrival and only partially excludable. It therefore carries the characteristics of a *public good* and the fact that it enters the production function introduces a *convexity*.[5]

Since the formal setup of this group of models is more relevant for the subject of this book, I will present it in more detail. The model to be presented is taken from Romer[1996]. It summarizes the models developed by Lucas[1988], Romer[1990], Grossman and Helpman[1991] and Aghion and Howitt[1992].[6] I will first present the model, then discuss its growth dynamics.

---

[5] See Musgrave and Musgrave[1973] for a discussion of the characteristics of public goods and Romer[1990] for a discussion of the application on R&D. Dowling[1992] defines a function $f(\cdot)$ as concave if $f' > 0$ and $f'' < 0$ i.e. it corresponds to condition 1 on page 6. Note that Romer refers to such a function as being *convex*.

[6] The theory of endogenous growth will not be presented in detail here since it is now summarized in a number of textbooks. See e.g. Aghion and Howitt[1998]. Verspagen[1992] gives a critical appraisal.

Suppose that the economy of a region i can be described with two sectors, a goods-producing sector and a sector that is engaged in research and development (R&D). Suppose also that the production of output in period t can be modelled by a Cobb-Douglas production function

$$Y_t = [\phi_K K_t]^\alpha [A_t \phi_L L_t]^{1-\alpha}, \quad (\alpha, \phi_K, \phi_L) \in [0, 1] \quad (2.5)$$

where K and L denote capital and labour respectively and A denotes the level of technology that is employed in the production of Y. The terms α and $(1-\alpha)$ are elasticities of production and ϕ_i are fractions of factors employed in the goods-producing sector. Note that for $\phi_i = 1$, the function degenerates to a Cobb-Douglas production function with labour augmenting (or "Harrod-neutral") technical change. Just as the production of goods, the output in R&D depends on the employment of K, L and A. However, there is a major difference, namely the R&D sector produces *ideas* or *blueprints*, whose stock does not decrease through consumption. Thus this sector can only *augment* the existing level of technology A. The following specification seems appropriate:

$$\dot{A}_t = B_t \left[(1-\phi_K) K_t\right]^\beta \left[(1-\phi_L) L_t\right]^\gamma A_t^\theta - \delta_A A_t, \quad (\beta, \gamma, \theta) \in [0, 1], \quad (2.6)$$

where B_t denotes the level of technology in the R&D sector at time t. Equation (2.6) is not restricted to constant returns to scale, i.e. augmenting all factors by λ increases output of R&D by $\lambda^{(\beta+\gamma+\theta)}$ which can be superior or inferior to λ. It is plausible that in R&D $(\beta+\gamma+\theta) > 1$ i.e. output increases more than proportionally. To derive the region's growth rate of capital in per capita terms[7] we follow the procedure that was introduced on pages 7.f. Thus we obtain[8] (skipping the subscripts for convenience)

$$g_k = \frac{\dot{k}}{k} = s \cdot \mu_k k^{(\alpha-1)} A^{(1-\alpha)} - \delta_K$$

where $\mu_k = \phi_K^\alpha \phi_L^{1-\alpha}$. Correspondingly we obtain

$$g_A = \frac{\dot{A}}{A} = \mu_A k^\beta L^{(\gamma+\beta)} A^{(\theta-1)} - \delta_A,$$

---

[7]Note that the concept of technological knowledge per capita – A/L – is not meaningful. Therefore A is expressed in absolute terms.

[8]Unlike the model of Romer[1996] we introduce depreciation δ_i for both factors, $i = K, A$. This makes the following presentation less elegant. However, it seems to be more realistic.

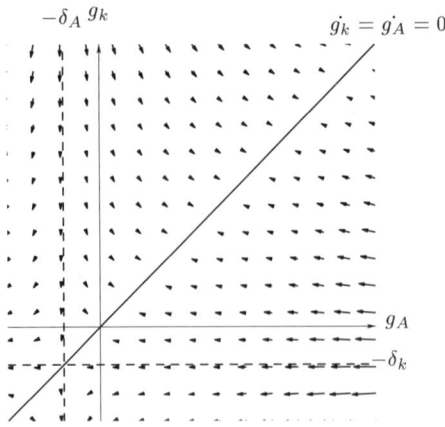

Figure 2.2: If $\beta + \theta = 1$ the region converges to a balanced growth path

where $\mu_A = (1 - \phi_K)^\beta (1 - \phi_L)^\gamma$. Note that μ_k and μ_A are independent of time. We see that g_k increases with A but decreases with k. On the other hand, g_A decreases with A but increases with the other factors. We see as well that both growth rates can obtain negative values, namely if the "gross accumulation" is inferior to depreciation. To state this formally we derive the dynamics of the growth rates. Using the chain rule we obtain

$$\dot{g}_k = (g_k + \delta_K)[(\alpha - 1)g_k + (1 - \alpha)g_A] \qquad (2.7)$$
$$\dot{g}_A = (g_A + \delta_A)[\beta g_k + (\gamma + \beta)g_L + (\theta - 1)g_A]. \qquad (2.8)$$

The economy is said to *grow endogenously* if g_k and g_A are positive and are not driven to 0 i.e. $\dot{g}_k, \dot{g}_A \not< 0$. We see from equation (2.7) that $\dot{g}_k = 0$ if $g_k = -\delta_K$ or $g_k = g_A$. Equally, $\dot{g}_k > 0$ if $g_k > -\delta_K$ and $g_k < g_A$ and vice versa. On the other hand, if we suppose for simplicity that $g_L = 0$, equation (2.8) shows that $\dot{g}_A = 0$ if $g_A = -\delta_A$ or $g_k = g_A(1-\theta)/\beta$; finally $\dot{g}_A > 0$ if $g_A > -\delta_A$ and $g_k > g_A(1-\theta)/\beta$ and vice versa.

Figures 2.2 and 2.3 depict these relations for different parameter constellations. Figure 2.2 shows that if $\beta + \theta = 1$ the economy converges to a balanced growth path, i.e. a path along which all variables grow at the same rate. There, the actual growth rate depends on the initial values of g_k and g_A. If however $\beta + \theta < 1$ the growth rates converge to the origin. Since we express capital endowment in per-capita terms this limit situation implies that growth of the region comes to a complete halt if population stays constant. This situation,

2.3 Implications of Neoclassical and Endogenous Growth Theories for Regional Growth

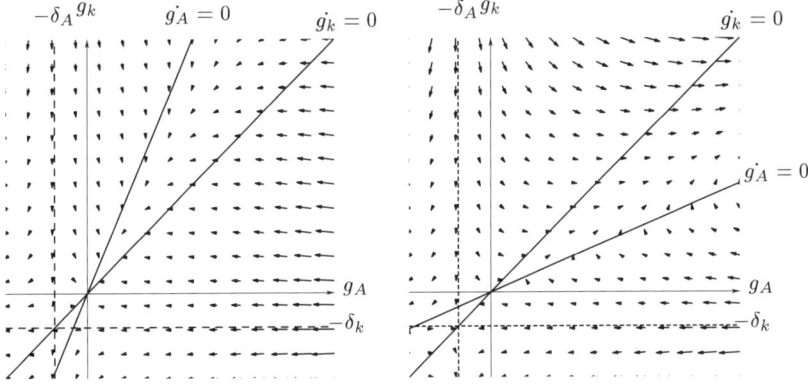

Figure 2.3: *If $\beta + \theta \neq 1$ the region either shrinks (left) or grows endogenously*

which is shown on the left hand side of Figure 2.3, is identical with the steady-state in the classical Solow model. Finally, if $\beta + \theta > 1$, the growth rates of k and A accelerate. This is shown on the right hand side of Figure 2.3. Hence, the region grows endogenously if $\beta + \theta \not< 1$

2.3 Implications of Neoclassical and Endogenous Growth Theories for Regional Growth

So far I have considered only single region economies. Therefore, of course none of the models presented in the previous sections – neither the Solowian nor the endogenous growth model – were able to explain regional disparities in growth or agglomeration. In this section I intend to analyze the ability of these models to explain regional disparities in a two-region setting. Namely, I will discuss 2 issues: the consequences of factor migration and the implications of the neoclassical growth model for the convergence of regional growth rates.

2.3.1 Factor Migration

In a detailed analysis, Bode [1996] considered the consequences of a) interregional factor migration and b) interregional trade on the regional convergence of growth rates in a two-region framework. I will partially follow his analysis here, though I will limit my arguments on factor migration since the model to be presented in chapter 4 will also consider migration.

2.3.1.1 Implications of the Solowian Growth Model

Assume two regions, both hosting a representative firm that produces with production function (2.1). Let k_i be the capital/labour ratio (or *capital intensity*) of region i. If we assume A_i to be identical for both regions then we see from equation (2.2) that if $k_1 > k_2 \Rightarrow y_1 > y_2$. Note (e.g. from 2.3) that $\dot{k}_1$ may be greater, smaller or equal to $\dot{k}_2$ depending the actual k_i i.e. on where regions are situated with respect to their equilibrium point k^* (see Figure 2.1).[9] In the end, every region will have converged to its proper equilibrium point k_i^* and if production parameters are assumed to be identical in both regions then both regions will converge to the same capital intensity.

If we allow for interregional factor migration the situation is accelerated. Assuming that factor wages equal their marginal product, i.e. $\partial f / \partial k = f_k = r/w$ we can deduce from the concavity of $f(\cdot)$ that the labour productivity of a region is superior if its capital intensity is superior. Therefore this region will offer higher wages and thus attract workers from the other region until this difference vanishes, which is the case if capital intensities in both regions are identical.[10] On the other hand, if capital intensity in a region is superior, its relative rent is lower and capital will migrate out of this region, which yields the same result. In the end, both regions have identical capital intensities, migration will have come to a halt and thus they will grow at identical rates. On their way to equilibrium, regional growth rates will differ: the region with lower capital intensity will grow faster (see section 2.3.2.1 for a proof).

The situation is different if the regional levels of technology (A_i) are not identical.[11] Suppose that $A_1 > A_2$. Now equation (2.3) tells us that $\dot{k}_1 > \dot{k}_2$ even if $k_1 = k_2$. Moreover the margial product of capital f_k in region 1 is superior even if $k_1 = k_2$. Thus, the capital intensity in region 1 will increase, which again will increase labour productivity – and thus wages – in this region and in turn attract workers. Thus the region with superior A will display *positive* growth rates, whereas the other region will display *negative* growth rates. In the end, region 1 – the region with the superior TFP – will host the total quantity

---

[9]In section 2.3.2.1, we will see that the statement is different for *growth rates* i.e. in the Solowian model, regions grow faster if their capital intensity is lower. See Figure 2.4.a.

[10]This argument neglects migration costs. Positive migration costs are consistent with a positive regional difference in wages.

[11]The effect of different saving rates is identical to the one of different A_i. I will not discuss this effect.

of factors, independend of its initial endowment. In a regional model we would call this outcome *agglomeration*. This is nevertheless not a satisfying model of agglomeration since the differences of TFP are simply assumed exogenously and the model does not offer an explanation *why A* is superior in the agglomeration.

2.3.1.2 Implications of the Endogenous Growth Model

As discussed above, endogenous growth theory models the accumulation of knowledge endogenously either considering it as a by-product or as the result of an intentional process. In a multi-regional framework the critical question is whether this knowledge remains only locally available or whether it is globally available, i.e. spills over to neighbouring regions.[12]

The implications of the *learning-by-doing* approach is that learning is bound to the stock (or the growth) of factors, either capital or labour (in the model of Arrow/Romer in section 2.2.2.1 it is bound to capital). This implies that (as Aghion and Howitt[1992] put it)

> *the models lead to the conclusion that the largest countries (simply measured in terms of population) should also experience the highest growth rates, a hypotheses that is not only implausible, but also not in accordance with the empirical facts.*

Note that learning by doing increases labour productivity and thus wages. Thus, if knowledge is only locally available and if factors migrate, this process is accelerated since larger regions accumulate knowledge faster, therefore the difference in labour productivity increases and workers are attracted to the biggest country. If the two regions stand for city and surrounding area, this model implies that the region with the higher pool of labour (the city) will attract *all* workers from the countryside (which equally cannot be observed in industrialized countries).

If on the other hand knowledge spills over between regions, a region will benefit from the learning by doing effect of its neighbours i.e. its capital or labour productivity will be higher compared to the situation where no spillovers exist. This effect will be more important for the smaller region since the stock of human capital is bigger in the bigger one. Assuming that wage equals marginal productivity, the smaller region will be able to offer higher wages and thus attract factors. Thus, the regions will converge to identical capital intensities. On

---

[12]The question of spatial spillovers of knowledge can be seen as a spatial interpretation of the discussion in section 2.2.2.2. For a discussion of regional spillovers, see section 4.1.

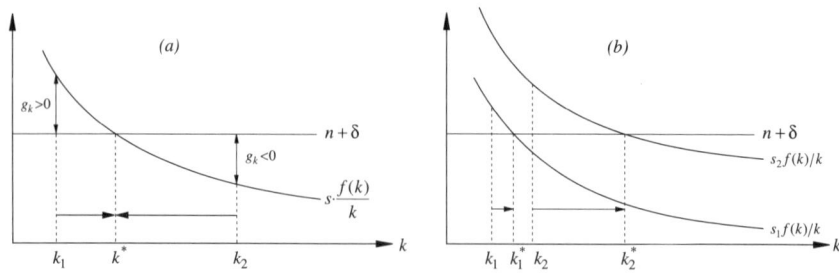

Figure 2.4: Growth rates and steady states for identical (a) and different economies (b)

the way to this equilibrium the region with low capital intensity will grow faster, once the equilibrium is attained, regions will grow at the same rate.

The implications of the *human capital oriented* approach are similar though it is now the endowment of human capital that will determine a region's growth rate. Thus, as long as no spillovers of human capital occur, the region with a higher endowment of human capital will c.p. grow faster and in the end will have attracted the stocks of capital and labour completely. If however human capital spills over, both regions will converge to the same capital intensity and then grow at the same rate.

2.3.2 The Convergence Debate

The discussion of the previous section has shown that the Solowian model predicts convergence to an equilibrium where capital intensity and thus regional per-capita income are identical. If regions are out of equilibrium, the regional income will differ but factor migration will lead to spatial equilibrium and thus regional per-capita income will *converge*.

The endogenous growth model has the same implications if knowledge spills over to other regions. However if knowledge remains local, the region with an initially higher level of knowledge (or human capital) will grow faster and subsequently attract the factors from the other region completely. In consequence regional per-capita incomes will *diverge*.

2.3.2.1 The Hypotheses of Convergence

The issue of convergence/divergence has taken considerable space in the literature. Barro and Sala-i-Martin[1992] showed that it is an inherent property (i.e.

2.3 Implications of Neoclassical and Endogenous Growth Theories for Regional Growth

this property holds even if *no migration takes place*) of the neoclassical growth model that regions will converge in *growth rates* of per-capita income. That is, poor countries will grow faster than rich countries. Moreover, they showed that this implies that regions will also converge in their per-capita *incomes*. In the literature the first type is referred to as β-*convergence*, the latter as σ-*convergence*. The proof involves consumer optimization in an infinite horizon model (the Ramsey model, see footnote 2 on page 7). I will suggest here a simplified proof of the convergence property which is based on the Solow-model alone.[13]

Consider growth equation (2.3) which is applicable for an aggregated economy as a whole but also for its spatial sub-aggregates, i.e. its different regions. Divide (2.3) by k to obtain the *growth rate* of capital in per-capita terms

$$\frac{\dot{k}}{k} = g_k = \frac{s \cdot f(k)}{k} - (n + \delta_K). \qquad (2.9)$$

Hence the capital stock of an economy (a region) grows if $s \cdot f(k)/k > (n+\delta_K)$ and shrinks if the relation is inverse. This is shown in Figure 2.4.(a), which depicts two regions identical in their (neoclassical) production function and in n, δ_K and s. From function (2.2) we know that region 1 has lower per capita income (it is *poorer*) than region 2 since its capital intensity (k_1) is lower than that of region 2 (k_2). However (from equation 2.3), since both economies are identical in their production parameters, they will converge to the same equilibrium point k^*.

β-*convergence* implies that the per-capita endowment of capital of poor countries (or regions) will grow faster than rich countries (regions). This means that they will *catch up* with richer ones, i.e. *converge* in terms of capital endowment per person. To show this property formally we derive

$$\frac{\partial g_k}{\partial k} = s \frac{f'(k)}{k} - s \frac{f(k)}{k^2} = \left(f'(k) - \frac{f(k)}{k} \right) \frac{s}{k}. \qquad (2.10)$$

In a neoclassical framework, this term is always negative since the marginal product of a concave function ($f'(k)$) is always inferior to its average product ($f(k)/k$). Thus g_k decreases with k. This is shown again in Figure 2.4.(a) where $k_1 < \bar{k}_2$. However, the growth rate of region 1 is superior to the one of region 2 and, both regions converging to k^*, the growth rates of both regions will converge.

---
[13] See also Barro and Sala-i-Martin[1995], p. 24.

The argument of convergence can be extended to per capita *income*. Using the chain rule we obtain from equation (2.2) $\dot{y} = f'(k)\dot{k}$. Then the growth rate of y is given by

$$\frac{\dot{y}}{y} \equiv g_y = \frac{f'(k)\dot{k}}{f(k)} = g_k \frac{f'(k)k}{f(k)} = g_k \cdot \epsilon_{yk},$$

where ϵ_{yk} is the production elasticity of capital per worker. Since $\epsilon_{yk} \in [0,1]$, g_y has the same properties as g_k, i.e. its derivative with respect to k is always negative. Therefore the neoclassical model predicts convergence in capital and income per capita. Since this theory implies that all countries will converge to the same steady state (i.e. the same output per capita) the situation is named *absolute convergence*.

Sala-i-Martin [1996b] argued that evolution of per-capita income of an economy i can be approximated by

$$\log(y_{it}) = a + (1-\beta)\log(y_{i,t-1}) + u_{it}, \qquad (2.11)$$

where a, β are constants. $\beta > 0$ implies β-convergence since then the annual growth rate $\log(y_{it}/y_{i,t-1})$ is inversely related to the initial value $\log(y_{i,t-1})$. Extending this approach to multiple periods Sala-i-Martin[1996a] suggests the following regression equation

$$\overline{g_{y,i}} = \alpha - \beta \log(y_{0,i}) + \varepsilon_i, \qquad (2.12)$$

where $\overline{g_{y,i}}$ is the average growth rate of income per capita in an observed time period in a region i and $\log(y_{0,i})$ is its initial income per capita. Here, regions of an economy are said to exhibit absolute β-convergence if a regression of equation (2.12) yields a negative estimate of β. Figure 2.5 shows a plot of the the annual mean of g_y against an inital value of y of the federal states of the U.S. We see that there is indeed a strong negative relationship between these two variables. A similar pattern can be obtaied for European Regions, for Japanese Prefectures or for OECD countries.[14] Crihfield and Panggabean [1995] gave evidence for significant β-convergence in a sample of 282 U.S. metropolitan areas. It is remarkable that the estimated gradient of the regression equation (β) varies throughoutly around 0.02, suggesting a convergence rate of 2% per annum.

---

[14] See Barro and Sala-i-Martin[1995], different chapters or Barro and Sala-i-Martin[1992].

2.3 Implications of Neoclassical and Endogenous Growth Theories for Regional Growth

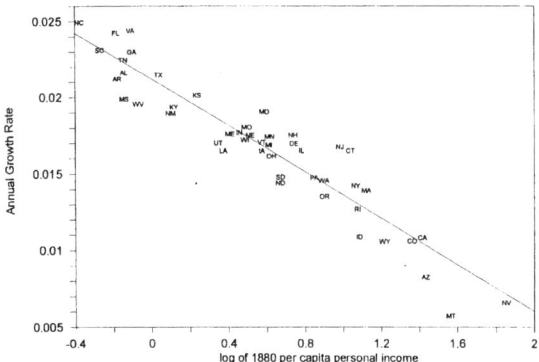

Figure 2.5: Average growth rate of per capita income of US states from 1880 to 1988 vs. 1880 initial value (from Barro & Sala-i-Martin, 1992)

An alternative concept of convergence is σ-convergence. Applying the variance operator to equation (2.11) we obtain[15]

$$\sigma_{y,t}^2 = (1-\beta)^2 \sigma_{y,t-1}^2 + \sigma_{u,t}^2, \qquad (2.13)$$

where $\sigma_{y,t}^2$ is the cross-sectional dispersion of per-capita income at time t. Solving this difference equation for the steady state income dispersion we obtain

$$\tilde{\sigma}_y^2 = \sigma_u^2 / \left(1 - (1-\beta)^2\right)$$

Thus equation (2.13) becomes

$$\sigma_{y,t}^2 = \tilde{\sigma}_y^2 + (1-\beta)^2 \left(\sigma_{y,t-1}^2 - \tilde{\sigma}_y^2\right)$$

i.e. if β-convergence holds, $\sigma_{y,t}^2$ will approach its steady state value $\tilde{\sigma}_y^2$, implying σ-convergence. Thus, β-convergence is a necessary condition for σ-convergence. For two reasons, the converse does not necessarily hold. First, an observed σ-convergence might be the consequence of a decreasing $\sigma_{u,t}^2$ alone. Second, if *leapfrogging* occurs, i.e. if a country overtakes another country in terms of GDP per capita, the variance of the sample might remain constant although considerable convergence processes may have occured. A time series plot of $\sigma_{y,t}^2$ of the US Federal States (Figure 2.6) supports the concept of σ-convergence. Again, a similar plot can be obtained for European countries and

---
[15]The following argumentation has been taken from Sala-i-Martin[1996b, p. 1329].

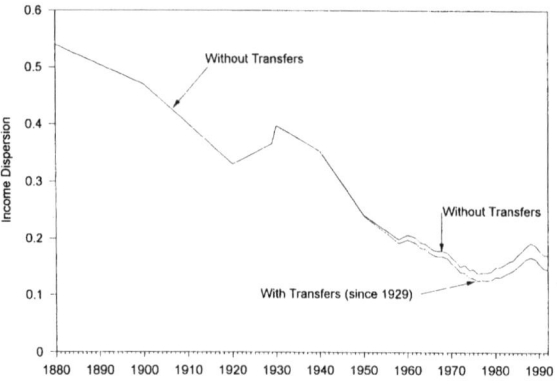

Figure 2.6: Dispersion of per-capita income across US states (from Sala-i-Martin [1996])

for Japanese Prefectures.[16] Note that convergence of growth rates implies that initial differences in capital intensity will vanish with time. Thus, evidence in favour of convergence is – at first sight – evidence against the theory of endogenous growth since the latter predicts constant or accelerating growth rates and thus increasing differences of growth rates.

2.3.2.2 Critics of the Convergence Hypotheses

Although there is evidence in favour of β and σ convergence, the concept of convergence has received considerable criticism in the literature. A first was that convergence can only be observed in a certain number or type of regions. Indeed, a plot of growth rates against initial per-capita values of a sample of 121 countries (excluding former central planned countries), presented by Mankiw, Romer and Weil [1992] and reproduced in Figure 2.7.a, strongly suggests *divergence* of growth rates. This is confirmed by regression results[17] which give evidence for *diverging* growth rates within the non-oil countries (though growth rates within OECD countries are *converging*). This finding is not in accordance with the convergence hypothesis.

---

[16] See Barro and Sala-i-Martin [1995, chapter 11].

[17] See Mankiw *et al.* [1992, Table III]. The authors give different estimates for three different regions, *non-oil* countries which include all but the oil producing countries (98 countries), *intermediate* countries which are 75 non-oil countries, excluding small countries and those whose data are supposed to include measurement error and finally 22 OECD countries.

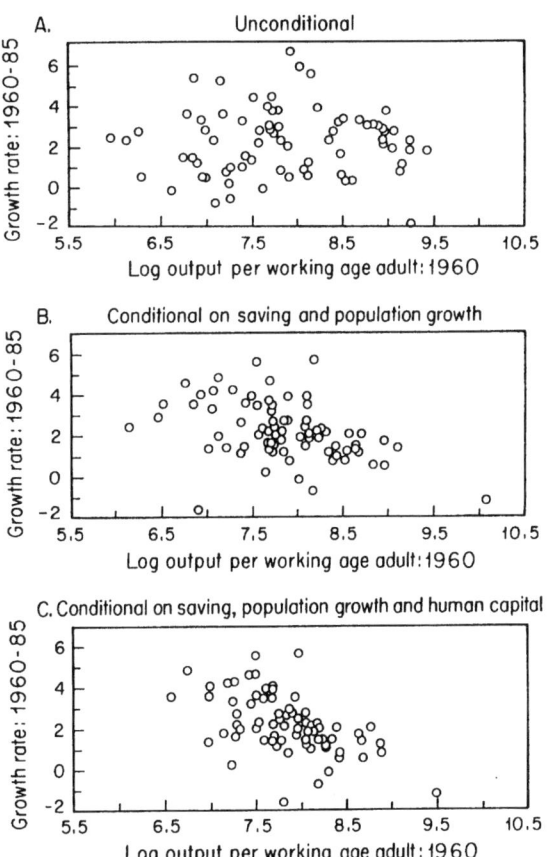

Figure 2.7: Different types of convergence behaviour (from Mankiw, Romer & Weil [1992])

In response, supporters of this theory suggest that this is the case since countries differ fundamentally in their basic economic variables. This includes not only economic institutions (note that the set of OECD countries with their similar institutions exhibit convergence) but also several measurable parameters such as human capital, innovation, saving rate, population growth etc. Thus, countries will converge anyway but to *different steady states*. Figure 2.4.b on page 16 sketches this. Consider two countries which differ in their saving rate; production parameters, n and δ are supposed to be identical. Country 1 has a lower capital intensity but nevertheless grows slower than country 2 and finally converges to a lower equilibrium k_1^*. Thus both countries converge to their proper equilibrium value. Convergence is therefore *conditional* on the initial parameters and Barro and Sala-i-Martin [1992, 1995], Mankiw et al. [1992] refer to *conditional convergence* when they allude to this phenomenon. Formally, conditional convergence implies that the convergence equation (2.12) is extended by the appropriate variables **X** to obtain the following regression equation

$$\overline{g_{y,i}} = \alpha - \beta \log(y_{0,i}) + \mathbf{X}\boldsymbol{\beta} + \varepsilon_i, \qquad (2.14)$$

i.e. the regression includes **X** as control variable. Indeed, when controlling for the above mentioned parameters, the picture (see Figures 2.7.b/c) as well as the regression results change. All countries now display significant convergence.[18] The economic interpretation of this finding is however difficult. Basically, conditional convergence means that a country converges to its own steady state which is determined by the above mentioned parameters. Another way to put it could be: *If*, say, Ethiopia had the same saving rate, population growth, production parameter, human capital endowment etc. as, say, the U.S. *then* the growth rates of these two countries would converge (in absolute terms). It is obvious that this is not a meaningful statement; rather we would be interested *why* we cannot observe convergence. As a consequence, the fact that conditional convergence regressions regularly yield an estimate around 0.02 for β is in my view not a meaningful result and the figure should rather be considered as a "second Solow residual". Or as Durlauf [1996] put it:

> *Interestingly, this paper* (D. refers to Sala-i-Martin [1996a]) *focuses more on the robustness of the conditional convergence finding than its economic interpretability.*

A number of authors have therefore sought to suggest approaches to convergence that go beyond the mere growth accounting approach presented above. Bernard and Jones [1996] suggest that the convergence literature overemphasizes the importance of capital accumulation and forgets almost completely the role of technology. In a sectoral disaggregated analysis they show that the cross-country dispersion of labour productivity in the manufacturing sector has increased (hence σ-divergence) and that this effect is mainly attribuable to the total factor productivity (which is represented by the parameter A in equation 2.1 on page 6). Quah [1996] argues that there exist two related but logically distinct aspects of economic growth – one is the mechanism with which agents in

---
[18] See Tables IV – VI of Mankiw et al. [1992].

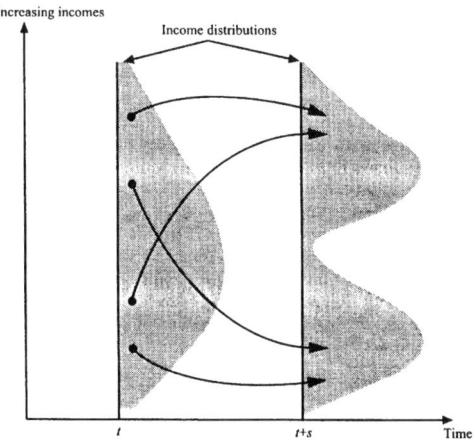

Figure 2.8: Twin-peaks distribution dynamics (from Quah, 1996)

an economy push back their technological and capacity constraints, the other refers to the relative performance of different (rich and poor) economies. The first aspect concerns the classical notion of growth, whereas the second concerns interaction between countries and (more generally) movements within the distribution of incomes. Quah then argues that different constellations of these two aspects are consistent with a convergence parameter β of 0.02. At the same time however, different constellations will lead to different evolutions of the cross-country dispersion of per-capita income. It is even possible that a *bimodal* income distribution emerges from a formerly unimodal one. This finding is confirmed by Galor[1996] who names this phenomenon *club-convergence* (referring to Baumol, 1986) as a third convergence type along with absolute and conditional convergence. Quah refers to the fact that a number of rich countries have remained rich, a number of poor countries have remained poor but some countries have shifted from rich to poor and vice versa (e.g. Korea and Phillipines for the latter). See Figure 2.8 for an illustration of this process.

Another line of criticism is implicit in the analysis of Seitz[1995a], who considered a set of 324 West German small statistical units (so called *Kreise*) where he distinguished three different types of regions: 92 cities, 112 surrounding areas (which are adjacent to cities) and 114 rural areas. These regions differ in a number of respects like e.g. population density or endowment of human

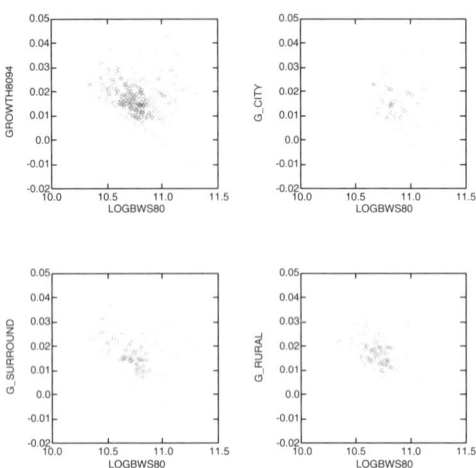

Figure 2.9: Plot of the average growth rate in the period 80–94 against Log(GDP80) for 324 West German regional statistical units (Kreise). Data from "Volkswirtschaftliche Gesamtrechnung" 1996.

capital or infrastructure[19]. Running a regression that tests for absolute convergence (equation 2.12) he obtained significant results for β for all three types of regions and for the set as a whole (see Table 2.1 for a reproduction of the results). This behaviour is evident in Figure 2.9. If however he controls for human capital endowment and for the regional saving rate[20] convergence is no longer significant for rural areas. Note however that cities and surrounding areas display stronger convergence behaviour. This result is confirmed when using 164 larger planning regions, so called "Arbeitsmarktregionen" which encompass functional spatial economic aggregates, i.e. regions that can be considered as *functional* rather than statistical units.

In a thorough analysis of the same spatial aggregate (Arbeitsmarktregionen)

---

[19] For a more detailed analysis see section 6.2.

[20] FHU measures the proportion of the working population with a college degree, the saving rate is proxied by INV, the per capita investment in the producing sector. Note that these control variables correspond to those chosen by Mankiw *et al.*[1992].

		cities	surround	rural	overall
absolute convergence	slope (β)	0.016	0.019	0.019	0.016
		(2.0)	(2.8)	(3.7)	(5.0)
	R^2_{corr}	0.061	0.153	0.154	0.125
conditional convergence	slope (β)	0.037	0.030	0.016	0.027
		(3.9)	(3.2)	(1.7)	(4.4)
	FHU	0.124	0.199	0.056	0.097
		(2.8)	(3.7)	(1.0)	(2.9)
	INV	0.004	0.002	-0.001	0.002
		(2.8)	(1.1)	(0.4)	(1.6)
	R^2_{corr}	0.247	0.181	0.101	0.213

Table 2.1: Results of convergence regressions for three different types of West German kreise (from Seitz, 1995, t-values in brackets)

Bode [1998, chapter D] rejected the hypotheses of convergence using several different approaches. Similar results have also been reported by Boltho, Carlin and Scaramozzino [1995] who ran convergence-regressions for Italian regions for six time periods (covering 1928 to 1991). They found "*little support to the view that Italian regions have converged over the last 60 years ...*" and conclude that the "*2 per-cent rule suggested by Barro* and *Sala-i-Martin [1995] does not seem to apply in the Italian case*". Apparently, the fact that Barro and Sala-i-Martin [1995, p.398] included not only the 20 Italian regions but 90 European regions in their regressions rendered this effect invisible. Basically, this implies that the *Mezzogiorno problem* remains.

Thus, there is no evidence for global convergence if we consider *different types* of regions. This result is somewhat puzzling. If conditional convergence is suggested as an approach to describe the behaviour of national states then it should also be valid at a lower level of spatial aggregation. Otherwise, the concept should be considered as somewhat arbitrary. It seems difficult to defend the concept of conditional convergence if it depends on the level of spatial aggregation and thus on arbitrarily drawn borders.

2.4 Summary and Conclusion

This chapter gives an overview of the neoclassical tradition of growth theory. In the origin of the neoclassical growth model (Solow, 1956) the *accumulation of factors* (i.e. capital and labour) was the driving force of neoclassical growth.

The model implies that an economy evolves towards an equilibrium capital intensity. As long as the economy is out of this equilibrium, capital accumulates faster or slower as labour, depending on where exactly the economy is situated with respect to the equilibrium point. Once the economy is in equilibrium capital grows at the same rate as labour, thus leaving capital intensity constant. Hence, the only driving force of economic growth is the growth of population – a rather unsatisfying result from a methodological point of view. Another issue of the model that has been strongly criticized is the fact that it does not give a statement as to the relevance of technological change. It rather treats it as a residual that grows "autonomously" every year.

To meet this shortcoming a number of extensions have been suggested which give an endogenous explanation of technological change. The two approaches that are suggested here – unintentional and intentional growth of knowledge – are summarized in the literature under the notion of *endogenous growth theory*. One of the implications of the models suggested in this literature is that growth may be self-sustaining and that therefore rich countries may stay rich and poor countries may stay poor.

In section 2.3.1 it is shown that these characteristics also hold in a multi regional setting. If, however, knowledge or human capital is considered as the driving force of economic growth and if we allow for spatial spillovers of this factor, the mechanics of the endogenous growth model are identical to those of the Solowian one. This section implicitely made clear that the neoclassical model makes no statement as to agglomeration. It simply predicts identical regional capital intensity and neglects the forces of agglomeration.

If we consider closed economies, the results of the endogenous growth theory contrast with those of its neoclassical counterpart which predicts that poor countries grow faster than rich countries, i.e. the latter predicts *convergence* of growth rates of capital intensity and therefore convergence of per-capita incomes. Therefore, the fact that convergence is a stylized fact that can be observed across a number of regions has been taken as evidence against endogenous growth theory. However, as I argue in section 2.3.2.2, convergence only applies to a certain type of regions and at a certain level of spatial aggregation. This holds even for the concept of *conditional convergence* which investigates convergence properties conditional on initial conditions. I give evidence that even the concept of conditional convergenve does not hold universally. Apparently it depends of the level of spatial aggregation whether regions display converging behaviour or not.

In chapter 4, I will suggest a model that is able to explain this behaviour i.e. why at a low level of spatial aggregation it is possible to observe *non-convergence* while a higher spatial aggregate displays *convergence*. This model will consider growth and convergence processes at an arbitrary low level of spatial disaggregation. A main hypotheses of this model is that once growth dynamics are considered at a spatially disaggregated level the *forces of agglomeration* have to be taken into account. The next chapter therefore surveys the literature that investigates spatial processes in the economy i.e. why industries agglomerate in space.

Chapter 3

Why and How Does Economic Activity Concentrate in Space? Another Overview of the Literature

Step back and ask, what is the most striking feature of the geography of economic activity? The short answer is surely concentration
PAUL R. KRUGMAN

3.1 Introduction

The notion of *space* is not a very present one in standard economic literature. Indeed, browsing an index of a standard textbook one will rarely find a reference to "space" or analogous concepts. In recent years however, the interest in spatial economics and – thus – the number of publications in major journals that deal with spatial issues has increased significantly. However, taking a closer look, one realizes that "space" is actually amongst the oldest subjects of economic analysis and has managed to occupy its niche pretty early and to stay there since.

This chapter will give an overview of some of the literature on spatial issues in economics. The models presented here will be distinguished between those which explain the "how" and those which explain the "why" in the title. Put differently, some models are *normative* in nature while others are *positive*. Of course, in the context of this work the question *why* the economy concentrates in space is more interesting. Once this issue is clarified, the consequences of spatial concentration may be investigated. The emphasis will be on models which investigate the location of *footloose industries*, in contrast to industries whose primary occupation is resource extraction or processing. It is obvious that the latter concentrate around the respective resource deposits in an attempt to minimize transport costs.[1]

One of the first systematic attempts to develop a taxonomy of the motivation of spatial concentration was given by Ohlin[1933].[2] He identified different forces which he subsumed under the concept of *agglomeration economies*. Namely he distinguished three categories:[3]

1. *Economies of scale* within the firm,

2. *Localization economies*, i.e. economies external to the firm and arising from the size of the local industry and

3. *Urbanization economies*, i.e. economies which are external to the industry and arising from the size of the local economy.

Let me briefly illustrate these three different types of economies before presenting the relevant literature in more detail. The role of the *first* type is straightforward.[4] If a certain mode of production is subject to economies of scale, then it is of course profitable to produce on a large scale and therefore – implicitly – concentrated in space. In principle, under economies of scale (or *increasing returns to scale* which is the dual viewpoint) it would be preferrable to concentrate the production completely in one factory, i.e. in one location. However, since shipping of goods is subject to transportation costs, there is a trade-off between concentration and distance (or, put differently, economies of scale vs. transportation costs). Some of the models (to be presented in section 3.2) will explicitly investigate this relationship. Once an economies of scale industry is established, (specialized) workers who are employed in this industry will need to buy certain goods and services to be able to work full-time. Hence, this industry will attract further economic activity and thus, an agglomeration emerges.

The *second* type, localization economies, is present when a firm of a certain industry takes an advantage of the fact that it is located near firms of the

---

[1]This has been discussed by Weber[1909]. See also Richardson[1969] or Schätzl[1996].

[2]One of the first to discuss this motivation was of course Marshall[1920] whose arguments will be presented in section 3.3.1.

[3]Cited from McDonald[1997, p. 37]

[4]See also the discussion in Mills [1967], where he proposed that an economy without economies of scale would be an economy with a uniform spatial distribution. An example of such an economy might be the medieval production of apparel.

same industry. E.g. new ideas on new products are developed and refined more quickly since local communication accelerates the exchange of knowledge. But also the access to a specialized pool of labour and technical expertise may be counted into localization economies. *Third*, urbanization economies are more general and arise if a firm takes an advantage of being located in an agglomeration rather than in a rural area. Examples are the access to a high variety of infrastructure like streets, harbours etc. Moreover, the access to a higher variety of technical expertise usually to be found in bigger cities might be an advantage.

Of course, if agglomeration economies exist, they will have a positive influence on the growth of a sector or of a city and therefore agglomerated areas can be expected to grow differently compared to rural areas. In chapter 4 I will develop a model that takes this effect explicitly into account.

In the following section I will present some of the literature that deals with spatial issues – as far as being relevant for the analysis of the subsequent chapters. One type of models refers to *transportation costs* to explain how and why economic activity concentrates in space. Thus, these models come from the branch of trade theory. Usually, they more or less explicitly assume economies of scale. Thus, these models refer to the first of the three agglomeration economies. Another strain of models refers to *spatial external effects* to explain the same phenomena, therefore rooted rather in production theory. They are presented in section 3.3. Results of this chapter are summarized in section 3.4.

3.2 The Role of Transportation Costs

3.2.1 Thünen's Rings

One of the oldest models of spatial organization (if not *the* oldest) was suggestet by von Thünen [1826].[5] He was interested in the spatial distribution of economic activity (which was mainly agricultural at that time) around an existing agglomeration in a featureless plain. He considered different crops (or different "sectors") since they differ in two respects, their *rent* (i.e price times harvested quantity) and their *transportation costs*. From these two factors Thünen derived

---

[5] A recent appraisal of Thünen's work is given by Samuelson [1983]. The Thünen model is however presented in a number of publications. See also Krieger-Boden [1994] or Krugman [1996, p. 9]. Although Thünen is usually named as the first economist who was concerned by spatial issues, Stull [1986] showed that even the work of Smith [1776] had an important spatial dimension.

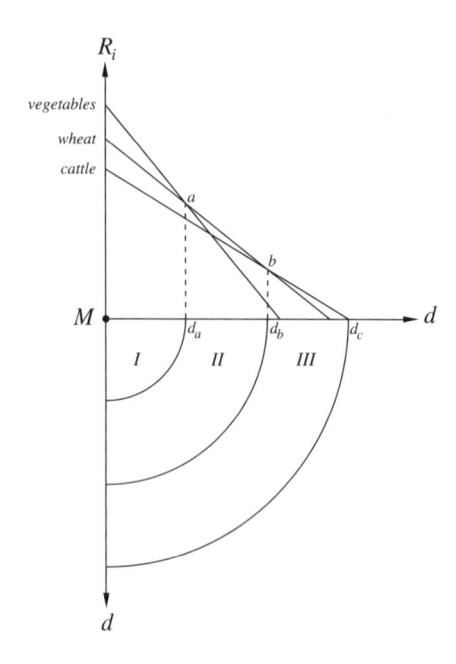

Figure 3.1: Emergence of Thünen's Rings for three different crops

the *locational rent* π_i for every crop i with the following simple function

$$\pi_i = (p_i - c_i - d \cdot \tau_i) \cdot Y_i$$

where p_i is the market price of crop i, c_i is its cost of production and τ_i is cost of transportation per unit including depreciation through quality losses; d is distance to the market (the agglomeration) and Y_i is yield of crop i. Thus, the locational rent decreases with distance d. Now, the higher the locational rent, the more intensive the economic activity can be. Therefore, the closer the area to the market, the higher the yield of the crop. This implies that crops are factor intensive and are subject to high transport cost will be produced in areas close to the agglomeration and crops that are factor extensive and subject to low transport costs will be produced in distant areas.

Thünen illustrated his arguments with three different kinds of product, vegetables, wheat and cattle. Figure 3.1 illustrates this example, where M is the position of the market. Vegetables require a high factor input and therefore will be produced near the market. Moreover, vegetables can obtain a high profit but are subject to high transport costs. Therefore the locational rent is high if distance to market is low but decreases quickly (the gradient of the locational rent function is steep). At point a (i.e. distance d_a), producers are indifererent with respect to the alternative i.e. wheat. Beyond d_a, producers prefer to produce wheat since now its locational rent is superior to that of vegetables. The same process applies to cattle which is produced beyond d_b up to d_c, where its locational rent is zero. Drawing circles around M, taking d_a, d_b and d_c as radii we obtain three rings which represent three zones of activity. Zone *I* is the vegetable-producing area, zone *II* is wheat-producing and zone *III* is cattle-producing – the least intensive activity. Beyond d_c Thünen assumed "deserted land". With this model, Thünen was able to explain the different zones as they could have been observed at the time. Seitz[1996] used this approach to explain the spatial segregation of a city in a central business district with high rents, a commercial district and a residential district. This illustrates that the Thünen rings are not limited to past economic activities. One point that should be criticized, however, is that the model simply *assumes* the existence of a market (or of a centre in its more recent version). Thus, it should be seen as a normative model of spatial organization (the "how" in the title) and not of emergence of markets or cities (the "why").

3.2.2 Central Place Theory

The theory of central places is attributed to Christaller[1933] and Lösch[1944], who published their work independently. The assumptions of this approach are that economic activity takes place in a featureless plain and that production is subject to economies of scale (the first of the three types of agglomeration economies outlined on page 30). Christaller extended the model of Thünen in two ways. First, he assumed that production takes places in the centre (the agglomeration) and transport of goods goes from the centre to the surroundings (rather than vice versa as in the Thünen model) to provide these regions with goods produced in the centre. These "exports" are subject to transport costs and therefore their price increases with distance form the centre. Since the propensity to buy decreases with increasing prices, the price of goods will attain a critical level at some distance $\bar{d}$ where the willingness to buy vanishes. This critical distance is the *maximum reach* of the product and a potential market ring emerges around the centre whose radius is given by this reach – quite similar to the one shown in Figure 3.1. This is a remarkable similarity to the Thünen

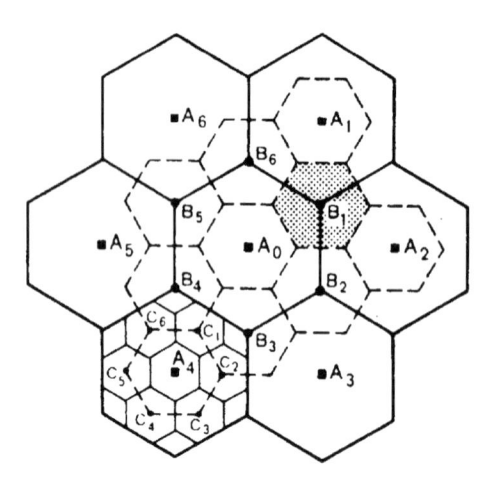

Figure 3.2: System of Central Places according to Christaller (from Schätzl, 1996, p. 74)

model since so far it differs only in the direction of transports. As in the Thünen model, Christaller allowed for different goods with different transport costs and thus different reaches.

Christaller's second – and more original – extension of the Thünen model is that through the assumed economies of scale there is a critical minimal market size for each product below which its profits are negative. In the assumed featureless plain, this critical market size can be expressed in terms of distance, hence the minimum market size determines the *minimum reach*.[6] From this assumption, a web of cities emerges across the plain, where the cities can be classified within a spatial hierarchy (see Figure 3.2). The process of emergence is as follows. Let $\mathbf{g} = (g_1, g_2, \ldots, g_n)$ be a vector of goods g_i which is sorted according to the minimum range of products. Thus g_1 is the good with the highest minimum range, g_2's minimum range is the next lowest and so on. Then major cities (cities A_0 to A_6 in Figure 3.2) produce the whole range of products $(g_1, \ldots, g_n)$. The next level of cities (cities at the B-level of Figure 3.2) imports g_1 from the nearest major city but produces itself $(g_2, \ldots, g_n)$ and so on down to the bottom level, where the smallest city produces only g_n. Since agents attempt to minimize transport costs, a *hexagonal* spatial structure

---

[6]In an attempt to limit this overview to the necessary aspects with respect to the following chapters, I am not going into details as to the production structure. See Christaller [1933] or Schätzl [1996].

3.2 The Role of Transportation Costs

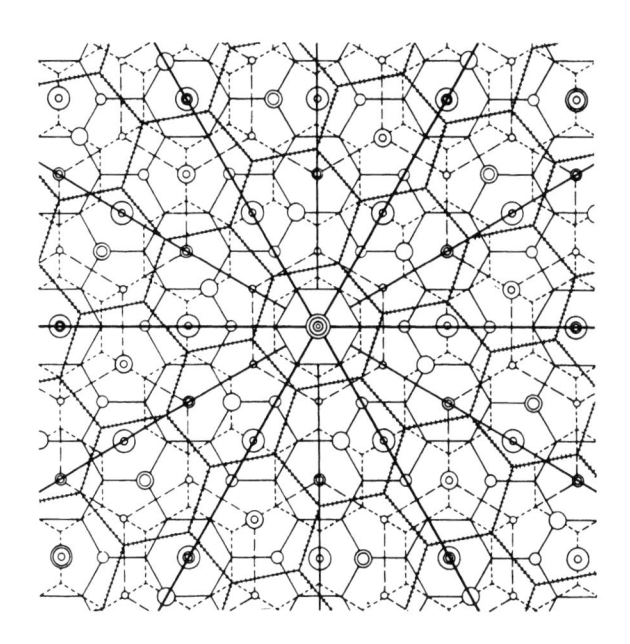

Figure 3.3: System of hexagonal layers of locational hierarchy according to Lösch (from Isard, 1956, p. 270)

emerges where layers of different density – according to the hierarchical level – coexist.

In his book, Lösch [1944] refined these arguments by introducing a more flexible hexagonal structure. In the model of Christaller, it is possible that some firms obtain monopoly rents or that some regions are without supplies due to the existence of minimum and maximum reaches: Imagine a product (say g'_2) whose maximum reach is smaller than those of g_1 while its minimum reach is higher than those of g_2. This product could be produced e.g. in places at the A-level, thus supplying then A and C-cities but leaving (in this example) B-cities without supply. Thus, there are unrealized profits, which is inconsistent within a framework of perfect markets. These profits could be realized by producing g'_2 in B'-cities which are closer together than A cities but not as close as B-cities. Thus we can think of an "invisible hand" that will create a new lattice of B'-cities.

A similar argument is as follows. Suppose a product (say g'_1) whose maximum reach is higher than the one of g_1 while its minimum reach is higher than the maximum reach of g_2. g'_1 will be produced in A-cities and g'_1-producers will obtain a locational rent. Again, this rent can be eliminated only by moving production of g'_1 to a new type of cities, say A'-cities, now on a lattice coarser than the lattice of A-cities. If this arguments are developed at all product levels $(g_1, \ldots, g_n)$ a continuum of lattices would emerge. Lösch assumed an existing regular distribution of places whose position in the hierarchy of agglomerations (i.e. whether they will be an A or a B etc. city) is determined by the above process. Under this assumption, a complex structure of hexagonal layers emerges, of which a graphical representation is given in Figure 3.3.[7]

Hence, Central Place Theory is able to explain why different types of cities exist. However, most of the interesting questions of spatial concentration of economic activity remain obscure. The role of increasing returns is for example not explicitly considered and it still does not explain *why* economic activity concentrates in space, since places were assumed to exist already. The authors of Central Place Theory are sometimes grouped together with Thünen and A. Weber[8] under the name of *German school of location theory*. A recent reformulation and extension of this school is given by the following approach.

3.2.3 Krugman's Core-Periphery Model

Krugman [1991b, 1995, 1996] suggested an approach along the lines of the work of Thünen and Christaller & Lösch. He restated these models in a general equilibrium framework and, allowing for labour migration, was able to explain the formation of cities endogenously. His model is a two-region, two-sector model (*agriculture* and *manufacturing*). Consumers derive utility from the consumption of both goods where the utility function is assumed to be of the form

$$U = C_M^\mu C_A^{1-\mu},$$

---

[7] See Schätzl[1996] or Lösch[1944] for details on this impressive picture.

[8] Weber[1909] investigates the optimal location of a production plant where deposits of raw materials and location of consumption (i.e. markets) are given. He is able to derive the optimal location of a tranporting plant where transport cost as a function of product weight play the major role. Weber's approach is not further considered here. See also Richardson[1969] or Schätzl [1996].

3.2 The Role of Transportation Costs

C_A being consumption of the agricultural good and C_M being consumption of the manufacturing good. The latter is defined as CES-aggregate

$$C_M = \left(\sum_{i=1}^{n} g_i^{(\sigma-1)/\sigma} \right)^{\sigma/(\sigma-1)}, \qquad (3.1)$$

where n is a large number of potential products (i.e. goods) g_i and $\sigma > 1$ is elasticity of substitution among them. Good i is produced by a single factor, L_{Mi} and is (as in Thünen and Christaller & Lösch) subject to economies of scale which Krugman specifies as follows:

$$L_{Mi} = \alpha + \beta x_i,$$

where x_i is the good's output and α, β are production parameters. Krugman further assumed that the single factor (labour) does not migrate if employed in agriculture but can migrate if employed in manufacturing.

Under the assumption of monopolistic competition, Krugman derived the zero-profit level of economic activity (i.e. the point beyond which no firm will enter the market) for every region. He further argued that real income in a spatial model will depend on transport costs since an imported good is c.p. more expensive than a domestic product. To capture these costs he introduced a parameter $\tau \in [0, 1]$ that describes them with an "iceberg metaphor". Namely, τ is the part that remains after shipment, i.e. the longer the distance of shipment, the lower the part of product to be delivered. Formally, this implies that the price of an imported good is p/τ and not just p. Thus, τ is an inverse of transport cost, low τ mean high transport cost (i.e. high losses during transport) and vice versa. Assuming that relative wages of both sectors equal relative prices of their products, Krugman derived relative demand for g_{ij}, the consumption of good g_i in region j. From that he could derive income of workers in both regions. The next step is to derive *real wages* which are

$$\omega_1 = w_1 P_1^{-\mu} \qquad \text{and} \qquad \omega_1 = w_2 P_2^{-\mu}$$

where $\mu \in [0, 1]$ is the share of workers that work in the manufacturing sector and P_i is a CES price indes for manufacuring goods for consumers in region i. These price indexes include transportation costs (cif prices).

It can be shown that the model depends on three parameters, σ, τ and μ as the only parameters that cannot be skipped by choice of units. From the perspective of this thesis it suffices to concentrate on parameter τ. The interesting

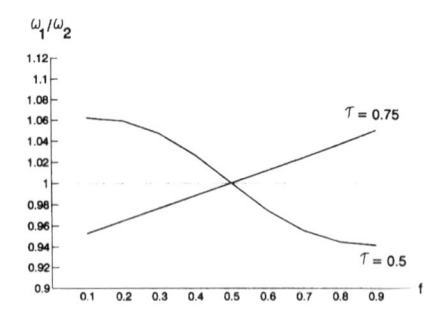

Figure 3.4: Critical threshold of migration as a function of transportation costs (Krugman, 1991, p. 493)

question is how the ratio of real wages w_1/w_2 behaves with a shift in the regional share of workers (where f is defined as the share of workers of region 1). If this ratio *decreases* while f *increases* (i.e. if we observe a negative feedback) regions will converge to a uniform spatial distribution of labour in manufacturing. On the other hand, if w_1/w_2 *increases* with f – positive feedback – the process is self-accelerating and the economy will end up in a *core-periphery pattern* where manufacturing is concentrated in one of both regions. *Which* of these cases applies depends on the three parameters.

Figure 3.4 depicts these dynamics for different values of τ. If transport costs are high ($\tau = 0.5$), real wages of region 1 decrease relative to those of region 2 with an increase in f. Therefore, the higher the regional share of workers, the lower the attractiveness of this region and this process will stabilize at $f = 0.5$. On the other hand, if transport costs are low ($\tau = 0.75$) a region is the more attractive, the higher its share of labour in manufacturing is, which yields a self-reinforcing process that stabilizes at $f = 0$ or $f = 1$.

The intuition behind this result can be found in the relation between returns to scale and transportation costs: if transport costs are low it is profitable to concentrate production at a maximum in one region to fully exploit these economies and then simply ship the products. With increasing transportation costs, these economies of scale are more and more exhausted and – beyond a critical threshold – spatial concentration is not profitable anymore. Krugman [1991b] further explores the role of σ and π, but since these parameters do not alter the behaviour of the model qualitatively, I will not go into detail here.

With his extension to a general equilibrium model, Krugman was able to

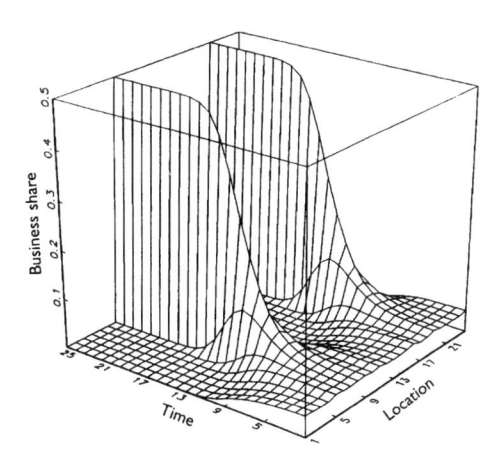

Figure 3.5: Emergence of spatial concentration in a self-organizing economy (Krugman, 1996, p. 25)

explain *why* the economy concentrates in space. Krugman [1996] further extended this analysis to a multiple region model. Since with this extension a general equilibrium framework would be extraordinarily tedious to deal with, he set up a simulation framework in which the economy is interpreted as a *self-organizing system*, i.e. a system, where economic agents interact in a decentralized way without being led by some benevolent dictator[9]. There, a chain of 24 locations interact with their direct neighbours (the first interacts with the 24th and vice versa). Hence the economy is interpreted as a circle. Figure 3.5 shows a simulation run with 25 iteration (=time) steps. We can see that economic activity concentrates on two opposite sites of the circular city. Thus, Krugman could show that a regular spatial pattern of economic activity emerges, i.e. the system is subject to *spatial self-organization*.

The contribution of this extension was to make explicit that an interesting model of spatial concentration should include *centrifugal* as well as *centripetal* forces, the first being given by economies of scale and the latter by transportation costs. The model can be seen as a two-dimensional version of the theory of Central-Places and indeed, Krugman assumed that a two-dimensional version of his model would yield a hexagonal pattern, just as Christaller and Lösch predicted. The next section presents an approach that illustrates the models

---

[9] I will examine self-organizing systems in chapter 5.

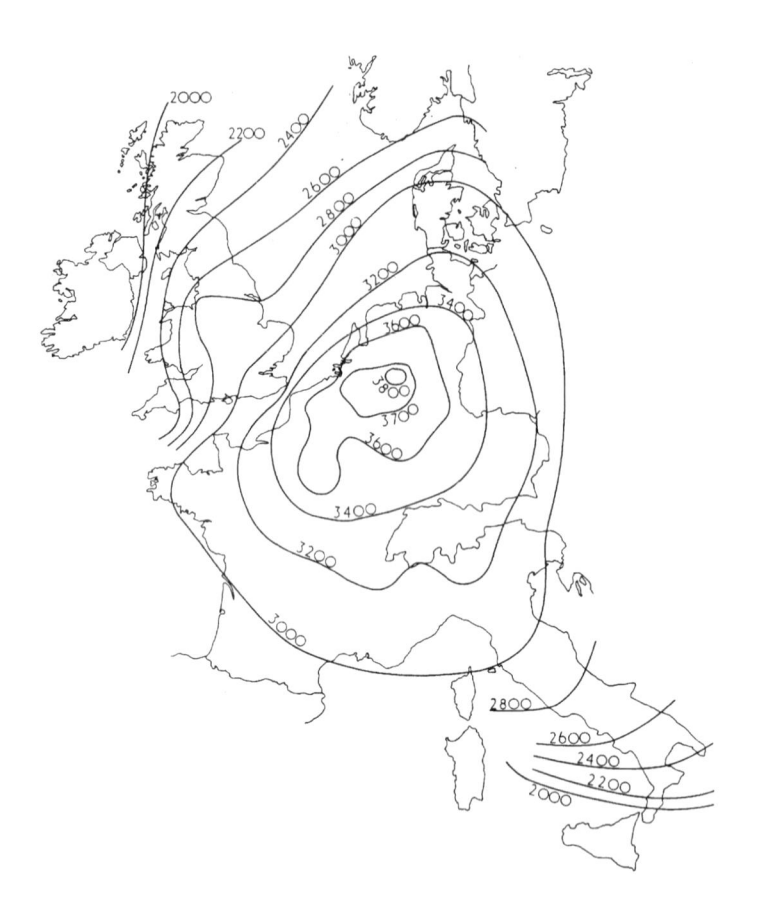

Figure 3.6: Economic potential of regions in an enlarged Common Market (EC[6] with Scandinavia, UK and Ireland. Clark et al. (1969), p. 205)

presented so far, though it does not refer directly to them and is rather ad hoc.

3.2.4 A Heuristic Approach: The Idea of Economic Potential

Let me finish section 3.2 with an approach that is *ad hoc*, i.e. it is not based on any of the above presented theories, since it comes from the field of geography, rather then economics. It nevertheless illustrates them very well. The idea goes back to Harris[1954] (a european version – to which I refer here – was published by Clark, Wilson and Bradley[1969]) and is simple but nevertheless very appealing. The economic potential of a region i is defined as weighted sum of the incomes of other regions j plus the potential of the domestic market. More specifically, the *index of market potential* Π_i is defined as

$$\Pi_i = \frac{I_i}{c_m} + \sum_{j=l}^{n} \frac{I_j}{c_m + t_{ij} + F}, \quad l \neq i,$$

where I is regional income, n is the number of regions that enter the index, c_m is some minimum cost of supply, t_{ij} is cost of transportation from i to j and F is some tariff (which is relevant in international studies). Clark *et al.*[1969] computed the economic potential for the European Community (which included 6 countries at that time) plus UK, Ireland and Scandinavia. They consider 5 scenarios which include different political statuses (Treaty of Rome, enlargement) and different types of transportation facilities (containers, channel tunnel). Figure 3.6 presents for the purpose of illustration the rings of economic potential in an "enlarged common market" (which is closest to the current situation). Three points are worth mentioning. First, the approach is consistent with the observation that peripheral regions in Europe are poorer. However, the approach does not offer an explanation for it, but rather describes the status quo with a certain index. Second, although Belgium belongs to the core of the rings of economic potential it is one of the poorer regions within EC(6). Finally, the index of market potential can only be computed for a certain point in time. The approach implies however that a high market potential in the centre (e.g. in Central Europe as shown in Figure 3.6) exerts an attraction on economic agents in the periphery (comparable to a suction of a whirlpool). This again would lead to an self-reinforcing process which is not captured by the theory. Therefore, this approach adds a descriptive tool to the geographer's toolbox but is rather irrelevant in economic theory. It nevertheless illustrates very well the relevance of transportation costs in the formation of markets.

3.3 The Role of Spatial Externalities in Production

The literature refers to the notion of *externality* (or *external effect*) if production or utility of an economic agent is a function of a variable that is determined by other agents.[10] It is useful to distinguish *technological* from *pecuniary external effects*.[11] The first type refers to externalities which are not necessarily transmitted by a price or by some costs. Think of the benefit a firm draws from the

---

[10] See section 4.2 on page 64 for a detailed treatment of externalities.
[11] This distinction has been introduced by Viner[1931].

presence of other firms, e.g. through the fact that it may hire more easily educated and specialized personnel from it (or of the disutility a person draws from pollution of these firms). Pecuniary externalities are transmitted by the market. Think of a market where the price of a product increases through increased demand. In the literature technological external effects are often simply referred to as "externalities".

In this section, I will present a family of models that is based on *production theory*. The difference to those of section 3.2 is primarily a formal one, the core of the models to be presented here being a production function of one or more sectors and interactions (between sectors or regions) that lead to some type of externalities. Moreover, transportation costs are not of main concern. I will first refer to the origins, i.e. to the works of especially two authors. Then I will present a number of existing formal models that deal with the question of spatial concentration. I classified these models into three categories: models that refer to increasing returns in production (i.e. economies of scale), models that use *density* as a proxy for Marshallian externalities and models that model *distance* explicitly. Although it is not always easy to classify a model into one of these three categories, the distinction aims to emphasize the different existing ways of implementing spatial externalities.

3.3.1 The Godfathers: Externalities in the Works of Alfred Marshall and Jane Jacobs

In his *Principles of Economics*, Marshall[1920] dedicated one chapter to the localization of industries (chapter *X* of Book *IV*). There, he identified "local trade secrets" and "localized skills" (what today might be referred to as "localized human capital") as central factors of the concentration of industries[12] and therefore implicitly the formation of cities. Marshall argued that these localized skills will be communicated *implicitly* by some local culture of trade or production and thus facilitate the emergence of localized specialization.

---

[12] Another main factor – also mentioned by Marshall (p. 223) – is of course the existence of natural resouces. Note however that the importance of natural resources in economic activity has decreased whereas the importance of localized human capital has not, despite improved means of communication and transportation. Recent essays which investigate the concentration of industries refer to the "Silicon Valley Effect" to illustrate the phenomenon.

> *When an industry has thus chosen a locality for itself, it is likely to stay there long: so great are the advantages which people following the same skilled trade get from near neighbourhood to one another. The mysteries of trade become no mysteries; but are as it were in the air, and children learn many of them unconsciously.* Marshall[1920, p. 225]

The emphasis on trade can probably be explained by its importance in England at that time. What is mentioned in this citation can of course be applied to "skilled production" as well as to "mysteries of production" and indeed, we still can observe that cities or regions specialize in certain products or technologies. Then, this local pool of knowledge is useful in production though it is free of charge. In contemporary terminology one would probably say that this "localized human capital enters the production function as a *positive (technological) externality of knowledge* or as *knowledge spillover*". Marshall continues:

> *If one man starts a new idea, it is taken up by others and combined with suggestions of their own: and thus it becomes the sources of further new ideas. And presently subsidiary trades grow up in the neighbourhood, supplying it with implements and materials, organizing its traffic, and in many ways conducing to the economy of its material.* Marshall[1920, p. 225]

These effects act at different levels. Some are external to the single firm but internal to the local industry (like the formation of new ideas), hence they refer to *localization economies*. Others are external to the local industry but internal to the local economy (like the formation of subsidiary trades and the organization of traffic), i.e. they refer to *urbanization economies* (see p. 30).

Beyond these *spatial spillovers of knowledge*, Marshall mentioned the tendency of firms to locate where the specialized labour is and vice versa[13] as a possible explanation of localization of specialized industries in one place:

> *Again, in all but the earliest stages of economic development a localized industry gains a great advantage from the fact that it offers a constant market for skill. Employers are apt to resort to any place where they are likely to find a good choice of workers with special skill which they require; while men seeking employment naturally go to places where there are many employers who need such skill as theirs and where therefore it is likely to find a good market.* Marshall [1920, p. 225]

Hence, we see from these arguments that local presence of firms of the same industry exerts positive externalities (sometimes referred to as *Marshallian Ex-*

---
[13]Krugman[1991a] used the term *labour market pooling* for this phenomenon.

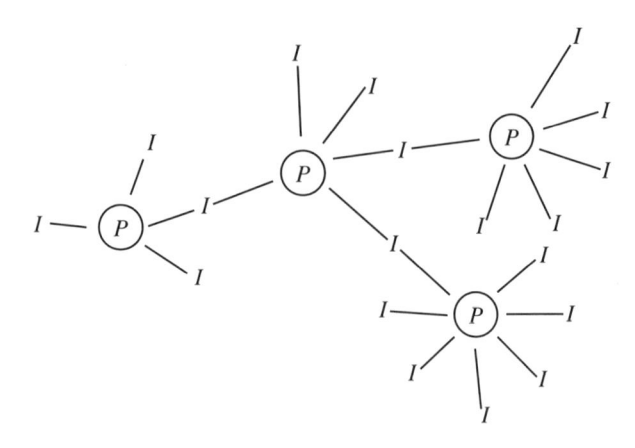

Figure 3.7: Innovation (I), development of new products (P) and increase of diversification according to Jacobs (p. 63 of the German translation)

ternalities[14]). As they are positive, they will foster growth of the sector which is able to incorporate them and if a city is specialized in that sector, the localized production secrets will foster the growth of that city. To put it in a brief way: *Specialization fosters growth*. However, besides the importance of localized special knowledge Marshall also mentioned the importance of *variety* of employment:

> *The advantages of variety of employment are combined with those of localized industries in some of our manufacturing towns, and this is a chief cause of their continued growth.* Marshall[1920, p. 226]

Here, Marshall points out that specialized cities (i.e. those with a low variety of employment) are liable to depression if the sector in which the city is specialized is in crisis.

A different view of variety has been developed by Jacobs[1969]. She argues that the discovery of new products or new technologies will create new kinds of specialized jobs. These new products will usually start as by-products and play an economically negligible role. Then, either the product is successful and a new branch will emerge or it is not and the branch will vanish. Once a new branch is established, the same process might start over again. Figure 3.7 illustrates this process, where *P* stands for product and *I* stands for innovation. Jacobs cites a number of products where this story sounds plausible. In her view, it is

---
[14] See e.g. David and Rosenbloom[1990].

variety of existing products or technologies that inspires people and thus allows them to develop new products. Put briefly: *Variety fosters growth*, which is the opposite view as compared to Marshall. Since this variety enters the production function of the city free of charge, this effect is sometimes referred to as *Jacobs externalities*.

Thus, at first sight, there is a contradiction between Jacobs and Marshall. However this contradiction vanishes once a closer look is taken. Consider the story of *Detroit* as told by Jacobs[1969, p.123][15]. At the beginning of the last century it has been a city dominated by agricultural industries, like mills, and was exporting refined agricultural products. Besides, there was a number of shipyards and workshops which were engaged in machinery and equipment, like repairing mills and transportation facilities. These branches were auxiliary to the dominant agricultural sector until the steam engine appeared, when these sectors quickly started to engage in these new technologies and to export their products. This decreased the relative importance of the agricultural sector. With the appearance of the combustion engine these firms could quickly adopt this new technology and today Detroit is known as *the* city of automobiles in the US if not worldwide. Therefore Detroit as we see it today is certainly one of the best examples of Marshallian externalities. The conclusion of this story is that it *depends on the stage of the life-cycle of a technology* whether Jacobian or Marshallian Externalities play the dominant role. This view is confirmed by empirical studies I will present in section 3.3.3 (p. 52).

How do these two concepts of externalities relate to the three types of agglomeration economies as discussed on page 30? The first of the agglomeration economies – economies of scale – results from cost degressions in production. Therefore, from an analytical point of view, it is a pecuniary externality but neither Marshallian nor Jacobian. However, it is possible that *empirically* we measure increasing returns to scale at the level of the firm if Marshallian externalities prevail.

Marshallian externalities are probabaly best matched by the second type of agglomeration economies – localization economies – since Marshall mainly argued at the level of the industry. Indeed, Henderson[1986] and Henderson *et al.*[1995] equate this type of externality to localization economies and Jacobian externalities to urbanization economies. This is however not an exact way

---

[15] JJacobs[1969, chapter 4] describes this process in much greater detail. I will only outline the basic process here.

to put it. It is true that most of the effects discussed by Marshall refer to the advantages of a concentration of an industry in one region, thus of localization economies. But (as shown above) Marshall was aware that the positive externality may quickly turn into a negative one if the sector is in crisis. On the other hand, urbanization economies are independent of the type of industry of a city. Therefore they will exist whether a city is specialized (say a "Marshallian" city) or its economic activity is diverse (say a "Jacobian" city). Hence, they can not be equated to urbanization economies either. Finally, Jacobian externalities are certainly not identical to localization economies since they refer to diversity.

Thus, strictly speaking, agglomeration economies and spatial externalities refer to the same phenomenon but to different concepts that do not match. Some of the models presented in the following sections do not make this distinction as clear as seems necessary. Rather, they sometimes model spatial external effects only implicitly, e.g. when they refer to "some kind of" agglomeration economy. Let me start with a class of models that refer to economies of scale.

3.3.2 Models that Refer to Increasing Returns in Production

One of the first to formally investigate agglomeration economies was probably Henderson[1974]. He specified the following production function for two representative industries (that he called sectors 1 and 3) in a representative city:

$$Y_i^{1-\rho_i} = K_i^{\alpha_i} L_i^{\beta_i} M_i^{\delta_i}, \qquad (3.2)$$
$$\text{where} \quad \alpha_i + \beta_i + \delta_i = 1, \ 0 \leq \rho_i < 1, \ i = 1, 3.$$

Y_i is output and K_i, L_i, M_i are capital, labour and land sites used by sector i respectively. Function (3.2) implies that each firm of industry i produces under *constant* returns to scale (since α_i, β_i and δ_i sum to unity) while the industry as a whole operates under *increasing* returns to scale as long as $\rho_i > 0$ (since then $(\alpha_i + \beta_i + \delta_i)/(1 - \rho_i) > 1$). Thus, if $\rho_i > 0$, the industry is subject to *localization economies*[16]. Thus, ρ_i captures the degree of increasing returns to scale. Henderson assumed that the two industries differ in their realization of ρ_i. Namely, sector 1 is a goods producing sector with $\rho_1 > 0$, sector 3 is a housing sector with $\rho = 0$ (i.e. no localization economies). Sector 2 is an intermediate

---

[16] If i in equation (3.2) means *firms* instead of industries, the equation models *economies of scale* at the firm level. On the other hand, if i means *complete cities* with all their respective industries, the model would capture *urbanization economies* instead of localization economies.

goods sector that produces production sites with *decreasing* returns to labour subject to the following production function[17]

$$(M_1 + M_3)^{1-\rho_2} = M^{1-\rho_2} = L_0,$$

where M is raw land not separately specified and L_0 is labour employed in this sector. $\rho_2 < 0$ represents the degree of decreasing returns to scale. Henderson closed the model using full employment conditions and setting up a utility function for a representative individual

$$U = y_1^a y_2^b y_3^c, \qquad (3.3)$$

y_i being individual consumption of Y_i. Individuals maximize their utility while two assumptions prevail: 1) consuming individuals are identical with capital owners and work as labourers and 2) capital owners are a separate group and do not work as labourers. Thus, maximization is subject to one of the two restrictions respectively: Individuals maximize their income subject to income $\mathbf{y} = p_L + p_K(K/L)$ (first assumption) or $\mathbf{y} = p_L$ (second assumption), where p_i are factor prices. Based on the following indirect utility function[18]

$$U = a^a b^b c^c \mathbf{y} q_1^a q_2^b q_3^c,$$

where q_i is price of output Y_i, Henderson derived the optimum city size, i.e. the city size that optimizes its utility level.

From the perspective of the work at hand, these optimum city sizes are not of primary interest and I will not go into detail here. Let me however discuss the way Henderson implemented externalities in his model. Localization economies (and thus spatial externalities) are captured by the parameter ρ_i and the result obtained is based on the assumption that this parameter differs between industries. Note however that Henderson did not *explain* how these externalities occur, but simply *imposed* their existence. Thus, his analysis is not useful if we search for an explanation of spatial externalities.

---

[17] From the perspective of equation (3.2), this function results from $Y_2 = M$ and $\alpha_2 = \delta_2 = 0$ and $\beta_2 = 1$. However, I will follow the notation in Henderson[1974], equation (3).

[18] The *indirect utility function* results from the combination of a utility function $U = f(\mathbf{x})$, where $\mathbf{x}$ is a vector of goods x_i, with the Marshallian demand functions $x_i = g(\mathbf{p}, I)$, $\mathbf{p}$ being a corresponding vector of prices and I being level of income of the representative agent. See e.g. Intriligator, Bodkin and Hsiao[1996, chapter 7] or Berck and Sydsæter[1993, chapter 26].

A similar approach was chosen by Abdel-Rahman[1988], who used a utility function of type (3.3) where he set $a + b + c = 1$. One of these goods is a CES aggregate of services, Q, that is produced in a central business district (CBD) with the following production function

$$Q = \left(\sum_{j=1}^{n} y_j [d]^\sigma \right)^{(1/\sigma)}, \qquad (3.4)$$

where y_j is the consumption of household j of good y, d is distance from the CBD and $\sigma \in (0,1)$ is a substitution parameter that represents consumers' preference for product variety. For $\sigma \to 0$, consumers derive more utility from variety and less for $\sigma \to 1$. The production side in Abdel-Rahman's model is characterized by monopolistic competition and decreasing average cost (i.e. economies of scale). Cities will form since a higher number of potential consumers allows for production of a higher variety of goods which again will attract more consumers if they prefer variety.

Again, it is possible to compute an optimal city size under different parameter settings. Therefore the approach of this model is very much in line with the approach of Henderson[1974], discussed above. The contribution of Abdel-Rahman's paper is the inclusion of variety as possible explanation of agglomeration economies. Since he included distance (hence transportation costs) in his model, it deals with space more explicitly and therefore can explain the existence of a CBD endogenously.

Rivera-Batitz[1988] chose a similar approach where he used a function of type (3.4) in consumption *and* production. Take function (3.4), replace "Q" by "M_i", "y" by "z" insert this function into (3.2) and we obtain the Rivera-Batitz model. His contribution was to show that increasing returns in production may emerge from this type of model. Assuming that factors z_j enter the production function symmetrically (i.e. they are used in identical quantity) he derived the following production function

$$Y_i = n^{\delta_i (1-\sigma)/\sigma} K_i^{\alpha_i} L_i^{\beta_i} z_i^{\delta_i}, \qquad (3.5)$$

where (similar to equation 3.4) z_i is $\sum_j z_j$ used in sector i. Thus, variety (expressed by n) can be interpreted as a production factor and the production function will display increasing returns to scale if the number of products n in the market is exogenous to the firm. Since variety is exogenous to the firm

3.3 The Role of Spatial Externalities in Production

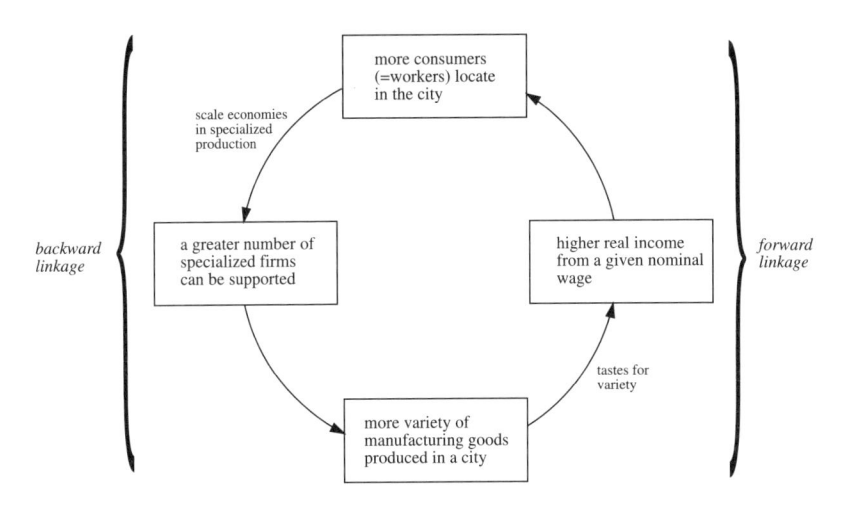

Figure 3.8: Circular Causality in Spatial Agglomeration of Firms and Workers (from Fujita, 1993)

but endogenous to the industry, this is a model for *localization economies*. The process of agglomeration is comparable to the one described by Abdel-Rahman (see discussion above), though Rivera-Batiz applied this process to production *and* consumption. Moreover he derived the optimum variety n and beyond that, Rivera-Batiz[1988] extended his approach to a two-region (i.e. two-city) model and was able to derive the equilibrium spatial distribution of households (i.e. of population) under different parameters of the utility function.

Finally, Fujita[1988] developed a model along the same lines (i.e. using a function of type 3.4) where he derived different patterns of spatial distribution of land rents. In another paper Fujita[1993] discusses the role of monopolistic competition in a rather informal way. Figure 3.8 reproduces his Figure 1 as a summary of the models discussed above. It illustrates the dynamic consequences of equation (3.5). Basically, it implies that if n grows endogenously, a process of *cumulative causation* leads to a spatial concentration of workers and thus to formation of cities (the "why" in the title of this chapter). Fujita used the term "forward" and "backward linkage" to characterize the way scale economies are transformed into increasing returns to scale at a city level.

3.3.3 Models that Refer to Spatial Density

The idea of using *spatial density* as a proxy to explain Marshallian externalities is straightforward. *If* Marshallian externalities matter, then a higher spatial concentration (density) of firms (capital, labour, innovation) will allow these spatial effects to manifest themselves more easily. *"After all"* (as Glaeser et al.[1992] put it) *"intellectual breakthroughs must cross hallways and streets more easily than oceans and continents"*. In this section, I will present a group of models that use different measures of density to capture this effect.

One of the first to investigate localization economies empirically was (again) Henderson[1986]. He estimated *localization economies* for different industries in a study based on the ideas developed earlier in Henderson[1974] (see discussion on page 46). The general approach was to specify a production function which allows to test for scale effects of the number of firms in a certain area

$$Y/L = A(\mathbf{S})Y(\mathbf{k}) \qquad (3.6)$$

where $Y(\mathbf{k})$ is a firm's constant-returns-to-scale production function of the vector of inputs $\mathbf{k}$ which are measured per-capita. $A(\mathbf{S})$ is an external shift factor whose arguments are scale and technology measures specific to an industry in an urban area. Henderson chose the following specification for $A(\cdot)$:

$$A(\cdot) = e^{\gamma/L} P^{\epsilon_P}$$

where

$$\epsilon_L = \frac{\partial(\log Y)}{\partial(\log L)} = -\frac{\gamma}{L}, \quad \text{hence} \quad g(\cdot) = e^{-\epsilon_L} P^{\epsilon_P}$$

where L is local industry employment in an urban area and P is the population of this area which is assumed to be fully employed. Since these variables are measured with respect to a constant unit of space (the urban area) they implicitly measure density. ϵ_L and ϵ_P are elasticities, i.e. an increase of the density of L (of P) of 1% leads to an increase of Y by ϵ_L% (ϵ_P%), holding the firms' input fixed. These effects are assumed to be Hicks-neutral (which is not rejected by the data), i.e. they leave the relative marginal product constant.

From function (3.6) Henderson derived two different approaches to econometric specification. The first is a translog production function and the second the dual translog cost functions. Both functions include $\log A(\mathbf{S})$ as additive term. He argues that *an aggregate production function* (i.e. one that comprises all industries) *can by definition have only urbanization economies represented in it* (Henderson, 1986, p. 48). In consequence, *localization economies* can be identified only if industry-specific production functions are estimated. With the simultaneous inclusion of industry-specific labour (L) and overall labour (P) in the regression he aims to measure both types of agglomeration economies simultaneously.

Based on data for 16 industries in the US and in Brazil he could identify eight which are subject to localization economies (Henderson, 1986, Table 2) but only one of these 16 industries was subject to urbanization economies. Henderson argued that these eight industries should cluster spatially and presented some evidence for this hypothesis. He concludes that agglomeration economies are in general *localization economies* rather than *urbanization* ones. However five of these eight industries are resource dependent and therefore it is possible that the model simply measures the fact that these industries cluster around the respective resource deposits. What is to be retained from this model is the fact that Henderson specified spatial density of labour (i.e. the number of workers per city) as proxy-variable for agglomeration economies.

A different approach was chosen by Glaeser *et al.*[1992]. Their objective was to examine whether industries are subject to *Marshallian*[19] or to *Jacobian* externalities[20]. They chose a simple econometric specification. Assuming that firms maximize profit function

$$\pi_t = A_t f(L_t) - w_t L_t$$

with respect to labour they obtain the first order condition $A_t f'_L = w_t$. A_t is a measure of total factor productivity (TFP) and w_t is wage at time t. The authors suggest a decomposition of A into two components

$$A = A_{\text{local}} A_{\text{national}}$$

---

[19] Marshallian externalities imply that agglomeration of firms of a certain sector *helps knowledge spillovers between these firms and, therefore, the growth of that industry and of that city* (Glaeser *et al.*, 1992, p. 1127). Since this is a spatial interpretation of the ideas of Arrow[1962] and Romer[1986, 1990] (see discussion in section 2.2.2) they refer to MAR-externalities.

[20] See discussion in section 3.3.1. Glaeser *et al.*[1992] actually investigate *three* different types of externality, the third being *Porter*-externalities. However, since the ideas of Porter[1990] differ only slightly from those of Marshall, I will not go into detail here. The essence of his ideas is that local competition between firms of one industry fosters growth rather than local monopoly.

where they specify the growth rate of A_{local} as

$$\log\left(\frac{A_{local,t+1}}{A_{local,t}}\right) = g\left(\begin{array}{c}\text{specialization, local monopoly,}\\ \text{diversity, initial conditions}\end{array}\right)$$

This specification reflects the fact that if Marshallian externalities are present, the local TFP will increase as a function of specialization. Thus an estimate of this factor should yield significant results. Alternatively, if an industry is subject to Jacobian externalities, A_t should grow as a function of diversity. The third factor, local monopoly, aims to capture Porter-externalities which are not further discussed here (see footnote 20 on the page before). Setting $f(L) = L^{1-\alpha}$ they derive the following econometric implementation

$$\log\left(\frac{L_{t+1}}{L_t}\right) = C_0 + \mathbf{X}\boldsymbol{\beta} + g\left(\begin{array}{c}\text{specialization, local monopoly,}\\ \text{diversity, initial conditions}\end{array}\right) + \varepsilon_{t+1}, \tag{3.7}$$

where $t = 1956$ and $t+1 = 1987$. $\mathbf{X}$ is a matrix of control variables and $g(\cdot)$ is a simple linear combination of the enumerated factors. *Specialization* of a city is measured as the city's share of employment of an industry relative to the share of employment of this industry in the US. Thus, Glaeser *et al.* use the same density measure as Henderson[1986] (discussed above), though relative to the mean. *Competition* is measured as firms per workers in the city relative to firms per workers in the US and finally *diversity* of a city is measured by fraction of employment accounted for by the city's largest five industries.

Using data for 1016 industries in 170 cities the authors present empirical evidence that local competition and diversity foster employment growth in cities. The coefficients for specialization were not significant, i.e. Glaeser *et al.* did not find empirical evidence for Marshallian externalities. However, they qualify their result since their dataset did not allow them to consider young industries, where Marshallian externalities can be expected to happen. Note that, again, Marshallian externalities were specified using a measure of density of industry employment.

With a similar target in mind, Henderson, Kuncoro and Turner[1995] use a similar approach but a different dataset to test for Marshallian and Jacobian externalities. For eight industries in 224 metropolitan areas they estimated a simple econometric model

$$L_{t+1} = f(w_{t+1}, MC_{t+1}, L_t, \rho_t, \Delta_t, \ldots) + \varepsilon_{t+1} \tag{3.8}$$

where $t = 1970$, $t+1 = 1987$, MC_t is marginal cost of industry i at time t, ρ_t is a measure of concentration of that industry (corresponding to specialization in Glaeser *et al.*) and Δ_t is a measure of diversity in the industry's location. ρ_t is to capture Marshallian externalities and Δ_t Jacobian ones. This latter variable is measured by the *Hirschmann-Herfindahl* index of concentration for two digit industry k:

$$HHI_{ik} = \sum_{j \neq k} s_{ij}^2, \quad HHI \in (0, 1],$$

s_{ij} being share of three-digit industry j in city i. Thus, HHI is an index for spatial density of an industry or of the *lack of diversity*, i.e. if Jacobian externalities are present, we expect a negative sign for this measure. Note, that function (3.8) differs from the one used by Glaeser *et al.* (3.7) only in the specification of the left hand side (Henderson *et al.* measure levels, while Glaeser *et al.* specify growth rates).

However Henderson *et al.* run their regressions seperately for five "traditional industries" and for three "new high-tech industries"[21]. For the five traditional industries, Henderson et al. find significant evidence for Marshallian externalities but no evidence for Jacobian ones. On the other hand, young high-tech industries seem to be sensitive with respect to diversity (i.e. they are subject to Jacobian externalities) and not to specialization. Thus, their results differ from those of Glaeser *et al.* Henderson *et al.* explain the difference with the fact that different periods have been used in their regression and that Glaeser *et al.* used different criteria to include an industry in their sample.

Although the results of Henderson *et al.* seem to confirm *both*, Marshall *and* Jacobs, it seems to be possible that the result reflects a simple statistical artifact. If young industries are small in size (which is usually the case) it is evident that they can be found in a diverse environment. On the other hand, if traditional industries are large, they can of course be found to be spatially concentrated if they are subject to economies of scale. Hence, possibly, the approach chosen by Henderson *et al.* shows simply that the industries in their sample are subject to economies of scale, which are not yet manifest in the young industries.

In an extension of this model, Henderson[1997] identified the lag structure of both types of externalities. Basically, the variables used in regression are the

---

[21]The tradtional industries are *machinery, electical machinery, primary metals, transportation* and *instruments*. New high-tech industries are *electronic components, medical equipment* and *computers*.

same as in equation (3.8), however augmented by the lags of ρ. Again, he found strong evidence for Marshallian externalities and he could show that they die out after six years. Jacobian externalties are significant but smaller. Nevertheless, they do not die out within the duration of the sample (eight to nine years).

A completely different approach was chosen by David and Rosenbloom [1990] who developed a model of *labour market pooling* which is one of the effects mentioned by Marshall[22]. To do so, they set up two equations of motion, one concerning labour and the other concerning capital. The first is

$$\frac{\dot{L}}{L} = M(K, L) = nF_L(K, L) + N(L) - C(\omega, \lambda), \qquad (3.9)$$

which is their equation (4). F_L is the marginal product of labour, which is assumed to equal wage rate. n is a constant and $N(\cdot)$ is an increasing sigmoid function which converges to some N^* as L increases. The behaviour of this function is to represent the boundedness of the labour market externality (i.e. the benefit from an increase of L is not infinite). Finally, $C(\cdot)$ is an increasing function of λ which represents the size of the largest equally accessible industrial employment centre, and of ω which represents the real wage rate offered at other equally accessible locations. Thus, the term $-C(\omega, \lambda)$ captures the effect that a region is less attractive if its size and its wages are inferior to other regions and therefore the growth rate of labour in this region will be lower. The corresponding equation for capital is (see equation (9) of David & Rosenbloom):

$$\frac{\dot{K}}{K} = B(K, L) = \{S(K)\}F_K(K, L) - g \cdot K, \qquad (3.10)$$

where $g \cdot K$ is a simple linear relation which describes congestion that increases with capital, F_K is the partial derivative of the production function with respect to K (assumed to equal interest rate r) and $S(\cdot)$ is a positive sigmoid function that describes the effect of *learning by doing*[23] and of the diversity of the range of investment projects. As above, $S(\cdot)$ converges to some S^* as K increases. Thus, the growth rate of K and L depend on the spatial *density* of capital and labour, i.e. density measures the level of spatial external effects.

Functions (3.9) and (3.10) define a two-dimensional dynamic system in the K, L-plane. Three possible outcomes emerge from these system which are reproduced in Figure 3.9. There we see that the city either dies out (see 3.9.a), it

---

[22] See citation and footnote 13 on page 43.
[23] See the discussion in section 2.2.2.1 or in Arrow[1962].

3.3 The Role of Spatial Externalities in Production

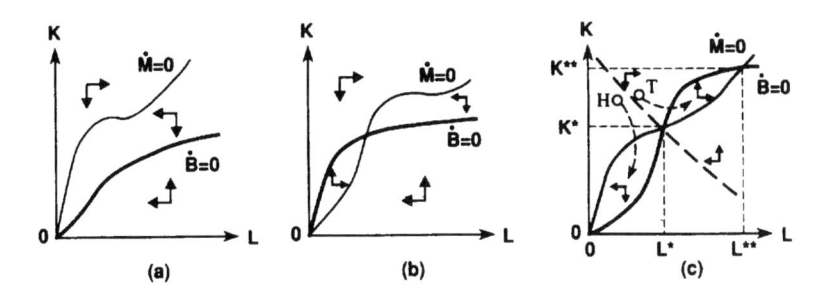

Figure 3.9: Three possible phase diagrams for the model of David & Rosenbloom [1990]

converges with probability 1 to some equilibrium point (see 3.9.b) or else it converges with probability 1 to some stable equilibrium point, either (K^{**}, L^{**}) or $(0,0)$, depending on the initial configuration of the city (see points T and H in Figure 3.9.c). Note, that in 3.9.c (K^*, L^*) is an unstable equilibrium, i.e. the city will move away from it if there is a small disturbance.

A similar argument was put forward by Ciccone and Hall[1996] although their formal setup is different. Like David and Rosenbloom they assume that density measures Marshallian externalities. In consequence, their production function models output in an acre of space (M):

$$Y = f(L, Y, M) = L^\alpha \left(\frac{Y}{M}\right)^{(g-1)/g}.$$

Hence Y is produced with labour, L and varies with density (Y/M) with elasticity $(g-1)/g$. Thus, if $g > 1$, output *increases* with density (positive Marshallian externalities) but if $g < 1$, output *decreases* with density. Thus the model is able to capture a congestion effect, i.e. the fact that high population density may lead to congestion of a given quantity of e.g. infrastructure. Note, that rearranging this production function we obtain

$$Y = L^{\alpha g} M^{1-\alpha g}$$

which is the classical constant returns to scale Cobb-Douglas production function with some flexibility added in the elasticities. Based on this function the authors develop a factor density index $D_i(\alpha)$ (see equation (4) of Ciccone & Hall) which they include in the following regression equation

$$\log \frac{Y_i}{L_i} = \beta_1 \log \phi + \beta_2 \eta \log h_i + \beta_3 \log D_i(\alpha) + \varepsilon_s$$

where Y_i/L_i is labour productivity in country i, ϕ, η and α are parameters estimated elsewhere and h_i is a measure for human capital of that country. Their results show that a doubling of the employment density increases the average labour productivity by 6 percent. Moreover, more than half of the variance of output per worker across states (!) can be explained by differences in the density of economic activity.

3.3.4 Models that Refer to Distance

The models presented in the preceding subsection used *spatial density* of labour as a proxy for the effects described by Marshall[1920]. Thus, they model spatial externalities *without referring explicitly to space* or *distance*. From a methodological viewpoint this is somewhat unsatisfactory. If proximity matters, distance should play a role in the theoretical set up. In this section I will present a group of models that explicitly considers some form of *distance*.

Jaffe[1989] investigated spatial spillovers of academic research in the US. For this purpose he implemented a spatial version of the *knowledge production function* suggested by Griliches[1979], which obeys a modified Cobb-Douglas structure:

$$\begin{aligned} \log(pat_{ikt}) &= \beta_{1k} \log(ind_{ikt}) + \beta_{2k} \log(uni_{ikt}) \\ &\quad + \beta_{3k} \left[\log(uni_{ikt}) \log(co_{ikt})\right] + \varepsilon_{ikt}, \end{aligned}$$

where i is units of observation (US-states) and k indexes technological areas which referred to 300 different patent classes that were grouped into 5 categories. *pat* is the number of corporate patents, *ind* is R&D performed by industry and *uni* is university research. *co* is an index of geographic coincidence of university and industrial research. This index is computed as a simple uncentered correlation between *uni* and the total professional employees enaged in private research across metropolitan statistical areas (MSA). The *measurement of distance* is implicit, since an observation is only included in the correlation if it is within the same MSA. In addition to the above production function, Jaffe assumed a recursive relationship between both types of research i.e. that university research depends on industry research and vice versa. Moreover he assumed that both depend on an overlapping but not identical set of characteristics ch_i, i.e.

$$\log(uni_{ikt}) = \beta_{4k} \log(ind_{ikt}) + \delta_{1k} ch_1 + \xi_{ikt}$$

and

$$\log(ind_{ikt}) = \beta_{5k} \log(uni_{ikt}) + \delta_{2k} ch_2 + \mu_{ikt}$$

As a whole, this yields a simultaneous system[24] that is estimated with 3SLS. Jaffe found evidence of the importance of spatial spillovers from universities to industries although these were more evident within specific technological areas and not across these areas. Thus his data provide evidence for Marshallian spillovers.

Anselin, Varga and Acs [1997] used the same formal model as Jaffe but suggested different measures for geographical coincidence *co*. Moreover, they employed spatial econometric methods to obtain more precise estimates of spatial spillovers.[25] Hence, distance is explicit in their theoretical setup but also in the econometric implementation. Their results confirm the findings of Jaffe.

Jaffe, Trajtenberg and Henderson [1993] refined the model of Jaffe [1989] and suggested an approach in which they investigated *where* R&D spillovers go *geographically*. Thus, they give a spatial interpretation of the endogenous growth literature.[26] To do so they measure the frequency of spatial citations of patents originating from a) universities, b) top corporates and c) other corporates. This frequency is compared with a control citation frequency that refers to the existing spatial distribution of technological activity. With this procedure, R&D-spillovers within an industry are measured implicitly since the citation of a patent means that the new patent is technologically related to the cited one and therefore originates from a related industry.

The authors measure this effect at three spatial levels a) the country (US) b) the state and c) the MSA level. They found that the higher the spatial disaggregation, the higher the relevance of space in patent citations. To avoid statistical artifacts, they distinguish between overall citation and citation excluding self-cites. They run a regression for data in 1975 and 1980 where university and corporate cites were pooled for all three levels of spatial aggregation using the

---

[24] Of course, the error terms of this system are not independent. Jaffe discusses this issue in section II.

[25] For a discussion of these methods see Anselin [1988] or section 6.4 of this book.

[26] Namely Jaffe *et al.* [1993] refer to Romer [1986, 1990] and to Grossman and Helpman [1991]. A non-spatial analysis of patent citations is given by Jaffe [1986]. See also the discussion in section 2.2.2.

following regression equation

$$g = \beta_1 cit + \beta_2 selfcit + \mathbf{D}\boldsymbol{\beta} + \varepsilon,$$

where g is geographic match between originating and citing patents, cit is log of citation, $selfcit$ is log of self citation and $\mathbf{D}$ is a matrix of dummy-variables. All estimates of $\beta_{1,2}$ (excluding the one for β_2 on the country level) were statistically significant. Thus, their approach gives significant empirical evidence that spatial externalities exist. Moreover, they could show that the citations diffuse spatially with age of the originating patent. Finally, they mention that quite an important proportion of citations (40%) are not confined to closely related regions of *technology* space. That is these citations come from firms outside the firm's immediate technological (as opposed to spatial) neighbourhood. This implies that *Jacobian externalities are also present*.

The results of Jaffe *et al.* were confirmed by Audretsch and Feldman[1996] although their paper had a different aim. Their objective was to analyze the *propensity for industrial activity to cluster spatially* and to investigate the role of local knowledge spillovers for it. This is of course very much in the spirit of Marshall[1920]. They computed *Gini coefficients* of the location of production and of innovation and regressed them against a number of variables – *natural resources, scale, transportation costs, industry R&D/sales, skilled labour, university research* and *Gini of innovation* or of *production* respectively. An interesting result was that there is no significant partial correlation between Gini of production and Gini of innovation. However, partial correlation between R&D and both Gini coefficients was significant, which means that industries with a high level of R&D tend to cluster spatially. Moreover, transportation costs, skilled labour and university research had a significant positive influence on the propensity of firms to cluster spatially. Taken together, the results of Audretsch and Feldman [1996] confirm the theories of Marshall[1920][27]. *distance* was implicit in their analysis in the construction of the locational Gini coeffients.

Finally Coe and Helpman[1995], who were interested in international R&D spillovers regressed (in a different perspective but similar formally)

$$\log A_i = \beta_i^{(0)} + \beta_i^{(d)} \log R_i^{(d)} + \beta_i^{(f)} im_i \log R_i^{(f)}$$

---

[27] In an interesting case study of local connections in the biotechnology industry, Audretsch and Stephan[1996] found significant local relations between university and industry researchers, although they were "anything but overwhelming".

where A_i is a measure of total factor productivity (TFP) of country i, $R_i^{(d)}$ is domestic R&D capital stock of this country and $R_i^{(f)}$ the foreign one which is weighed by im_i, the share of imports in GDP.[28] Although admittedly *distance* is not an important variable in this model, it is at least implicitly included in m_i as trade with near countries is probably more intensive than with remote countries. I included the model of their paper since it indicates that foreign R&D has beneficial effects on domestic TFP which and thus that Marshallian externalities also exist at an international level.

3.4 Summary and Conclusion

In this chapter I presented some economic literature that deals with the issue of spatial factor allocation and its consequences for regional development. We saw that the "traditional" models of spatial organization leave the question *why* economic activity concentrates in space unanswered. However an extension of these models (Krugman, 1991b, 1995, 1996) was able to tackle this problem.

Then I discussed spatial externalities in a production theoretical framework. I argued in section 3.3.1 that agglomeration economies and spatial externalities refer to the same phenomenon but are two different concepts that do not match. The literature presented thereafter highlighted and implemented different aspects of spatial externalities more or less explicitly. The oldest family of models implements increasing returns to scale in production to explain agglomeration of economic activity. Thus, they refer to the fact that it is profitable to concentrate an increasing returns to scale activity spatially i.e. in a strict sense, these models do not refer to spatial externalities.

A second – more recent – group of models uses density of labour (either in the same industry or in general) to implement Marshallian externalities. The idea here is that if spatial proximity matters in communicating ideas, then the higher the density of labour, the better these externalities can manifest. All models which are estimated empirically provide evidence in favour of Marshallian externalities though some papers also report evidence in favour of Jacobian externalities.

---

[28] Engelbrecht [1997] seemed to be unsatisfied with this model. He suggested an extension of the regression equation which then included human capital and a dummy variable for G7 countries. His estimates were somewhat smaller than those of Coe and Helpman [1995] but still statistically significant and positive.

Finally, a third approach uses distance to implement spatial externalities. From a methodological viewpoint this approach seems to be the most justifiable one since if space matters in communication of knowledge distance will play a predominant role. Although these models differ formally, their econometric results confirm the conclusion of the above models i.e. Marhsallian externalities are found to be significant but there is also some evidence in favour of Jacobian externalities. Overall, section 3.3 gave ample evidence that knowledge spillovers exist and that they have a spatial dimension

Some of the models presented in this chapter (namely Glaeser *et al.* [1992] and David and Rosenbloom [1990] who consider the consequences of spatial spillovers for factor growth) implicitly touched the growth literature without explicitly investigating the consequences of spatial spillovers on regional growth. Others were completely silent on this issue. In my view, *if* Marshallian externalities (or positive technological spatial spillovers) exist, they will not only foster concentration of economic activity but also the dynamics of regional growth. That is, forces that are responsible for the agglomeration of economic activity will also influence the growth dynamics of agglomerated regions. The growth dynamics of cities can therefore be expected to differ from those of rural areas. After all, agglomeration and growth can be interpreted as two sides of the same coin, growth being accumulation of factors in *time* and agglomeration being accumulation in *space*. In the following chapter I suggest a model that aims to make a link between these two forces.

Chapter 4

Spatial Knowledge Spillovers and the Dynamics of Agglomeration and Regional Growth

> *What can people be paying Manhattan or downtown Chicago rents for, if not being near other people?*
> ROBERT E. LUCAS

4.1 Introduction

As shown in chapter 2, the classical model of growth predicts regional convergence of growth rates of per-capita income. Indeed, on a *regionally aggregated* level – such as different countries or large administrative subregions of countries as e.g. the federal states of the US – we could observe regional convergence.[1] These regions have in common that they are similar in structure, i.e. they usually have rural and agglomerated areas and even some kind of capital that is the administrative centre of the country (or the region). However, as we took a closer look at *spatially disaggregated subregions* (in section 2.3.2.2) such a homogenous convergence patterns could no longer be observed. It is true that we observe convergence between agglomerated areas and their surrounding less densely populated areas. Rural areas however display a *non-converging* behaviour regarding their growth rate of per-capita income.[2] This is a puzzling observation which is not conform with the neoclassical growth theory. Apparently, the *character* of a region, i.e. whether it is a rural area, a suburb or a city deter-

---

[1] See Figure 2.5 on page 19.
[2] See the discussion in section 2.3.2.

mines its growth trajectory. This would imply that spatially aggregated analysis would simply average away the effects of regional factor accumulation and thus of regional growth.

In this chapter I will suggest a formal model for the analysis of these phenomena. The model will be developed in a production theoretical framework. The underlying hypothesis upon which it will be based is that once I consider regions at a spatial disaggregated level, I have to consider not only the dynamics of growth but also the dynamics of *agglomeration* since both types of dynamics can be described as dynamics of *factor accumulation*; growth being factor accumulation in *time* and agglomeration being factor accumulation in *space*.

* * *

The discussion in section 2.2.2 (page 8) has shown that factors used for production by some economic agent obeying a public good characteristic have the potential to spill over to other economic agents.[3] In section 2.2.2.1 we saw that *technological knowledge* (i.e. *human capital*) has this potential. Another possible candidate is *R&D-output* (as discussed in section 2.2.2.2). It is a main hypothesis underlying the approach of this chapter that *the process of spilling over* (as described in the endogenous growth literature) *has a spatial dimension.* The importance of this spatial dimension is given by the fact that what we call "spill over" is a result of *personal communication* i.e. exchange of knowledge between persons. The importance of personal contacts is not (or only slightly) altered by the use of telecommunication means since only knowledge that is entirely formalized (e.g. in form of a blueprint or an article) can be transmitted in this way. An important aspect of knowledge, however, whether in production or in research, consists in *unformalized knowledge*, acquired by practice and learning by doing. As Dosi[1988] puts it:

> *There are elements of being a 'good engineer', a 'good designer' or even a 'good mathematician' that cannot be entirely transmitted in an explicit algorithmic form.* (Dosi, 1988, p.224)

Dosi refers to *tacit knowledge* when alluding to this phenomenon. In this context it seems reasonable to distinguish between *information* that can be formalized and *knowledge* that may be culturally bound, partly tacit and therefore cannot be formalized completely. Several studies (e.g. Henderson, 1974, Audretsch

---

[3]This is due to the fact that these factors are (at least partially) nonrival. See the discussion in Section 2.2.2.2 or Romer[1990, p.S75].

and Feldman, 1996 or Audretsch and Stephan, 1996) show that unformalized knowledge may play a major role in the innovation of new products.

Now *if* unformalized knowledge is communicated personally, *distance* will be an important variable in this process, since the intensity of contacts between persons can be expected to be negatively correlated to the *distance between them*. In the discussion of section 3.3.1 (page 42) we saw that it was this aspect of localization that Marshall had in mind when he was alluding to "local trade secrets".[4] Note that if this spatial dimension of communication between agents exists, it is possible to transfer it to *regional aggregates* of agents: the closer two regions, the more they will be able to profit from the respective pool of human capital (R&D-output etc.) of the other region. This argument gives a spatial interpretation of the literature on endogenous growth.[5] Now *if* these spillovers have a spatial dimension then it follows from the discussion in chapter 3 that they will be one driving force in the dynamics of agglomeration.

With the model to be developed in this chapter I will investigate the hypothesis that *it is these forces of agglomeration (i.e. spatial spillovers of nonrival goods or factors) that are responsible for the inhomogeneous pattern of growth convergence*. To analyze this phenomenon, I consider different types of regional aggregates and different distances in the model.

The remainder of the chapter is organized as follows. I first discuss properties of positive external effects and how they can be implemented in a production function. In section 4.3 I present the model and discuss its consequences on regional factor allocation. In the subsequent section, the regional convergence dynamics of the model is analyzed. Section 4.5 summarizes the findings. Let me emphasize again that the aim of the model is to investigate how economic activity will be organized in space and the consequences of this spatial organization for regional growth dynamics rather than to analyze welfare distortions from spatial external effects. The latter is possible by a straightforward modification of the approach in Romer[1990, p.S96] and has been done thoroughly by Bode [1998] in the context of regional knowledge-spillovers.

---

[4]Indeed, in its Survey of Silicon Valley, the *Economist* [1997] identified *meetings in bars* as important for new ideas to be developed and disseminated. This effect is usually difficult to catch and this is why such reports (just like Marshall, 1920, p. 225; see citation on page 43) often refer to expressions like "something in the air" etc. Basically this expression circumscribes *unformalized localized technological knowledge.*

[5]See the discussion in section 2.2.2 or Romer[1986, 1990], Lucas[1988] as well as Mankiw et al.[1992] and Romer[1996].

4.2 Positive External Effects in Production. Properties and Implementation

4.2.1 Externalities: General Definition and Properties

The notion of *external effect* was (again) introduced by Marshall[1920] although he was solely concerned with external *economies*, i.e. positive external effects. According to Marshall (p. 221) an external economy arises from the development of the industry as a whole but also from the degree of organization of firms, which fosters communication and thus the exchange of relevant information. This definition corresponds mainly to what has been said in section 3.3.1.

Later, Pigou[1932] showed that externalities appear as "*one of the chief causes of divergencies between 'private net product' and 'social net product'*". Thus external effects will result in a suboptimal allocation of resources, i.e. to a deviation from the welfare optimum.[6] In the 1970's and 1980's, external effects had been rediscovered to explain the welfare consequences of environmental pollution and to derive economic instruments to reduce it.[7] Baumol and Oates' [1988, p. 17] definition of external effects includes two conditions

> 1.) An externality is present whenever some individual's (say A's) utility or production *relationships include real (...) variables, whose values are chosen by others (...) without particular attention to the effects on A's welfare. (...)*
> 2.) *The decision maker, whose activity affects others' utility level or enters their production functions, does not receive (pay) in compensation for this activity an amount equal in value to the resulting benefits (or costs) to others.*

A more formal definition is given by Buchanan and Stubblebine[1962] or Mishan[1971]. Let $F(\cdot)$ be a production function of an agent g such that

$$Y_g = F(\mathbf{i}, \mathbf{x}),$$

$\mathbf{i}$ being a vector of factors internal to g and $\mathbf{x}$ being a vector of factors external to g but internal to another agent, say h. h is said to *exert an external effect* on g if he chooses the level of $\mathbf{x}$ (his $\mathbf{i}$) and thus influences the output of g without involving compensation. Since I assume throughout this book that economic

---

[6]To improve this situation Pigou[1932, p. 224] suggested imposing a tax on negative externalities or to pay a subsidy for positive externalities. This approach has been extended by a number of authors. See e.g. Baumol and Oates[1988] or Mishan[1971] for a survey of the literature.

[7]See Baumol and Oates[1988] or Endres[1994].

activity of a region exerts a *positive* external effect on its neighbours, I will discuss the properties of this type of externality at a formal level. Based on these properties I will determine the functional form to be used in the analysis of the subsequent sections.

1. If an externality is present, we should expect that the properties of the internal factors be unaffected. Thus, Inada conditions 1.) and 3.) of page 6 should still hold. Condition 2.) will hold if we account only for internal factors, it will be violated however if we include both, internal and external factors.

2. The primary condition for **x** to be an externality is of course

$$\partial F / \partial x_j \neq 0, \quad \forall j,$$

where x_j is the jth element of **x**. x_j is said to exert a *positive* externality if

$$\partial F / \partial x_j > 0, \quad \forall j.$$

3. It also is plausible that a positive external effect increases the marginal factor productivity of internal factors. That is

$$\frac{\partial^2 F}{\partial i_k \partial x_j} > 0 \quad \forall j, k$$

where i_k is the kth element of **i**.

4. In a regional interpretation of spillovers we can expect output to rise if the external factor immigrates into region A, i.e. if it is *internalized*. This is due to the fact that only part of the factor of a region B spills over to A. Once it is internalized however (i.e. $x \to i$), it will fully contribute to the output of A (and now spill over to B). Suppose that i_k and x_j be *functionally separable* from the other elements of **i** and **x**, i.e. they can be aggregated.[8] Then we can set $i_k = \phi G$ and $x_j = (1 - \phi)G$, ϕ being a share parameter. Migration of x_j into region A now implies that ϕ increases. Then the condition

$$\partial F / \partial \phi > 0$$

---

[8] For a discussion of separability see e.g. Berndt and Christensen[1973].

should hold. The intuition behind this condition is that if x_j and i_k are, say, human capital, then an immigration of x_j increases i_k and thus should increase output. This is not automatically the case, since an immigration decreases x_j, thus the positive externality and therefore Y_A will decrease as well. Hence the condition states that the *net effect* of immigration be positive.[9]

5. The implication of immigration on the marginal productivity of **i** depends on the separability of the immigrating factor with respect to **i**. Take again x_j and i_k as functionally separable from other factors. Then it follows from the Inada conditions (page 6) that

$$\frac{\partial^2 F}{\partial i_k \partial \phi} < 0 \quad \forall k$$

since now two mechanisms intervene. First, an increase in i_k (from the immigration of x_j) decreases its marginal product. Second, since now x_j decreases, we see from condition 3 that $\partial F / \partial i_k$ decreases.

The situation is different if x_j is *not* functionally separable from a second internal input, i_l. Then an immigration of x_j, which increases i_k will induce a net increase of the marginal productivity of i_l, i.e.

$$\frac{\partial^2 F}{\partial i_l \partial \phi} > 0 \quad \forall l$$

The justification of this behaviour corresponds to the one given in condition 4.

6. Finally, we expect that if no externality is present (i.e. only internal factors are used), the output is nevertheless positive.

4.2.2 Functional Implementation of Externalities

A number of forms of production functions are used in the literature. In this section I will discuss four of these. Specifically, I will analyze which of the above conditions fulfil. As a general form I use a three factor function $Y_A = F(i_1, i_2, x_1)$, where i_1, i_2 are internal factors and x_1 is an external factor that spills over to region A.

---

[9] The opposite effect $\partial F / \partial (1 - \phi) < 0$ follows immediately.

1. The simplest functional form is the *additive* production function where

$$Y_A = \alpha i_1 + \beta i_2 + \gamma x_1.$$

   Note however, that neither condition 1 is fulfilled nor exists any cross derivative. Thus, this functional form is not appropriate.

2. A functional form often used in theoretical analysis is the *Cobb-Douglas* production function:[10]

$$Y_A = i_1^\alpha i_2^\beta x_1^\gamma.$$

   This function fulfills all conditions but 6. This is due to the fact that x_1 is a necessary input, i.e. if $x_1 = 0$, the whole function degenerates to 0. This is somewhat implausible if x_1 is an external effect.

3. A combination of the two previous functions which avoids the problem of the pure Cobb-Douglas type would be

$$Y_A = (i_1 + \gamma \cdot x_1)^\alpha \cdot i_2^\beta$$

   However, with this functional form, condition 3 is violated and thus this form cannot be used.

4. A generalization of the additive and the Cobb-Douglas type is of course the CES-function.[11] Here, we obtain

$$Y_A = (\alpha i_1^\varrho + \beta i_2^\varrho + \gamma x_1^\varrho)^{1/\varrho},$$

   which becomes additive if $\varrho = 1$ and Cobb-Douglas for $\varrho \to 0$. For any $\varrho \in (0, 1)$ we obtain a function that meets all of the above requirements.

Hence, the CES implementation seems to be most appropriate for an analysis of externalities. Later however, in a multiple region setting, I will need to build and analyze spatial aggregates of output, which is not possible with the CES-function since partial factor derivatives cannot be built. Thus, I will approximate it with the Cobb-Douglas function, knowing that the boundaries (where $\mathbf{x} = \mathbf{0}$) are not included.

---

[10] First published in Cobb and Douglas[1928].
[11] Published by Arrow, Chenery, Minhas and Solow[1961].

4.3 The Model

In the model that follows I consider two regions (A, B), each region hosting an exogenously given number of firms. Each firm is subject to external effects (or *knowledge spillovers*) from the other firms and will itself generate such effects.

The analysis of the model will be as follows. I first investigate the consequences of spillovers between the firms of one of the two regions. For simplification purposes, I will limit the analysis to two firms (in appendix A.1 I extend the analysis to an arbitrary number of firms). In a next step (section 4.3.2), I consider the consequences of different levels of knowledge spillovers between both regions. As to the dynamics of spatial factor allocation, the results of this model do not differ fundamentally from existing models based on *new trade theory* (e.g. Krugman, 1991b, 1995, 1996). However, since my approach is based on production theory, it allows me to extend the analysis and to investigate the dynamics of regional growth and convergence (which is done in section 4.4).

4.3.1 The Incidence of Spillovers Between Firms of One Region

Consider two firms $i = 1, 2$ situated in region A which both employ specific production factors – capital, labour and technological knowledge – to produce some output Y_i. As argued above, some part of the technological knowledge (or "human capital") used by one firm will spill over to the other firm situated in the same area, hence nearby. For the sake of simplicity we incorporate this factor into capital, thus employing a "broad concept of capital"[12] Let both firms be endowed with identical Cobb-Douglas technology. Then, a simple specification of this relationship would be[13]

$$Y_i = \left(K_i \cdot K_j^\delta\right)^\alpha L_i^\beta \qquad (4.1)$$
$$\text{with } i, j = 1, 2;\ i \neq j;$$
$$\alpha, \beta, \delta \in [0, 1],$$

---

[12]This is to reduce the dimensionality of the model. An extension would increase the dimension of the phase space but not the behaviour of the model. The same concept was used e.g. by Barro, Mankiw and Sala-i-Martin[1995].

[13]I we assume instead a part of *R&D output* to spill over, a possible specification would be

$$Y_i = \left(K_i \cdot Y_j^\delta\right)^\alpha L_i^\beta.$$

However, its dynamic properties can be shown to identical to the one of eq. (4.1)

Thus the total factor endowment of region A is $K_A = K_1 + K_2$, $L_A = L_1 + L_2$ and the spatial factor distribution of this region can be described using *share parameters*:

$$K_1 = \phi K_A; \quad K_2 = (1-\phi) K_A,$$
$$L_1 = \theta L_A; \quad L_2 = (1-\theta) L_A,$$

Rewriting equation (4.1) we obtain

$$\begin{aligned} Y_1 &= [\phi K_A]^\alpha [(1-\phi) K_A]^{\alpha\delta} [\theta L_A]^\beta \\ Y_2 &= [(1-\phi) K_A]^\alpha [\phi K_A]^{\alpha\delta} [(1-\theta) L_A]^\beta \end{aligned} \quad (4.2)$$

Assume for a moment the quantity of K_A and L_A to be fixed (an assumption that will be relaxed in the subsequent section). Then the firms' output $Y_i, i = 1, 2$ is a function of ϕ and θ alone. The use of factor shares, rather than absolute factor quantities allows me to clearly distinguish the effect of migration *between the firms of one region* (which will affect factor-shares) and the effect of factor-immigration *from outside region A* which does not necessarily affect factor shares. If factors migrate between firms, shares will of course change which will change the ratio of marginal factor products, but will leave the factor aggregates (K_A and L_A) untouched. If factors immigrate from outside (e.g. through labour migration, private or public investment) the factor aggregates will grow, which does not affect the ratio of the firms' marginal factor products unless the factor shares are affected by this immigration.

Suppose that both factors can move freely between firms of region A, then they will move to the firm that offers higher wage or rent. Hence, the capital share of firm 1 (ϕ) increases if firm 1 offers a higher capital rent, it will decrease (i.e. $1 - \phi$ increases) if the rent is lower. It will finally remain constant if both firms offer identical capital rents. The share of labour (θ) will behave correspondingly for differences in wage. Assume that factor wages equal their marginal product of production function (4.1). This implies that factor revenues might differ from the private marginal product (i.e. the one without external effects). Basically, this assumption reflects the fact that all factors will benefit from economies of agglomeration and is consistent with the fact that they receive higher wages in agglomerated areas. This statement is reflected e.g. in the citation at the beginning of this chapter. Based on this assumption we can state the following equations of motion for the factor shares (ϕ, θ):

$$\begin{aligned}\dot{\phi} &= \pi\left(\frac{\partial Y_1}{\partial \phi} - \frac{\partial Y_2}{\partial (1-\phi)}\right) \\ \dot{\theta} &= \tau\left(\frac{\partial Y_1}{\partial \theta} - \frac{\partial Y_2}{\partial (1-\theta)}\right),\end{aligned} \quad (4.3)$$

where π, τ are functions that describe the degree of response of factor migration with respect to wage differences. I will assume that no migration occurs if the wage difference is zero. Then π and τ are homogeneous functions. Moreover I will assume that π and τ are increasing functions, i.e. a higher wage in a certain region will lead to increased immigration. It can be shown that with these assumptions the behaviour of the phase space (i.e. the number and characteristics of the zero-growth loci and the behaviour of $\dot{\phi}$ and $\dot{\theta}$ outside them) is identical for all π, τ. Therefore, in the following analysis I set π, τ as identity functions for simplicity. Then, the share of K_A (L_A) employed by firm 1 (by firm 2) will increase as long as the marginal product of capital (of labour) is higher in firm 1 (firm 2).

Inserting equations (4.2) into (4.3) we obtain a two-dimensional dynamic system of order one in ϕ and θ. Region A will be in *spatial equilibrium* if none of the factors has an incentive to migrate, i.e. if $\dot{\phi} = 0$ and $\dot{\theta} = 0$. Solving this system numerically we obtain the solutions

$$\phi = \theta \text{ if } \delta = 0 \quad \text{and} \quad \phi^* = \theta^* = 0.5 \text{ if } \delta > 0$$

The phase space of this system is given in Figure 4.1; the dashed line represents the zero-growth loci of $\dot{\phi}$ and the solid line is where $\dot{\theta} = 0$. Hence, the system is in spatial equilibrium where these two lines intersect (note that if $\delta = 0$ these two lines degenerate to a single one). We see from the phase space that the solutions represent *stable attractors*, i.e. the system *converges to* the zero-growth loci. Note, from equation (4.1) that the case of $\delta = 0$ corresponds to the neoclassical case. We see from Figure 4.1.a that this model does not make a statement as to spatial factor distribution since it simply predicts equal factor proportions in both regions i.e. shares might converge to every $\phi = \theta \in [0, 1]$. If $\delta > 0$ the model predicts identical factor endowment for every firm in the equilibrium (see Figure 4.1.b for an illustration). This result is known from the literature on agglomeration economies (e.g. Rivera-Batitz, 1988) though obtained by a different approach.

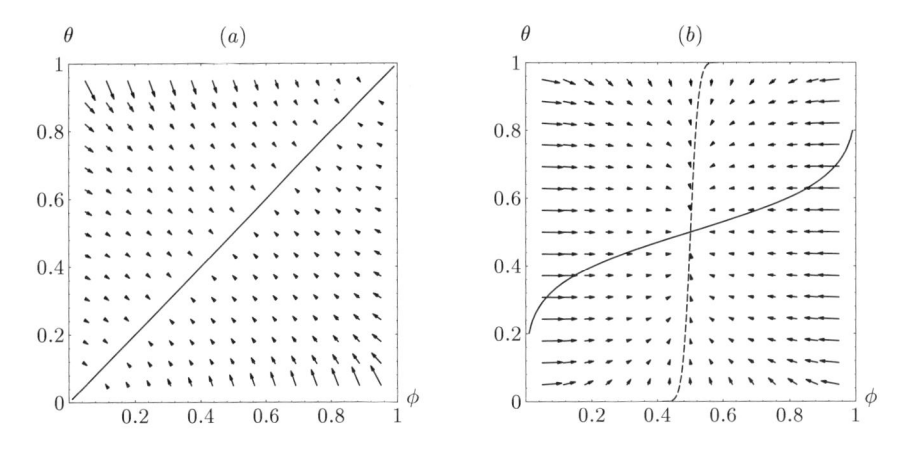

Figure 4.1: Dynamics of factor migration between two firms if $\delta = 0$ (a: no spillovers between firms) and $\delta > 0$ (b: spillovers between firms)

4.3.2 The Incidence of Spillovers Between Regions

Above, I argued that distance matters if we consider spatial phenomena. In the case of spatial factor spillovers this implies that the further apart regions are, the weaker the spillover interactions between them. Let us consider in this section *two regions A, B*. Assume that both can be described by the model discussed in the previous section, i.e. by a set of two of firms that interact via spillovers. Think of region A and B as two more or less remote areas of a city, as a city and its suburb or the rural area that surrounds it, as the Silicon Valley vs. Route 128, or as a country in Europe vs. a country in Africa. The output of region A can now be described as

$$Y_A = Y_1 + Y_2 = K_A^{\alpha(1+\delta)} L_A^{\beta} \cdot \underbrace{\left(\phi^\alpha (1-\phi)^{\alpha\delta} \theta^\beta + (1-\phi)^\alpha \phi^{\alpha\delta} (1-\theta)^\beta \right)}_{\mu},$$

whereas μ simplifies considerably if the equilibrium is attained.[14] Assume that a similar function exists for region B and that spillovers exist as well between regions A and B that will be captured by a parameter Δ.

To take distance into account, assume that Δ increases with the technical parameter δ but decreases with distance. Thus, if the technical parameter δ

---

[14] μ can be interpreted as parameter that embodies level-effects of the factor-distribution under Marshallian Externalities. If $\delta > 0$ and $\phi = \theta = 0.5$ then $\mu = 2 \cdot 0.5^{\alpha(1+\delta)+\beta} < 1$ (note that in the neoclassical case $\mu = 1$). However, the following analysis holds for arbitrary $\phi, \theta \in [0, 1]$.

(which describes spillovers between firms) is high, spillovers between regions A and B might potentially be high as well. On the other hand, the more the regions are remote, the lower the actual spillovers between A and B will be under a given δ. It follows that Δ cannot be superior to δ since δ is determined by technical conditions. We specify this relation as follows

$$Y_i = \mu \left(K_i \cdot K_j^\Delta\right)^{\alpha(1+\delta)} L_i^\beta \qquad (4.4)$$
$$i, j = A, B, \ i \neq j, \ \Delta \in [0, \delta].$$

Note the similarity to equation (4.1). To analyze the consequences of distant spillovers we distinguish two cases: $\Delta = 0$ and $\Delta > 0$.

4.3.2.1 Dynamics of Factor Allocation if the Coefficient of Spillover $\Delta = 0$

Suppose there are no spillovers between two remote regions i.e. $\Delta = 0$. Think of two regions distant enough to eliminate all possible spatial externalities or of knowledge that is not useful for the respective regions.[15] Although, the assumption of zero spillovers might be somewhat restrictive I will nevertheless discuss it and use it as a benchmark for the subsequent analysis. Setting $\Delta = 0$, equation (4.4) simplifies and we obtain

$$\begin{aligned} Y_A &= \mu K_A^{\alpha(1+\delta)} L_A^\beta \\ Y_B &= \mu K_B^{\alpha(1+\delta)} L_B^\beta \end{aligned} \qquad (4.5)$$

Production functions (4.5) are homogeneous of degree $\alpha(1+\delta)+\beta$, i.e. each region A, B obeys increasing returns to scale in capital and labour if $\delta > \frac{1-\beta-\alpha}{\alpha}$. Hence if $\alpha + \beta = 1$ (i.e. production has constant returns to scale to the private factors of each firm) we have increasing returns if $\delta > 0$ (i.e. if spillovers occur). Note, that the production function may display increasing returns even for $\alpha + \beta < 1$ if the spillover coefficient δ is sufficiently high.

To analyze the spatial allocation of capital and labour for remote regions we follow the procedure of the previous section. Suppose that the quantity of capital and labour in the economy is fixed, i.e. $\mathbf{K} = K_A + K_B$ and $\mathbf{L} = L_A + L_B$. Let me describe the spatial distribution of these two factors by two

---

[15] This might be a reasonable assumption if we consider spillovers between rural areas and cities. A part of the human capital that is useful in a city might simply be useless in the countryside and vice versa.

4.3 The Model

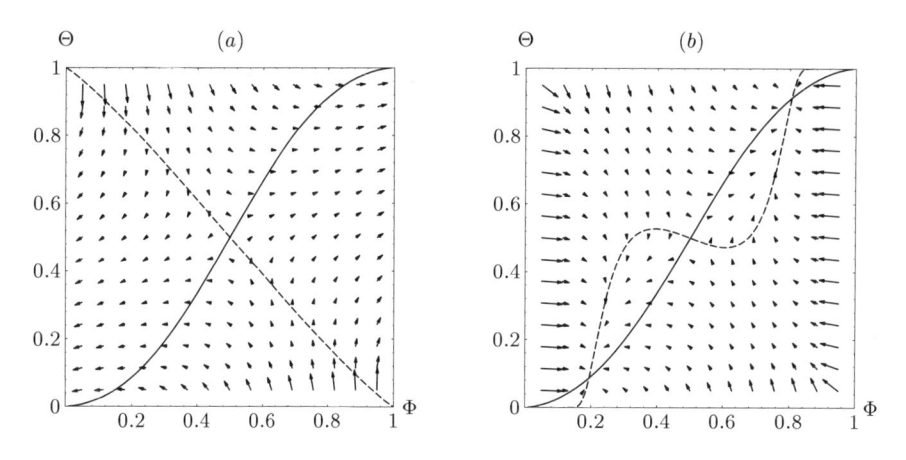

Figure 4.2: Dynamics of factor migration between two remote regions if $\delta > 0$ and $\Delta = 0$ (a) or $\Delta > 0$ (b) respectively

share-parameters $\Phi, \Theta \in [0, 1]$

$$K_A = \Phi \mathbf{K}; \quad K_B = (1 - \Phi)\mathbf{K},$$
$$L_A = \Theta \mathbf{L}; \quad L_B = (1 - \Theta)\mathbf{L}.$$

Rewriting equations (4.5) using these share parameters we obtain

$$\begin{aligned} Y_A &= \mu[\Phi \mathbf{K}]^{\alpha(1+\delta)}[\Theta \mathbf{L}]^\beta \\ Y_B &= \mu[(1-\Phi)\mathbf{K}]^{\alpha(1+\delta)}[(1-\Theta)\mathbf{L}]^\beta \end{aligned} \quad (4.6)$$

Assuming again that factors migrate to regions that offer higher wages we state the equations of motion

$$\begin{aligned} \dot\Phi &= \Pi\left(\frac{\partial Y_A}{\partial \Phi} - \frac{\partial Y_B}{\partial(1-\Phi)}\right) \\ \dot\Theta &= \mathrm{T}\left(\frac{\partial Y_A}{\partial \Theta} - \frac{\partial Y_B}{\partial(1-\Theta)}\right) \end{aligned} \quad (4.7)$$

where Π and T are again identity functions for simplicity. Solving the system numerically for $\dot\Phi = \dot\Theta = 0$ we obtain a set of two solutions

$$(\Phi^*, \Theta^*) = (0, 0) \quad \text{and} \quad (\Phi^*, \Theta^*) = (1, 1),$$

i.e. either region A or region B will receive the entire factor share. Figure 4.2.a shows the phase space for this system of differential equations. We can see that the system converges to either of both possible solutions. Figure 4.2 also allows us to identify these points as stable equilibrium. If $\Phi = \Theta = 0.5$, regions A and B have identical marginal returns to capital and labour. Therefore there is no incentive for factors to migrate, i.e. $\dot{\Phi} = \dot{\Theta} = 0$. However we see from Figure 4.2 that this point is an *unstable equilibrium*, i.e. the system (4.7) will evolve to one of the stable solutions if a small deviation of this point occurs. In our context such a small deviation could be the migration of one worker or one unit of capital. *Which* of the stable solutions will be obtained cannot be predicted since this first move of one factor is a random event. Thus, the system possesses multiple equilibria and is *path-dependent*.[16]

4.3.2.2 Dynamics of Factor Allocation if the Coefficient of Spillover $\Delta > 0$

To assume no spillovers between two regions is probably somewhat strict, even if they are very distant. Think of two remote centres of the same branch (e.g. the Silicon Valley and Route 128 for the computer industry). It is obvious that the exchange of ideas is more lively between firms *within* one area but such an exchange certainly also exists, though less intensively, between firms of both regions. It is probably just as strict to assume zero knowledge spillovers between city and countryside (think e.g. of agricultural research in universities, i.e. in cities). It seems therefore reasonable to analyze the case of $\Delta > 0$. Equation (4.4) now becomes

$$Y_A = \mu K_A^{\alpha(1+\delta)} K_B^{\Delta\alpha(1+\delta)} L_A^{\beta}$$
$$Y_B = \mu K_B^{\alpha(1+\delta)} K_A^{\Delta\alpha(1+\delta)} L_B^{\beta}. \quad (4.8)$$

As above we rewrite equations (4.8) using share parameters to obtain

$$Y_A = \mu[\Phi \mathbf{K}]^{\alpha(1+\delta)}[(1-\Phi)\mathbf{K}]^{\Delta\alpha(1+\delta)}[\Theta \mathbf{L}]^{\beta}$$
$$Y_B = \mu[(1-\Phi)\mathbf{K}]^{\alpha(1+\delta)}[\Phi \mathbf{K}]^{\Delta\alpha(1+\delta)}[(1-\Theta)\mathbf{L}]^{\beta} \quad (4.9)$$

The equations of motion are of course identical to the ones given in equation 4.7. However, solving (4.7) for $\dot{\Phi} = \dot{\Theta} = 0$ yields different solutions in the case of $\Delta > 0$ and therefore the system behaves differently. In the phase space

---

[16] For a discussion of path-dependence in agglomeration see Arthur [1994] who discussed it within a formal context different to the one suggested here.

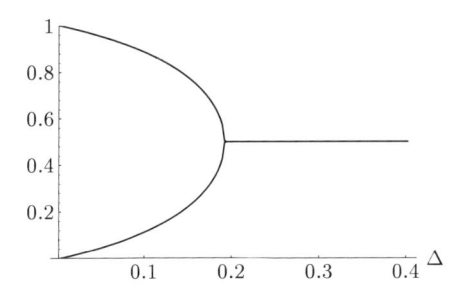

Figure 4.3: Bifurcation diagram: stable attractors of Φ, Θ as a function of Δ

we observe two different types of behaviour: for "low" Δ the system converges to either of two pairs $(\Phi, \Theta) \neq (0,0); (1,1)$. An example is given in Figure 4.2.b. If Δ increases towards δ, these two points converge to $(0.5, 0.5)$ and the phase space is then comparable to the one given in Figure 4.1.b on page 71[17]. Hence if $\Delta > 0$ the vertices $(0,0)$ and $(1,1)$ are not a stable solution anymore (as in the case of $\Delta = 0$). The bifurcation diagram of Figure 4.3 shows the stable attractors as a function of Δ (for given values of α, β and δ). Here the notion of "low" Δ becomes more operational: it simply means "below the bifurcation point". This point varies with α, β and δ. Since an increase of Δ can be interpreted as the two regions becoming integrated, this property of the model is consistent with the fact that factors migrate out of a city to a surrounding area if communication between both regions is facilitated.

To summarize, the model so far predicts that under existence of knowledge spillovers an agglomeration pattern (a spatial concentration of factors)[18] will be established and that within one region firms tend to an equal factor distribution. Let me now turn to the analysis of convergence dynamics that follows from this process.

4.4 Marshallian Externalities and the Convergence of Regions

As shown in section 2.3.2, the question of convergence has been widely discussed in recent years. Section 2.3.2.1 has made evident that the neoclassical model of (exogenous) growth predicts decreasing growth rates of income per

---

[17]The movement ($\Delta \to \delta$) can be interpreted as the *two regions becoming integrated*.

[18]On a larger regional level the outcome of the model can be seen as a spatial interpretation of the ideas developed in Lucas[1990].

capita when its level increases. This implies that regions are predicted to converge to their steady state value. Equation (2.10) on page 17 showed that this property holds for all production functions that are concave. β-convergence, means that poor regions tend to grow faster than rich ones, which implies that poor regions tend to *catch-up* with the per-capita income of richer ones. We also saw in section 2.3.2 that this prediction is far from being uncontroversial. I will argue in this section that it might depend on the *spatial level of analysis* whether the regional unit considered tends to display divergent or convergent behaviour.

The proposition that only convex function imply β-convergence has also been challenged by a literature that stands in the tradition of real business cycles[19] and that assumes a stochastic evolution of the technology parameter A as used e.g. in equation (2.2) is stochastic ("technology shocks"). The assumption of the form of stochastic disturbances is however often unrealistic[20]. Moreover, it is unsatisfying to assume stochastic evolution of technology when the technology is to be modeled. Thus, from the point of view presented in this book, this critique cannot falsify the approach taken by Barro and Sala-i-Martin [1992] to measure convergence. To proceed with the analysis, le me define a region as *displaying converging behaviour* if

$$\frac{\partial g_k}{\partial k} < 0, \qquad (4.10)$$

i.e. if the growth rate of capital per worker k decreases with an increase of its stock.[21] To investigate the behaviour of g_k on different regional levels I will assume that the stock of labour is constant (i.e. $g_L = 0$). This simplifying assumption will help to keep the analysis tractable. I will nevertheless carry out the analysis in the complete K, L-space (or in the ϕ, θ-space), i.e. for different values of L. A numerical analysis suggests that the qualitative behaviour of the model does not change with this simplification. Then, the condition for converging behaviour becomes $\partial g_K / \partial K < 0$, i.e. the growth rate of capital should be negatively correlated with the capital stock.

I will study this condition for a single region and for the aggregate of both regions. To analyze the behaviour of a single region I will first look at the convergence behaviour of its smallest unit – the firm – considering different levels

---

[19] See Kelly[1992], Kocherlakota and Yi[1995] and Leung and Quah[1966]. For the approach of real business cycles see Long and Plosser[1983].
[20] See the discussion in Aghion and Howitt[1998].
[21] See the discussion in Barro and Sala-i-Martin[1995, p. 26].

of δ. Then I will look at region A (resp. B), i.e. the aggregate of both firms distinguishing two cases: firms are out of spatial equilibrium (i.e. if $\dot\phi$ and $\dot\theta \neq 0$) and firms are in spatial equilibrium. in the first case it is interesting to look at the convergence dynamics of region A while firms converge to spatial equilibrium, in the second case it will be interesting to analyze an increase of K_A (resp. K_B). Finally I will take a look at the convergence dynamics of the spatial aggregate of regions A and B again distinguishing a) different levels of Δ and b) situations out of equilibrium and in equilibrium.

The motivation to investigate the convergence property of different spatial aggregates as predicted by the model is to receive some hindsight on what we can expect to observe if we analyze empirically the convergence properties of real life spatial aggregates.

4.4.1 Convergence Properties of Firms

1. Let me start with the smallest regional unit, the firm, and the simplest case: no spatial spillovers. Let F be a production function of this firm. If we assume $g_L = 0$ we obtain from the fundamental differential equation of the neoclassical growth model

$$g_K = s \cdot F(K, L)/K - d.$$

If we express the function using factor shares, the following expression is equivalent

$$g_\phi = s \cdot F(\phi, \theta)/\phi - d.$$

Deriving this equation with respect to ϕ we obtain

$$\frac{\partial g_\phi}{\partial \phi} = \frac{s}{\phi} \cdot \left[F_\phi(\phi, \theta) - \frac{F(\phi, \theta)}{\phi} \right]$$

i.e. a firm displays converging behaviour if the marginal product of capital is smaller than its average product. For a production function of Cobb-Douglas type – like function (4.2) where $\delta = 0$ – we know that $F_\phi = \alpha \cdot F/\phi$, i.e. marginal product is not higher than average product if $\alpha \leq 1$ (which is the case by definition). Thus, a firm will display converging behaviour in this simple case.

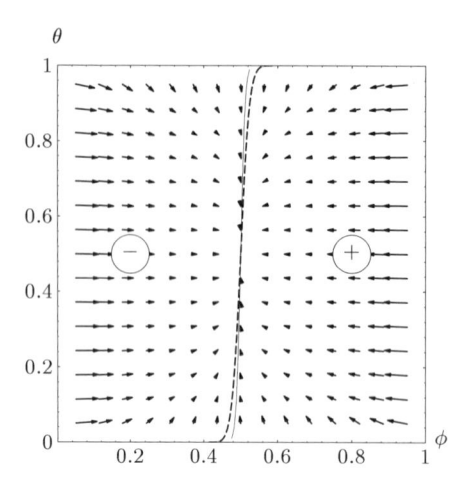

Figure 4.4: Convergence property of the aggregate of two firms. "−" denotes convergence with increasing ϕ and "+" denotes divergence

2. If $\delta > 0$, the situation is more complex since now the firms are interdependent, an increase of ϕ implying a decrease of $1 - \phi$. However, it is rather easy to show that the convergence condition (4.10) is fulfilled if

$$\underbrace{\frac{\alpha - 1}{\phi}}_{<0} - \underbrace{\frac{\alpha\delta}{1 - \phi}}_{>0} < 0$$

which is the case by definition as can be seen from the signs. Firms will therefore converge no matter the level of spillovers.

4.4.2 Convergence Properties of the Regional Aggregate of Firms

1. I define the growth rate of the regional aggregate to be the arithmetic mean of the growth rates of both firms. Let me first consider the implication of a change in the capital share of the firms, leaving the stock of capital in region A constant. Then

$$g_A = \frac{1}{2}(g_\phi + g_{1-\phi}) = \frac{1}{2}\left(\frac{\dot{\phi}}{\phi} - \frac{\dot{\phi}}{1 - \phi}\right).$$

The derivative of this term with respect to ϕ is too complex to be presented here. Figure 4.4 presents the result graphically. We see that the convergence property is not uniform. If ϕ is below some critical level, the aggregate displays convergence (denoted with "$-$"), above that level it shows divergent ("$+$") behaviour. However, since $\dot{\phi}$ is negative in the divergence-region, the system displays convergence on its way to spatial equilibrium. Note that there is a small corridor, where some trajectories might enter such that the system displays temporarily divergent behaviour. On the largest part of the (ϕ, θ)-space however, the system will converge and therefore we can expect to observe convergence if we look at spatial aggregates of firms.

2. If the firms are in spatial equilibrium, and $\Delta = 0$ (no spatial externalities exist between regions), the aggregate production function is given by equation (4.4). Following the discussion above, the aggregate will now display *divergence* in growth rates if $F_K > F/K$, i.e. if $\alpha > 1/(1 + \delta)$. Thus if – in an empirical analysis of growth rates – we look at spatial aggregates of firms we can expect to observe divergence.

It would of course be interesting to consider both effects simultaneously: a shift in ϕ and an increase in K_A. I expect that the dynamics is a simple additive combination of the two types discussed above and leave this question for further research.

4.4.3 Convergence Properties of an Aggregate of Regions

To analyze the behaviour of an aggregate of regions, I suppose that the firms of each region are in spatial equilibrium. This will help to keep the model tractable. The convergence properties then are as follows.

1. If the subregions are in spatial equilibrium, and $\Delta = 0$ we have divergence if $\alpha > 1/(1 + \delta)$ (see discussion above).

2. If $\Delta > 0$, i.e. spatial spillovers between regions exist, the aggregate production function is now described by equation (4.8). Using the same criterion as above, we find that region A (or B symmetrically) displays *diverging* behaviour if

$$\Phi < \left(\frac{\alpha(1+\delta)\Delta}{\alpha(1+\delta) - 1} + 1 \right)^{-1} \quad \text{as long as} \quad \alpha > 1/(1+\delta)$$

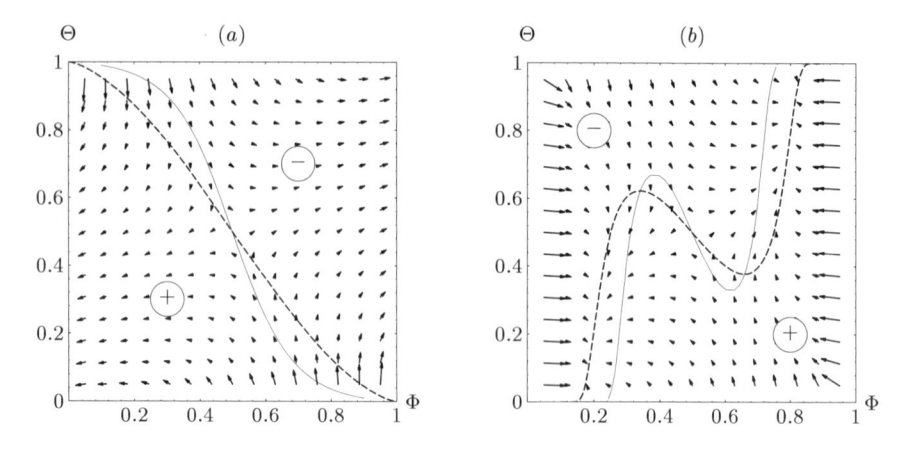

Figure 4.5: Convergence property of the aggregate of two regions where $\Delta = 0$ (a) and $\Delta > 0$ (b)

or with the relation signs inverted. Thus region A (resp. B) displays divergence until a critical level is attained, then it will display convergence. Thus we will have *temporary divergence*.

3. Let us finally take a look at the aggregate on its way to spatial equilibrium. As above we have

$$g_{A\cup B} = \frac{1}{2}(g_\Phi + g_{1-\Phi}).$$

Let me again present the convergence property graphically. In Figures 4.5.a and 4.5.b we see that in the largest part of the phase space $g_{A\cup B}$ decreases with $\dot{\Phi}$, i.e. where $\dot{\Phi}$ is positive, $g_{A\cup B}$ is negative and vice versa. Thus in these areas the systems displays converging behaviour. Note however, that in both cases there are areas where $\dot{\Phi}$ and $g_{A\cup B}$ have the same sign. This implies that although the regions might display divergence, their spatial aggregate will display convergence. Nevertheless, the spatial aggregate might temporaily display divergence, depending on the intial distribution of shares.

Thus, if we analyze empirically the dynamics of regional convergence, though we can expect convergence at the level of firms, their spatial aggregate might display diverging behaviour but an aggregate of regions will again converge. Table 4.1 summarizes these findings.

Table 4.1: *Convergence properties on different levels of spatial aggregates*

Firms	Convergence
Spatial Aggregate of Firms	*Divergence, Convergence* or *Temporary Divergence*
Regional Aggregate	*Convergence*

4.5 Summary and Conclusion

In this chapter I suggest an approach that analyzes the dynamics of factor allocation under spatial externalities in a production theoretical framework. The model is able to explain a number of phenomena. First, the model is able to explain the emergence of cities from a self-reinforcing dynamics of knowledge accumulation. The model thus gives a formal account of the theories suggested by Marshall[1920]. So far, the model confirms findings of other approaches which are based on a different theoretical background, namely trade theory. If the variables in the model are inerpreted as factors of one industry, the model can be considered as one of the formation of *industrial districts*. Moreover, the model is able to explain why some of the factors move out of the city to a surrounding area when both regions become integrated. The model finally can explain why a countryside-agglomeration dichotomy persists despite the self-reinforcing dynamics of spatial knowledge accumulation.

The fact that the model in this section is based on production theory allows me to extend the analysis and to consider the convergence dynamics of growth rates. I can show that, depending on the spatial level of analysis, regions will display either converging or diverging behaviour. However in the spatial aggregate, regions will converge although they might temporarily diverge. Thus, the model is able to explain why we observe convergence in a regionally aggregated dataset (Federal States or countries) whereas in a regionally disaggregated dataset the growth dynamics is more heterogeneous.

The model can be extended in several ways. An interesting direction would certainly be to disintegrate factor shares and regional factor stocks, i.e. to formulate the model with actual factor quantities. However, this will alter the modelling approach considerably, since the size of the phase-space will increase with the accumulation of factors. I will leave this for further research and in the next chapter extend the model to a multi-region model with local recursive interaction.

Chapter 5

Marshallian Externalities, Spatial Self-Organization and Regional Growth – an Agent Based Approach

> *economic life (...) consists of millions of relations or flows between individual firms and households. We can establish certain theorems about them but we can never observe all of them.*
>
> JOSEF A. SCHUMPETER

5.1 Introduction

The aim of the model set up in the previous chapter was to investigate the spatial allocation of production factors and its consequences for the dynamics of regional growth under the hypotheses of Marshallian externalities. Some of the phase spaces of the model displayed multiple equilibria, it was therefore not possible to predict where the factors will settle, although out of equilibria, the model implied a deterministic movement of the variables. Also, the model was limited to two regions, of course a strong simplification. One aim of this chapter is therefore to enlarge the model of the previous section to an arbitrary number of regions. Then the analysis cannot be done in the same way anymore since the number of regional interactions increases more than linearly. The analysis thus becomes technically too complex. Once, more than two regions are considered, the movements out of the equilibria points become merely unpredictable. The process of allocation and convergence to a stable pattern in these kind of models has therefore been described as *self-organization*. Another aim of this chapter is to make the model's property of self-organisation explicit.

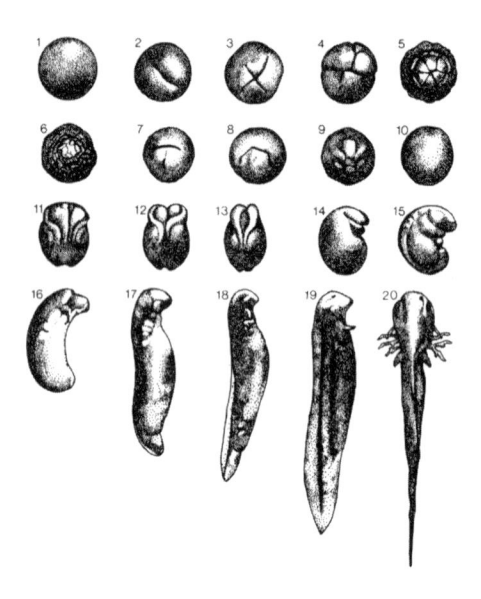

Figure 5.1: Metamorphosis from ovum to newt (from Eisenhardt et al, p.132)

5.2 Who Organizes the Economy?

Self-Organization is certainly one of the more popular catchwords in recent work on nonlinear dynamics[1] ("chaos" theory), complexity theory[2] or artificial life[3] etc. Since there seems to be no commonly acknowledged definition of "self-organization", let me start with a definition of this notion. According to Krugman[1996, p.3], those systems are self-organizing which

> ... *even when they start from an almost homogeneous or almost random state, spontaneously form large scale patterns.*

It is mainly the notion of *spontaneity* which makes it meaningful to refer to self-organization since it excludes the organization by some external agent, e.g. a benevolent dictator or central policy maker. The concept of self-organization stems from biology and has been used to describe complex phase transitions like the development of an embryo or the metamorphosis from ovum to newt (as depicted in Figure 5.1). Both are examples where the ordered development

---

[1] See e.g. Gleick[1988]
[2] See e.g. Nicolis and Prigogine[1989], Kauffman[1996] or Waldrop[1993].
[3] See e.g. Levy[1993] or Testatsion[1997].

of the macro-system is guided by interactions between agents at the micro-level – the cells in these cases. Given the number of agents involved, their transactions are extraordinarily difficult to investigate so that these phenomena have been called *complex systems*. The notion of self-organization is usually seen in conjunction with these kind of systems.[4]

It is straightforward to apply the concept of self-organization to economic systems. In this light, a market is interpreted as a self-organized phenomenon that describes transactions between micro-agents – sellers and buyers – and what we see as the outcome – GDP – is the result of innumerable such transactions. I assume that it was this concept that Smith[1776] had in mind when referring to the *invisible hand* to describe how supply and demand is coordinated. Note that the concept of self-organization is strictly opposed to the concept of the *Walrasian auctionator* that can be found in all major microeconomic textbooks[5] and that constructs a centralized agent who is responsible for the simultaneous clearing of markets.

One of the first contributions that explicitly investigated self organized processes in the economy was probably Schelling[1978]. Based on very simple assumptions on the behaviour of individuals he showed that the the dynamics of the macrosystem can differ fundamentally from what can be expected from the behaviour of the microunits. In his chapter 4 he set up a model where individuals of different races live together in a uniformly distributed pattern (i.e. mixed) in space (e.g. in a city). Then, he showed that although all individuals are tolerant toward individuals of the other race, the city will end up as a segregated one (i.e. with "ghettos" of white and black families) if an initial perturbance occurs. This is one example that shows that *Micromotives and Macrobehaviour* can differ fundamentally in complex systems.

* * *

The orthodox economic approach to describing complex systems is to *reduce their dimensionality*. Thus, markets – and even the macroeconomy – are described by what is called a *representative agent*. Here, the system under consid-

---

[4]The research into complex systems is not a new phenomenon that is e.g. bound to the use of computers (as one is tended to think when reading the dominating literature). See e.g. Hayek[1972] for a completely different approach. Horgan[1995] identified some 40 definitions of *complexity* and concluded that the research into complex systems failed to find a unifying approach.

[5]See e.g. Sher and Pinola[1981] or Varian[1996].

eration (the market, the macroeconomy) is considered as behaving like a single agent who adjusts parameters so that some target variable is optimized (like e.g. the representative agent's – i.e. the society's – utility etc.) Although this concept has proven to be useful to describe macroprocesses statistically (e.g. in an attempt to predict its behaviour) it has been strongly criticized. Kirman[1992] argued with Morishima[1984] that

> *even a correctly derived general equilibrium model ... should it lack the institutional backing to realize an equilibrium solution, then* (will) *amount to no more than a utopian state of affairs which bears no relation whatsoever to the real economy*

Kirman[1992] argues further that

> *if one rejects a particular behavioural hypothesis, it is not clear whether one is really rejecting the hypothesis in question, or rejecting the additional hypothesis that there is only one individual,*

a statement that he demonstrates through example. The point these citations make is that the representative agent is a theoretical concept that does not help us to understand *how the system* under consideration, its internal communication and its result as a self-organizing process *actually works*. Economists therefore turn more and more to alternative approaches, models that are inductive in their reasoning e.g models that start from individual behaviour and try to mimic stylized facts that can be observed in real life. Examples are *Game Theory* and *Evolutionary Economics*[6] to name a few.

Under the name of *Agent-Based Computational Economics* (ACE), a field is evolving that aims to connect these different approaches and to implement models as computer simulations to test them. Leigh Tesfatsion, who maintains an Internet-page on ACE[7], characterizes this field ("roughly") as

> *the computational study of economies modelled as evolving decentralized systems of autonomous interacting agents. A central concern of ACE researchers is to understand the apparently spontaneous formation of global regularities in economic processes, such as the unplanned coordination of trade in decentralized market economies that economists associate with Adam Smith's invisible hand. The challenge is to explain how these global regularities arise from the*

---

[6]See Nelson[1995] for a recent overview.

[7]See http://www.econ.iastate.edu/tesfatsi/ace.htm. I took the following citation from this page.

> bottom up, through the repeated local interactions of autonomous agents channeled through socio-economic institutions, rather than from fictitious top-down coordination mechanisms such as imposed market clearing constraints or an assumption of single representative agents.

Technically speaking, the approach is to implement agents together with their hypothetical behaviour on the computer and see whether the simulation results mimic actual stylized facts and if not to investigate why. In this sense, this approach can be seen as a *test* of the hypothesis implemented although the notion of test is not as strictly defined as the one used in statistics. Computational approaches to implement agents and some aspects of their behaviour are *Genetic Algorithms*[8], *Artificial Neural Networks*[9] or *Cellular Automata*[10] to name a few. In the following sections I attempt to extend the model of chapter 4 to an agent based approach to discuss the self-organizing properties of this model.

5.3 Cellular Automata as a Tool for Modelling Local Economic Interaction

The theory of *self-reproducing automata* goes back to von Neumann[1966] who developed a model for a real-life self reproduction robot that is able to gather the resources needed for self-reproducing from its environment. Since the ability to self-reproduce is one characteristic of living beings, these ideas can be seen as a starting point of the work that is now grouped under the notion of *artificial life*. Although in practice von Neumann's automata proved to be impossible to construct[11] the idea of automata where a number of microunits ("cells") interact with others by means of simple rules has been retained and further developed at a formal level. According to Wolfram[1994, p. 412],

> Cellular Automata are simple mathematical idealizations of natural systems. They consist of a lattice of discrete identical sites, each site taking on a finite set of, say, integer values. The values of the sites evolve in discrete time steps according to deterministic rules that specify the value of each site in terms of the values of the neighbouring sites. Cellular Automata may thus be considered as discrete idealizations of the partial differential equations often used to describe natural systems

---

[8] See e.g. Holland[1992] and Riolo[1992].
[9] See e.g. Herbrich, Keilbach, Graepel, Bollmann and Obermayer[1999] for a survey.
[10] See e.g. Wolfram[1994].
[11] See the discussion in Levy[1993, chapter 2].

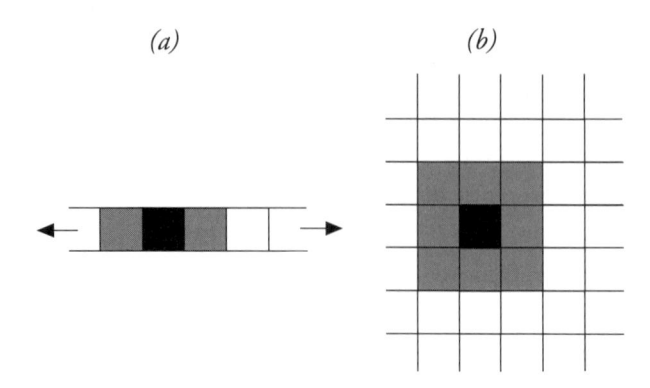

Figure 5.2: Structure of neighbourship in a 1-dimensional (a) and in a 2-dimensional CA (b)

Thus, according to this definition, cellular automata (CA) build a class of discrete dynamic systems that are discrete in *space, time* and *state*. Of course, an extension from natural systems (as referred to in the definition) to social systems seems to be natural.[12] Typically, CA are modelled as an n-dimensional array of sites. A one-dimensional CA is an array that forms a line of sites of finite length whereas a two-dimensional one has sites arranged within a lattice according to a given pattern of neighbourhood (See Figure 5.2 for a graphical presentation). A two-dimensional CA is very often presented as a quadratic lattice. However it can adopt any two-dimensional form. Also, the form of its cells is not limited to quadratic forms, and other forms, e.g. hexagons, have been used.

Let me restate Wolfram's definition more formally since this will be useful in the further discussion. CA are an n-dimensional array of sites whose state in $t+1$ is determined by the state of the system (the CA) in t via *local rules*[13], i.e. rules under which neighbouring sites interact. In each time step each site takes one state out of a (usually) finite set of states S. $S^{(k)}$ can be considered as a k-dimensional alphabet

$$S^{(k)} = \{0, 1, \ldots, k-1\}. \tag{5.1}$$

Let $2r$ be the number of neighbours then a rule defines a mapping

$$\mu : S^{(2r+1)} \to S.$$

---

[12] Indeed, Gaylord and Wellin[1995] and Gaylord and D'Andria[1998] use cellular automata to describe social systems.

[13] Later on I will consider global rules.

For example in a two dimensional CA where each site $a_{i,j}$ has 8 neighbours the general form of a rule is

$$a_{i,j}^{(t+1)} = \mu(a_{i,j}^{(t)}, a_{i,j+1}^{(t)}, a_{i+1,j}^{(t)}, a_{i+1,j+1}^{(t)}, \qquad (5.2)$$
$$a_{i,j-1}^{(t)}, a_{i-1,j}^{(t)}, a_{i-1,j-1}^{(t)}, a_{i-1,j+1}^{(t)}, a_{i+,j-1}^{(t)}),$$

where i, j determine the coordinates of the site, $\mu(\cdot)$ is a deterministic function. The state of the system in $t = (1, 2, \ldots, T)$, emerges if the rule $\mu(\cdot)$ is applied iteratively and simultaneously on each site in every time step. Note that via these rules, sites (cells, agents) are mutually interconnected. That is while the neighbours of a cell $a_{i,j}$ have an influence on $a_{i,j}$, the state of cell $a_{i,j}$ *simultaneously* influences its neighbours. It is this property of *parallel processing* that makes CA attractive for the modelling of processes where a high number of interactive processes are run simultaneously – like economic systems. Note that in principle the state of a CA is perfectly predictable from these rules. However – as Haken[1977] argued – this could prove to be incalculable due to the high dimension of the process and the mutuality of the rules.

A very simple and well-known cellular automaton is the *Game of Life* as conceived by Conway[14]. The Game consists of a 2-dimensional CA where the cells can be in two states (zero – one or "death"–"alive") and will change into the respective other state according to simple rules which account for the respective number of neighbours. Although rules are simple and deterministic, the systems displays "complex" global behaviour i.e. behaviour that cannot be predicted. Thus, the Game of Life can be used as a model of (computational) complexity. Conway's *Game* can probably called the hallmark of complexity theory (maybe comparable with the Mandelbrot Set in Chaos theory) and is available for virtually all computer systems.

Other applications are Wolfram[1994] who used CA as a device for modelling complex dynamical systems, and classifying them into different categories according to their complexity. The EvCA project of the Santa-Fe Institute (New Mexico) sets up CA driven by genetic algorithms to understand *"in detail the evolutionary mechanisms giving rise to the discovery of global coordination in such systems"*[15]

---

[14] For a description of the Game and a reference to Conway see e.g. Gardner[1983] or Schulman and Seiden[1978].

[15] Cited from http://www.santafe.edu/projects/evca/.

The motivation to use CA in a model of *spatial economics* is twofold. First, it is a very elegant and through the possible specification of localized rules a natural approach to model a multi-region economic system with local interactions. Second, all agents (regions) update their investment decisions *simultaneously* in every time step. This multi-processing capacity is what we observe in "real life economies". If, however, we use CA in economic modelling we have to extend Wolfram's definition (that was set up for physical or natural systems) in three ways:

1. we have to allow for *non-discrete states*. This enables us to deal with indexes of factor endowment. The same argument applies if we use relative terms or probabilities. Thus the set of states (5.1) becomes

$$S \geq 0 \quad \text{or even} \quad S \in \mathbb{R}.$$

2. Apart from local rules we have to allow for *global rules*, i.e. rules which define an influence of some aggregated variable of the CA on each site. This is necessary since a part of the relevant information in the economy is globally available like information on prices or economic institutions.[16] Finally,

3. We should allow equation 5.2 to be *stochastic* to capture the parts of the agents' behaviour that is not explicitely given by the rules of the automaton. Thus, from these two last points, function (5.2) will be extended to

$$a_{i,j}^{(t+1)} = \tilde{\mu}\left(\mathbf{a}_{i,j}^{(t)}, \Theta^{(t)}, \varepsilon^{(t)}\right)$$

where $\mathbf{a}_{i,j}$ represents the vector of $a_{i,j}$ and its neighbours, Θ represents a set of relevant global parameter (prices...) and $\varepsilon \sim i.i.d.$ Possibly, $\Theta = \nu(\mathbf{A})$ where $\mathbf{A}$ is the set of all sites of the automaton and $\nu : m \to n$ is an arbitrary function that maps the m-dimensional space of the state of the sites into the n-dimensional space of the global parameter.

In the following section I will implement the model of chapter 4 on a cellular automaton.

---

[16] Wolfram[1994, p.470] conceives global rules as well.

5.4 Local Interaction and the Dynamics of Agglomeration

5.4.1 A Hybrid Model

The model to be developed in this section will be a hybrid of a disaggreated version of tthe model of chapter 4 and the model of Romer[1996] that has been discussed in section 2.2.2.2. That is I will depart now from the broad concept of capital, as used in chapter 4 and include *human capital* in the production function. Thus the hybrid model for region i becomes

$$Y_i = [\varphi_K K_i]^\alpha [\varphi_L L_i]^\beta [\varphi_H H_i^{\text{eff}}]^{1-\alpha-\beta}$$
$$\dot{H}_i = [(1-\varphi_K)K_i]^\gamma [(1-\varphi_L)L_i]^\eta [(1-\varphi_H)H_i^{\text{eff}}]^\pi - d_H H_i,$$

φ_j being the part of factor j that is used in the goods-producing sector and d_H being depreciation rate for human capital. H_i^{eff} is the *effective* amount of human capital in region i. It might differ from H_i via spillover effects (see equation (5.3) for a formal specification of this effect). If we implement this approach in more than one region we can expect at least the following two mechanism to intervene:

1. Unlike in the Romer-model (section 2.2.2.2), savings are not necessarily invested in the region where they arise. Rather they are invested in regions with superior capital rent.

2. Regions are interconnected locally through local spillovers. This has been discussed extensively in the previous chapters (see e.g. section 4.1)

The next section discusses the technical implementation of the model.

5.4.2 The Rules of the Automaton

- Each site of the automaton represents a region of the economy. The resolution of the grid does not correspond to statistical units but to a fine grid that divides economic space into regions of identical size.

- Each site has an identical number of neighbours, i.e. no border-effects exist. Thus, for a one-dimentional CA, the economy can be thought of as a circular city (see Hotelling, 1929; Tirole, 1988; Krugman, 1995), for a two-dimensional CA, it can be thought of as a bagel or as a ball with

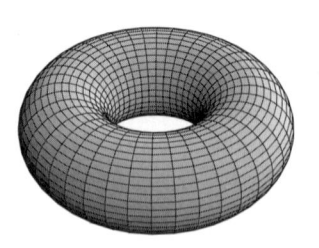

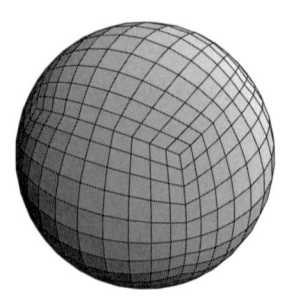

Figure 5.3: Two ways of connecting a two-dimensionsal quadratic Cellular Automata

the sites having the form of an irregular quadrilateral (see Figure 5.3 for an illustration).[17]

- Regions' initial endowment with capital and labour is identical with K and L and set to 1. The regions' initial endowment of A is random, following a uniform distribution with mean 1 and variance 1/2.

- Regions have identical saving rates $s = 0.2$. Depreciation rates are set $d_K = 0.1$ for capital and $d_H = 0.02$ for technological knowledge.

- Neighouring regions will profit from a region's stock of human capital, i.e. H spills over to the neighbouring regions. This process is specified as follows:

$$H_i^{\text{eff}} = \frac{1}{n\delta + 1}H_i + \sum_{j=1}^{n}\frac{\delta}{n\delta + 1}H_j, \quad \delta \in [0,1], j \neq i \quad (5.3)$$

j being the neighbours, and n being their number. δ is the degree of spillover, i.e. for $\delta = 0$ there is no spillover and for $\delta = 1$ the endowment of the neighbouring regions j counts to 100% in region i.[18] The

---

[17] In the case of the sites forming a ball, the form of the underlying automaton is not identical to a square.

[18] The main advantage of the suggested method of aggregation is computational convenience. A simple addition of factor endowments would lead to a quicker computational overflow.

mechanism of spillovers is highly nonlinear, since it is simultaneous, i.e. the endowment of a site i spills over to its neighbouring sites but at the same time, the neighbours' endowments spill over to site i. Thus, a web of spillovers is created i.e. although the actual factor endowment of a site might be rather low, its effective endowment might be superior to those of the neighbours.

- Capital migrates globally, i.e. its movement is not restricted to adjacent regions. The idea here is as follows. In every period, investors of every site check the investment opportunities of all the other sites simultaneously. More specifically, we suppose that investment opportunities are expressed through marginal product of capital, MPK, and savings are reinvested in regions whose capital productivity is superior to the mean capital productivity of the economy, $\overline{MPK}$. Hence, we have the following law of motion

$$\dot{K}_i = \lambda_i \left(\sum_j s_j Y_j \right) - d_K K_i$$

where

$$\lambda_i = \begin{cases} 0 & \text{if } MPK_i < \overline{MPK} \\ \frac{MPK_i^\varrho}{\sum_j MPK_j^\varrho} & \text{if } MPK_i, MPK_j > \overline{MPK}, \end{cases}$$

ϱ being a coefficient of elasticity that weighs the difference of MPK. For $\varrho = 1$, the money is invested according to the actual difference in MPK, for $\varrho = 0$, every region with superior MPK receives the same amount of money. This parameter captures the fact that people might not have complete information about MPK of each region. Then, they simply invest in a region if its MPK is superior although it might not be the region with the highest MPK. Note that this is a *global rule*.

- Unlike capital, labour migrates only locally and only a given proportion migrates every time step. With this behaviour we try to capture the fact that persons are more attached to a certain region due to personal preferences. If some neighbouring regions j offer a higher wage, then a proportion of θ of the population of region i moves to these regions. The actual redistribution is determined by the wage difference of the regions that offer superior wages. Similarly, if other neighbouring regions k offer lower wages, then a part of their population will move into region i or into one of the regions j that offer wages superior to those of region i. Thus we have the following law of motion

$$\dot{L}_i = \theta \left(\xi \sum_{j=1}^{l} L_j - \zeta \sum_{k=1}^{h} L_k \right),$$

where h is the number of neighbours that offer higher wages and l is the number of neighbours that offer lower wages compared to i. Note that $h + l \leq n$, the total number of neighbours. If i is the region that offers the highest wage within its pool of neighbours, then $\zeta = 0$, if it offers the lowest wages, then $\xi = 0$. Else, these variables are $\xi, \zeta = 1$

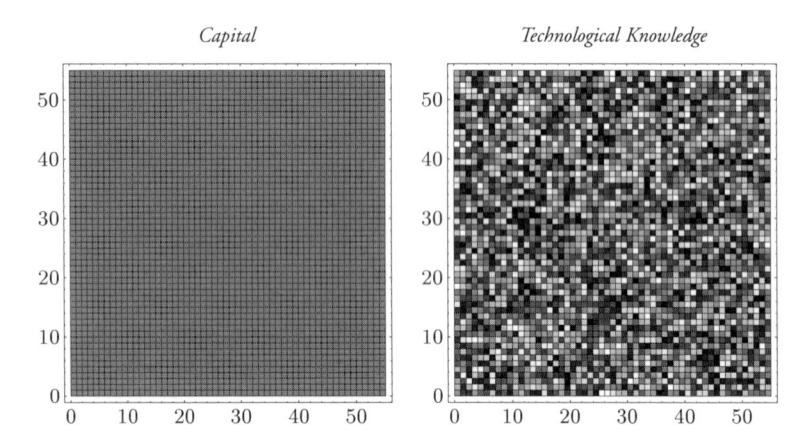

Figure 5.4: Initial factor endowment a two-dimensional economic space

5.5 Simulation Results

The simulations were carried out for two types of automata, a one-dimensional and a two-dimensional CA. This enables me to display the results in two ways. For the *one-dimensional* automaton I will depict the sites of the automaton on one axis and *time* on a second axis. The vertical axis depicts capital or labour density which is the way I describe agglomeration. Thus, this type of plot shows the evolution of factor density of each site with time. The *two-dimensional* version of this automaton will give a more intuitive perception of the spatial agglomeration process. Here, I will present graphically the spatial factor-distribution after $t = 50$ iteration steps.

The one-dimensional automaton will entail 80 sites and the two-dimensional ones will entail 55×55 or 30×30 cells respectively. Thus, the latter represent countries with 3025 or 900 regions. I will present simulation results of two different automata, one where labour is immobile and another where this factor migrates according to the rule set up above.

If we define agglomeration as the spatial concentration of production factors, we can describe it with a with a spatial Gini-coefficient. Moreover, in a model that uses a fine spatial grid (as corresponds to cellular automata) the formation of cities can be described as the formation of local *clusters* of production factors. Then, agglomeration implies *spatial autocorrelation*. I therefore consider this measure which has the value added that it will help us to distinguish agglomeration from mere random distribution. I therefore will consider these two measures to describe the degree of agglomeration obtained by the simulations. Note that these parameters are computed for the one-dimensional case only.

5.5.1 Results When Labour is Immobile

As in section 2.2.2.2 I will distinguish three different constellations in the parameter space: decreasing, constant and increasing returns to scale in the R&D-sector. If labour is immobile, the parameters β and ν are not to be considered.

5.5.1.1 Evolution of the Automaton Under Decreasing Returns in the R&D-Sector

If $\gamma + \pi < 1$, the R&D-sector displays *decreasing returns to scale*. As we saw in section 2.2.2.2, in this case a single region will converge to a zero-growth steady state. Figure 5.5 depicts the simulation results.
We see that the spatial distribution of capital is random and does not converge to an agglomeration pattern. The peaks that can be seen in the one-dimensional plot show the inflow of capital that occur in a certain point of time. The two-dimensional economy displays a random pattern as well. Indeed, both parameters, the spatial Gini-coefficient and the spatial correlation coefficient are decreasing. Hence, the economy tends towards a spatially uniform random distribution, i.e. if decreasing returns prevail, no agglomeration will occur.

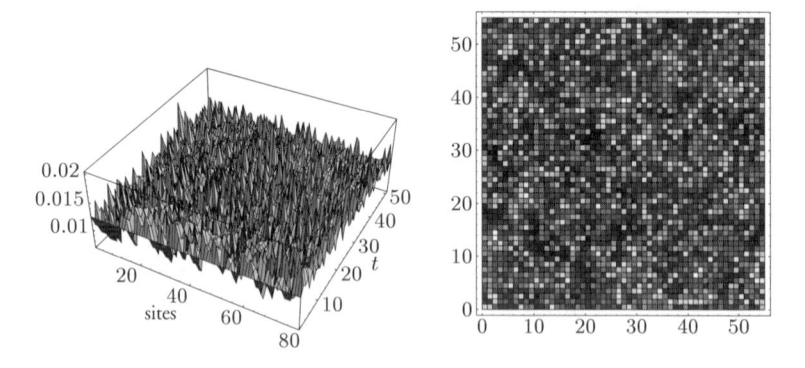

Figure 5.5: Spatial distribution of capital under decreasing returns ($\gamma + \pi = 0.4$) in a one- and in a two-dimensional country after $t = 50$ iteration steps.

5.5.1.2 Evolution of the Automaton Under Constant Returns in the R&D-Sector

If $\gamma + \pi = 1$, the R&D-sector displays *constant returns to scale*. The economy still does not display a city-countryside dichotomy (see Figure 5.6). Also, as in the previous case, spatial Gini-coefficient and spatial correlation converge to 0, although much more slowly than in the previous case. Visually however, we observe what we might call a "smoothing" effect, i.e. temporary clusters of high or low spatial concentration of capital. This becomes apparent in the plot of the one dimensional automaton, but also if we compare the two-dimensional automaton with the one of the next section.

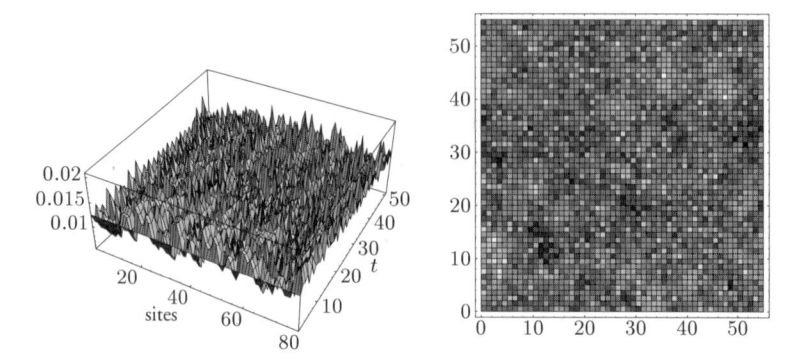

Figure 5.6: Spatial distribution of capital under constant returns ($\gamma + \pi = 1$) in a one- and in a two-dimensional country after $t = 50$ iteration steps.

5.5.1.3 Evolution of the Automaton Under Increasing Returns in the R&D-Sector

If $\gamma + \pi > 1$, the R&D-sector displays *increasing returns to scale*, i.e. an increase of all factors involved in research by λ would increase the rate of change of H by more than λ. Therefore the increase of capital productivity is greater than in the previous cases. This attracts more capital and thus increases capital productivity further. Hence we observe a mechanism of positive feedback, i.e. a *self-reinforcing* structure. Figure 5.7 shows that in this case a clear agglomeration pattern emerges. The one-dimensional economy converges towards a state with five agglomeration centres (in the two-dimensional economy we can identify 8 agglomeration centres). In this case, both parameters, the spatial Gini-coefficient and the spatial autocorrelation tend towards their maximum (towards 1), i.e. we have increasing concentration of capital (agglomeration). Hence, we see that in the context formulated by the model an agglomeration pattern occurs only, if increasing returns prevail in the R&D-sector.

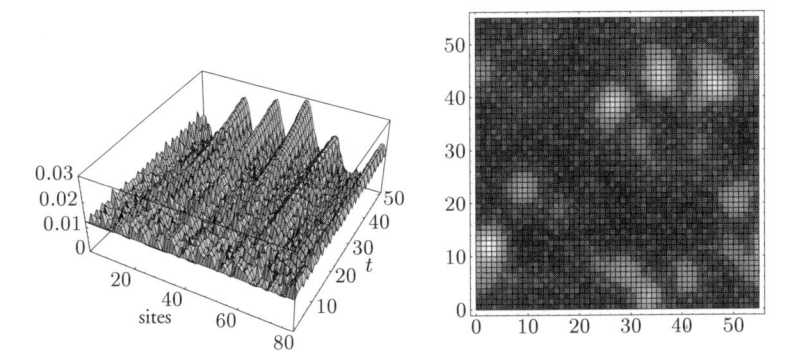

Figure 5.7: Spatial distribution of capital under increasing returns ($\gamma + \pi = 1.4$) in a one- and in a two-dimensional country after $t = 50$ iteration steps.

5.5.1.4 Consequences for the Convergence of Regional Growth Rates

In the previous section we could show that agglomeration occurs only if increasing returns prevail. What are the consequences for regional growth rates? And will regions converge in income per capita, and if not, why is convergence an empirical regularity within regions of a country?

To analyze this, we use the methodology described in section 2.3.2.1. There, the data was said to exhibit absolute β-convergence if the regression

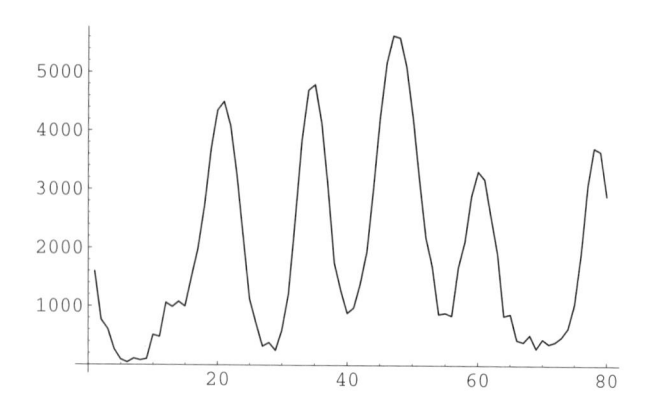

[GRAPH: Spatial distribution curve showing capital values ranging from ~500 to ~5000 across positions 0 to 80]

Figure 5.8: Spatial distribution of capital in a one-dimensional automaton after $t = 50$ iteration steps

$$\overline{g_{y,i}} = \alpha - \beta \log(y_{0,i}) + \varepsilon_i, \qquad (2.12, \text{repeated})$$

yields a positive estimate for β. Otherwise, the data is said to exhibit absolute β-divergence. $\overline{g_{y,i}}$ is the average growth rate of income per capita in the observed period in region i and $\log(y_{0,i})$ is its initial income per capita. Both variables can easily be computed from our simulation results. Table 5.1 shows regression results for the one-dimensional automata for the three scenarios, i.e. decreasing, constant and increasing returns in the R&D-sector. We see that in the case of decreasing and constant returns the economy displays converging behaviour. However, if increasing returns prevail, regions *diverge* in terms of income per capita.

	$\gamma + \pi = 0.6$	$\gamma + \pi = 1.0$	$\gamma + \pi = 1.4$
constant (α)	0.105	0.122	0.181
	(247.9)	(201.7)	(91.96)
slope (β)	0.0423	0.0351	-0.06
	(13.22)	(7.662)	(-4.267)
R^2	0.691	0.425	0.189

Note: t-values in brackets

Table 5.1: Results of linear convergence regressions for three different parameter constellations in a regionally disaggregated economy

This finding is of course uncomfortable, since in reality we observe regional agglomeration as well as regional convergence. Note however that we introduced a fine regional disaggregation with the imposed grid. This does not correspond to the usual statistical unit of observationwhich contains at least one major city and its surrounding countryside[19]. If we aggregate correspondingly, we obtain *five* regions (referring to Figure 5.8). Running the same regression procedure again, we obtain the results given in Table 5.2.

	$\beta + \theta = 0.6$	$\beta + \theta = 1.0$	$\beta + \theta = 1.4$
constant (α)	0.102	0.126	0.220
	(33.85)	(27.30)	(7.728)
slope (β)	0.000472	0.00376	0.0209
	(0.4156)	(2.1564)	(1.9332)
R^2	0.054	0.608	0.555

Note: t-values in brackets

Table 5.2: *Results of linear convergence regressions for three different parameter constellations in a regional aggregated economy*

It can be seen that in all three cases the five regions display *converging* behaviour. This suggests that convergence should be considered as a statistical artifact, i.e. convergence is not robust as to the choice of regional disaggregation. Rather, we observe divergence at the level of different countries, convergence of different aggregated regions of a country and again divergence if regions are disaggregated. This again suggests that convergence is not a meaningful concept to describe the growth dynamics of regions. Note that with the spatial aggregation we obtained *convergence* in an endogenous growth model which usually would *diverge* in its growth rates.

5.5.2 Results When Labour Migrates

5.5.2.1 Evolution of the Automaton

To present the simulation results in a more concise way I will only present the evolution of the spatial Gini-coefficient (which measures the spatial concentration) and the spatial correlation (which enables us to distinguish between systematic agglomeration an noise) for *labour* and *labour productivity*. In the next chapter, we will see (see Table 6.3 on page 110 and the corresponding discussion) that labour is more productive in agglomerated areas and therefore only a

---

[19]This holds for all the regional convergence studies as presented by Barro and Sala-i-Martin [1995].

parameter constellation that leads to the concentration of labour and of labour productivity is able to capture the phenomena observed in reality.

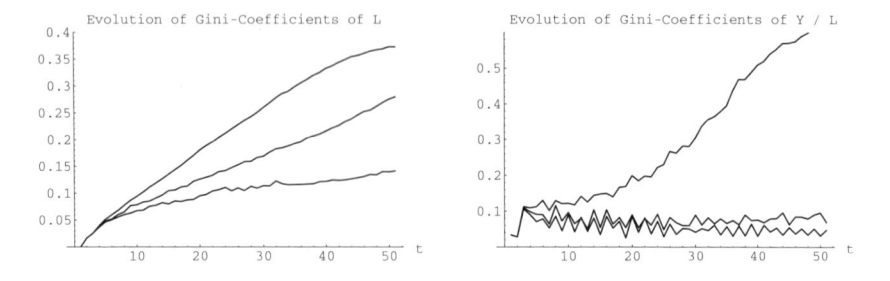

Figure 5.9: Evolution of spatial concentration of labour and its productivity under decreasing, constant and increasing returns to scale in the R&D-sector

From Figure 5.9 we see that labour agglomerates no matter what the level of returns to scale although it agglomerates quicker, the higher the returns to scale. From the evolution of the Gini of labour productivity we see that only if returns to scale are increasing the automaton displays agglomeration. Diagnostics are similar if we consider spatial correlation (which is measured an a way that corresponds to autocorrelation of time-series to the first lag) of L and Y/L (Figure 5.10). Spatial correlation increases independently of the level of returns to scale. This expresses a "spatial smoothing effect". However, for the case of labour productivity, it seems that a significant pattern of agglomeration only emerges for increasing returns.

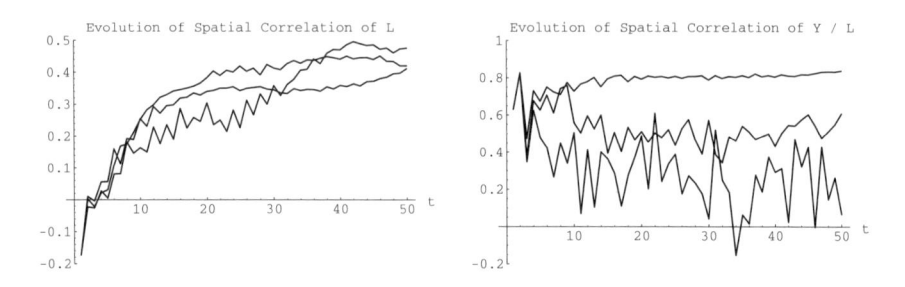

Figure 5.10: Evolution of spatial correlation of labour and its productivity under decreasing, constant and increasing returns to scale in the R&D-sector

Figure 5.11 gives plots of the spatial distribution of labour and its productivity after $t = 50$ iteration steps for increasing returns in the R&D-sector. We see a pattern of agglomeration for both labour and its productivity. We can therefore conclude that a constellation where the R&D-sector is subject to increasing returns is able to mimic real-life behaviour.

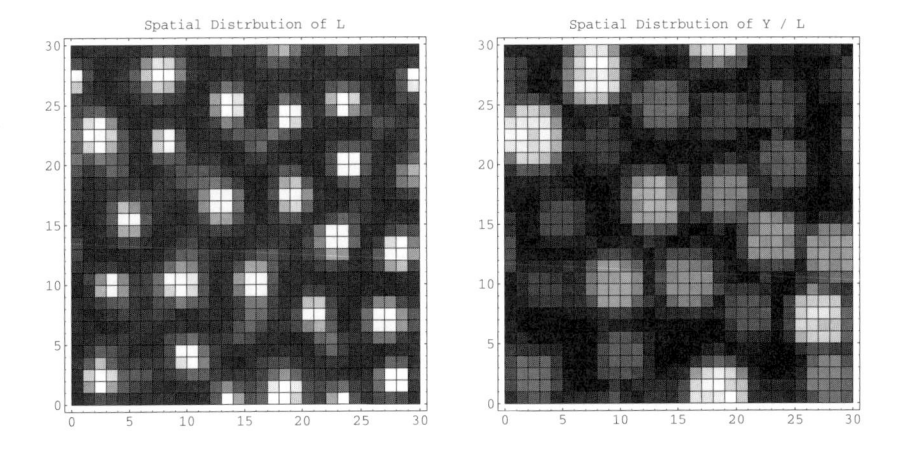

Figure 5.11: Spatial distribution of L and Y/L after $t = 50$ *iteration steps if increasing returns prevail in the R&D-sector*

5.5.2.2 Consequences for the Convergence of Regional Growth Rates

As an outcome of the discussion above I will limit the presentation of convergence regressions to the case where $\mu + \eta + \pi > 1$, i.e. increasing returns prevail in the R&D-sector. Running again the regression

$$\overline{g_{y,i}} = \alpha - \beta \log(y_{0,i}) + \varepsilon_i, \qquad (2.12, \text{repeated})$$

yields the results given in Table 5.3. Results correspond to those discussed in section 5.5.1.4 (note however the t-values). Let me therefore skip a further interpretation and summarize the findings of this chapter.

5.6 Summary and Conclusion

The aim of this chapter was to implement the model developed in the previous one into an interactive multi-region setting. To do so, I first discussed the paradigm of *self-organization* and in how far it could be relevant to model economic systems. I then presented the framework of *cellular automata* and extended it such that it can serve as a tool for the implementation of an economic

	non-aggregated	aggregated
constant (α)	0.2944 (49.5312)	0.4334 (7.351)
slope (β)	-0.0098 (-0.7338)	0.0190 (1.0233)
R^2	0.0054	0.2075

Note: t-values in brackets

Table 5.3: *Results of linear convergence regressions for a non-aggregated and an aggregated automaton when R&D-sector displays increasing returns to scale*

system. Based on a hybrid model I investigated the link between agglomeration and regional growth for different levels of spatial aggregates. What can be learned from this exercise is that

- Cellular Automata allow consistent modelling of processes of regional interaction like spatial spillovers and migration. With their multidimensionality and mutuality they are able to model simultaneous interaction.

- Agglomeration – in an empirically meaningful sense – occurs only under increasing returns to scale, i.e. under spatial spillovers of human capital.

- Under increasing returns, regions display divergence as to their growth rates of per capita income (β-divergence). However, when aggregated in an "empirically meaningful way" (i.e. such that regions host a capital and some countryside) the regional aggregates display β-convergence.

Hence I could reproduce the findings of chapter 4 in a different setting. I interpret this as evidence supporting the model developed there. Note that the model of this chapter displays converging behaviour in an environment with increasing returns to scale. Against the background of the discussion in section 2.3.2 this is remarkable. Possibly, this behaviour can help to explain the contradiction between the behaviour of endogenous growth models and the empirical evidence of β-convergence. However, I leave this for further research and will present some empirical evidence in the next chapter.

Chapter 6

Spatial Processes in the Economy – an Empirical Investigation

> *Everything is related to everything else, but near things are more related than distant things*
> WALDO TOBLER

6.1 Introduction

Like in the economic literature (see discussion in 3) *space* does not play an important role in the *econometric* literature. Although geographers and regional scientists have been interested in the quantitative analysis of spatial processes for quite a long time[1], econometricians (if we distinguish between econometrics and statistics as the first being driven by economic models whereas the latter is driven rather by data) discovered the phenomenon of space only recently and (as is true for virtually all economic textbooks) *space* is absent in all major econometric textbooks. Anselin[1988] is one of the first comprehensive textbooks that discusses the problems the inclusion of *space* will cause in econometric analysis and suggests different methods to tackle them.

The aim of this chapter is to investigate whether spatial economic processes as discussed in the previous chapter can be identified in the data. To do this I will first investigate whether spatial spillovers can be detected in the data on the basis of simple descriptive statistics. To prepare for a more in-depth analysis, I will give in the subsequent section 6.4 an overview of the problems that occur

---
[1]See Garrison[1967], Berry and Marble[1968], Cliff and Ord[1972, 1973, 1981] or Upton and Fingleton[1985].

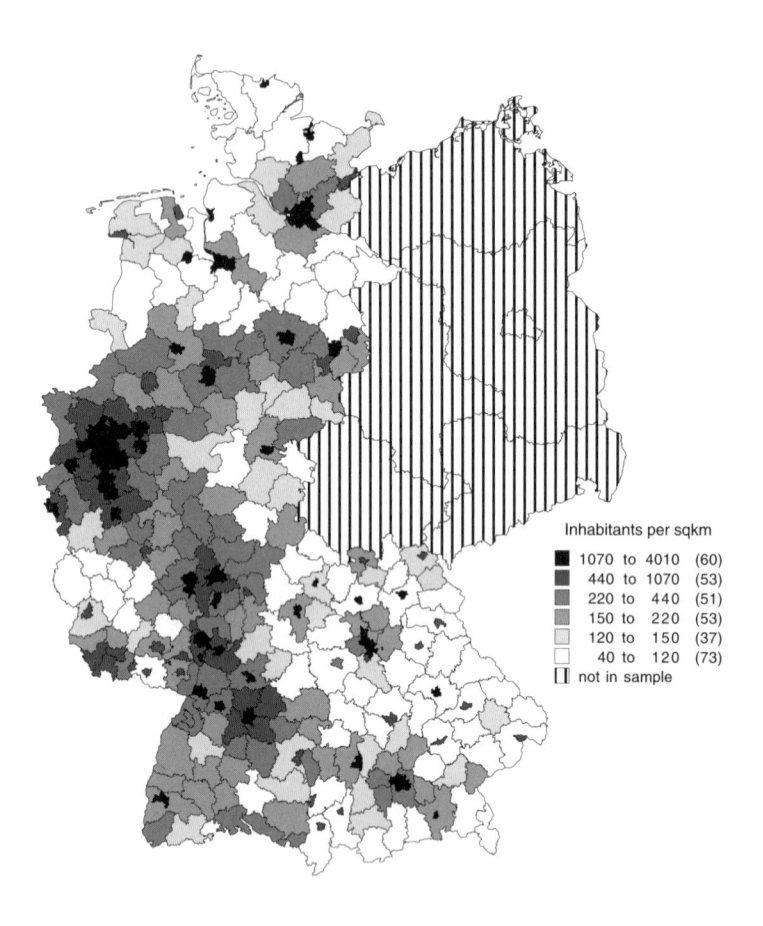

Figure 6.1: Population density of West-German Kreise

if *spatial dependence* exists in the data and consider different methods that deal with that problem. This section will draw heavily – though not exclusively – on the analysis in Anselin [1988]. In section 6.5 I will develop the empirical implementation of the model developed in chapter 4 and present the estimation results. Section 6.6 will summarize the findings of this chapter. To start however, I will describe how the dataset has been constructed.

6.2 Data: Sources and Construction

To test the model developed in chapter 4, I will run regressions at two levels: one for of 327 West-German *Kreise* (i.e. regional statistical sub-units) and one at the level of national states. For the latter case, I will use the data published by

6.2 Data: Sources and Construction

Mankiw *et al.* [1992]. This has the advantage that the data is publicly available and that the results in Mankiw *et al.* can be used as a benchmark. Since the construction of this dataset is described in their paper I will limit the presentation of the data to the dataset on West German counties, collected for the purpose of this analysis. *All* the data is reproduced in appendix C (page 155 f.).

For Germany I have collected data on the *producing sector of West-German Kreise*. East-Germany has been left out since data on annual investment (and thus on capital stock) could not be obtained for a sufficiently long time interval. *Kreise* are rather small regional administrative units that can be classified into different types: cities, suburban and rural areas (See Figure 6.1 for a graphical presentation of German *Kreise* with their population density.) This level of spatial aggregation has been chosen since it is the smallest administrative unit for which a sufficiently large dataset could be obtained. Berlin has been left out because of its special status at the time of the analysis. The data encompass the mining, construction and manufacturing sectors. Apart from *output* and the "classical factors" – capita (K) and labour (L) – I will use *R&D-personnel*, *human capital* and *infrastructure* as factors in the regressions. These latter have in common that they obey a public goods characteristic and can thus spill over to the neighbouring regions (see the discussion in section 4.1, page 61). *Human capital* is used as a proxy for the stock of technological knowledge of a region. *R&D-personnel* is used as a proxy for the R&D-intensity of a region. *Infrastructure* has a potential to spill over that is usually not considered in the literature on endogenous growth. The idea behind the inclusion of infrastructure is that a region's infrastructure will be used by individuals of other regions for transportation of goods etc. without compensation. Of course, the less distant two regions are, the more intensively they will use the other region's infrastructure, since their economies are potentially more integrated by flows of exchange. Another candidate to describe spatial knowledge spillovers could have been *output* of R&D. However, on the level of *Kreise*, there is no data available on that topic.

The sample will consist in a *cross-section* of the West-German *Kreise* for the year 1992 if not indicated otherwise. Sources and construction of the data is as follows.

Output is measured as Gross Value Added corrected for purchases of goods and services, VAT and shipping costs. Statistics are published every two years for *Kreise* by the Working Group of the Statistical Offices of the German

Länder, under "Volkswirtschaftiche Gesamtrechnungen der Länder".

Capital: The stock of capital used in the manufacturing sector of the *Kreise* has been estimated using a perpetual inventory method. Basically, this method cumulates annual investment and corrects these figures with a survival function to get an estimate of the capital stock still in use[2]. In the estimates I used a β-distribution with $p = 9$ and a mean age of $q = 14$. Type of survival function as well as these parameters have been provided by the Federal Statistical Office in Wiesbaden. This way, I attempted to obtain maximum coherence with the estimates of the capital stock of the German producing sector as a whole as published by the Federal Statistical Office.

Data on investment in the manufacturing sector at the level of German *Kreise* is published annually by the Federal Statistical Office in the series "E I 6". These figures however are limited to firms of the producing sector, excluding the mining industry, which have more than 20 employees. The vector of the producing sector as a whole has been estimated by multiplying these values such that the value of the capital stock of Western Germany – as published in the Statistical Yearbook – was attained. This procedure implies that estimates for *Kreise* with a high proportion of mining might be biased. For protection purposes, some *Kreise* did not publish data on investment (like e.g. the city of Wolfsburg, whose producing sector is dominated by Volkswagen). Therefore five *Kreise* are treated as missing.

Labour: Data on labour is published by the Federal Labour Office, Nürnberg which reports number of employees liable to social insurance by *Kreise*.

R&D is expressed as *number of employees engaged in R&D* in the public sector (1992) as well as in the private sector (1991). Data have been communicated by the *Stifterverband für die Wissenschaft* under obligation of secrecy. I will however give some summarizing statistics and present the data graphically (see Figure C.1 on page 155). The data does not distinguish between R&D-employees in the producing and non-producing sectors. Regression results therefore will implicitly include spillovers from R&D

---

[2]See Lützel [1971], Deitmer [1993] or Keilbach [1993] for a detailed description of this method.

of the non-producing sector to the producing sectors. I presume however that this effect is rather low.

Human Capital is expressed as the percentage of employees with a high level of qualification (university or polytechnical degree). Data on qualification levels of employees are published for 1989 by the Federal Research Institute for Regional Geography and Regional Planning (Bundesforschungsanstalt für Landeskunde und Raumordnung) in their Volume 47. Unfortunately, data for 1992 could not be obtained. I will therefore use data for 1989 as a proxy. Note that the data refers to the *Kreis* as a whole, i.e. the figures do not refer to the producing sector alone. Thus (as in the case of R&D - personnel) estimates implicitly include spillovers of human capital from the non-producing to the producing sectors.

Infrastructure: Data on infrastructure is published every four years by the Federal Statistical Office in the Series 3.5.1. I took data from 1989 since the use of data of 1993 cannot reasonably be interpreted if the remainder of the sample is from earlier dates. Figures include not only streets but also rural field paths and public places, all measured by surface. Assuming that it is streets that contribute to the local economic productivity[3] rather than field paths or public squares this data is to be used with caution. The contribution of infrastructure, as measured here, is therefore probably biased for rural areas and cities.

With the exception of R&D-personnel, data are reproduced in Appendix C. Table 6.1 gives some summarizing statistics. Figure 6.2 gives a set of scatterplots of the Log of these variables and Table 6.2 reports corresponding Pearson correlations. Corresponding years of obeservation are given in the index. In the following tables these indices will be dropped for ease of notation. We see from Table 6.2 that the simple correlation between input factors and output is positive. The relation between capital and output is nearly linear – one of the Kaldorian stylized facts (see e.g. Barro and Sala-i-Martin, 1995, p.5), though found here in a cross section of data, not in time series as usual. In this crosssection analysis the same type of relationship exists between capital and labour.

---

[3]This assumption has been investigated in a number of studies. See e.g. Seitz[1993], Seitz [1995b], Seitz and Licht[1995] or Mas, Maudo, Perez and Uriel[1996].

Table 6.1: Summarizing statistics of variables used in regression

	Y_{92}	K_{92}	L_{92}	R_{92}	I_{89}	H_{89}
N	327	322	327	323	327	327
Min.	95.000	211.202	2562.000	4.000	240.000	1.100
Max.	22258.000	37295.645	171938.000	42213.000	12935.000	18.100
Mean	2351.887	4269.550	27022.480	1502.115	3530.284	4.048
Med.	1486.000	2584.031	19249.000	378.000	3202.000	3.400
Std. Dev.	2621.773	5065.085	24080.324	3439.586	2256.167	2.280

Table 6.2: Pearson correlation matrix of variables used in regression

	$\ln(Y_{92})$	$\ln(K_{92})$	$\ln(L_{92})$	$\ln(R_{92})$	$\ln(I_{89})$	$\ln(H_{89})$
$\ln(Y_{92})$	1.000 (0.0)					
$\ln(K_{92})$	0.940 (0.000)	1.000 (0.0)				
$\ln(L_{92})$	0.962 (0.000)	0.948 (0.000)	1.000 (0.0)			
$\ln(R_{92})$	0.748 (0.000)	0.716 (0.000)	0.721 (0.000)	1.000 (0.0)		
$\ln(I_{89})$	0.159 (0.003)	0.153 (0.005)	0.220 (0.001)	-0.114 (0.049)	1.000 (0.0)	
$\ln(H_{89})$	0.347 (0.000)	0.337 (0.000)	0.283 (0.000)	0.572 (0.000)	-0.265 (0.000)	1.000 (0.0)

Note: p-values of χ^2-test for $H_0 : \rho = 0$ in brackets

Note that the log of these variables follow a normal distribution with the exception of infrastructure, whose distribution is negatively skewed. This might possibly be interpreted as evidence that this vector is biased due to the inclusion of city places and field paths.

6.3 Spatial Spillovers of Knowledge – First Evidence from the Data

6.3.1 How Do Spillovers Appear in the Data?

One result of the discussion in chapter 3 was that *if* spatial spillovers matter, production factors will be more productive in densely populated areas than in rural ones since the former allows for more intensive personal contacts, i.e. more

6.3 Spatial Spillovers of Knowledge – First Evidence from the Data

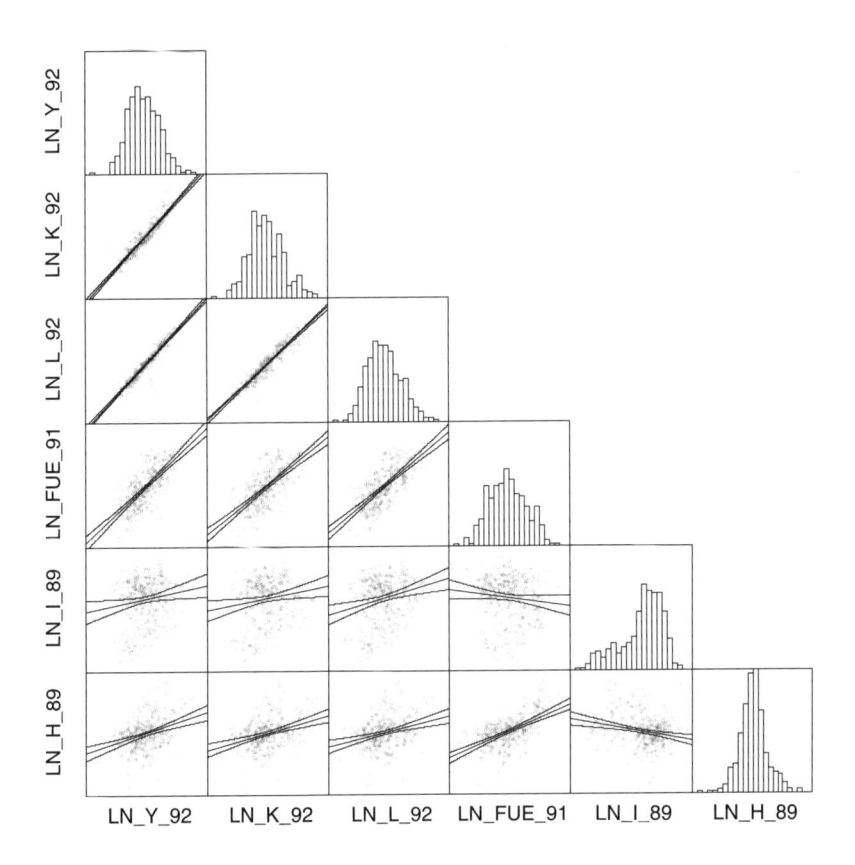

Figure 6.2: Scatterplot matrix of variables used in regression. Lines give a descriptive linear fit and a 95% confidence interval of the regression line

intensive exchange of ideas. Thus, we would expect to observe a positive relation between population density and factor productivity. Table 6.3 reports Bravais-Pearson correlations of these variables[4]. Indeed, we observe (in the first column) positive correlations between population density and the productivities of labour, infrastructure and human capital. The productivity of capital is uncorrelated while the productivity of R&D-personnel is negatively correlated with population density. This latter result is puzzling at first sight. Note however that Y/R is probably not the appropriate measure of R&D-productivity. Rather some more direct kind of measure of R&D-output (e.g. patents) would

---

[4] Factor productivity has been measured by $Y/factor$. Data of population density have been taken from a CD-ROM published by Macon GmbH, a firm that offers regional data and GIS systems.

Table 6.3: Pearson correlation matrix of population density and factor productivities

	$\ln(PD)$	$\ln(Y/K)$	$\ln(Y/L)$	$\ln(Y/R)$	$\ln(Y/I)$	$\ln(Y/H)$
$\ln(PD)$	1.000					
	(0.0)					
$\ln(Y/K)$	-0.075	1.000				
	(0.179)	(0.0)				
$\ln(Y/L)$	0.308	0.529	1.000			
	(0.000)	(0.000)	(0.0)			
$\ln(Y/R)$	-0.373	0.142	0.007	1.000		
	(0.000)	(0.011)	(0.906)	(0.0)		
$\ln(Y/I)$	0.861	0.100	0.539	-0.341	1.000	
	(0.000)	(0.074)	(0.000)	(0.000)	(0.0)	
$\ln(Y/H)$	0.477	0.100	0.561	-0.288	0.655	1.000
	(0.000)	(0.073)	(0.000)	(0.000)	(0.000)	(0.0)

Note: p-values of χ^2-test for $H_0: \rho = 0$ in brackets

be warranted. At the level of *Kreise* however patent statistics are not reliable since two mechanisms are likely to intervene: firms register their patents at the location of the head of the firm or even if patents are registered by residence of the inventor spatial allocation of patents will be biased by migration.

Another way of considering spatial spillovers is to look at the geographic distribution of these factor productivities. *If* spatial spillovers of knowledge exist, we can expect to observe spatial clusters of high and low factor productivity. This is due to the fact that localized communication of skills will increase the productivity of the factor in question. Think of firms that might be able to use their machines more efficiently or workers (R&D-personnel) who might be more productive if they could use a locally available pool of technological knowledge.

Let us first take a look at the spatial distribution of capital productivity, expressed as Y/K. We see on Figure 6.3 that there exist indeed spatial clusters of this variable. A look at Figure 6.1 reveals that these clusters are the strongest in less populated areas, a fact that has been described already by the negative (though insignificant) correlation between population density and capital productivity (see Table 6.3). This insignificance can be detected in map of Figure 6.3 since some cities have low and others have high capital productivity. A look at Figure 6.4 reveals clusters for labour productivity Y/L as well although these clusters are smaller, i.e. the reach of spatial spillovers seems to be lower. Note

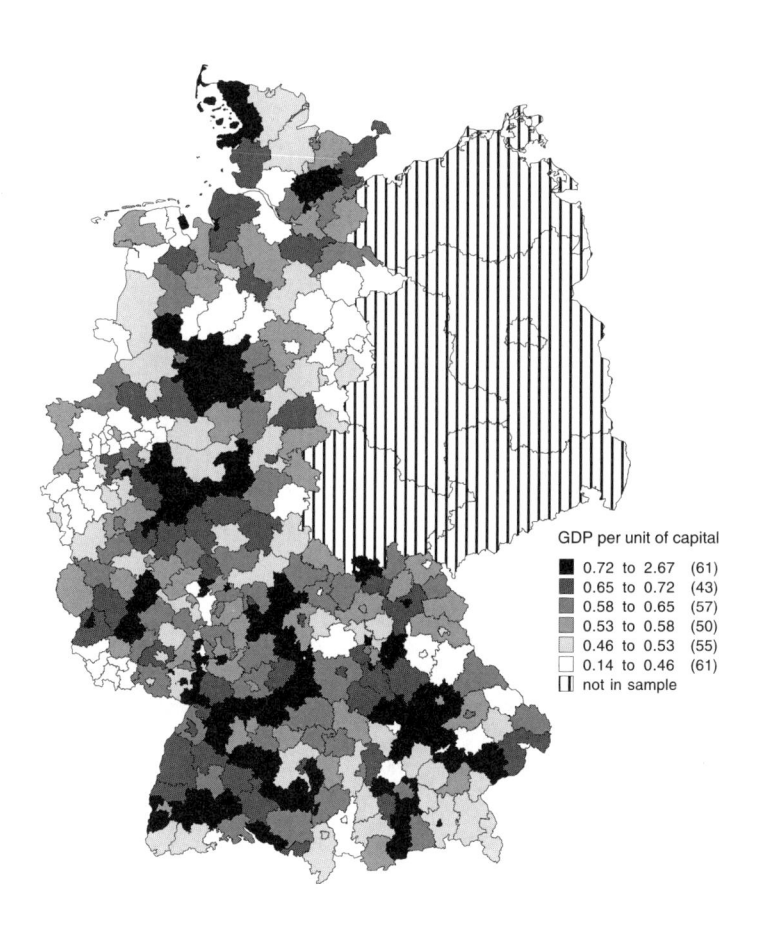

Figure 6.3: Capital Productivity of West-German Kreise (1992)

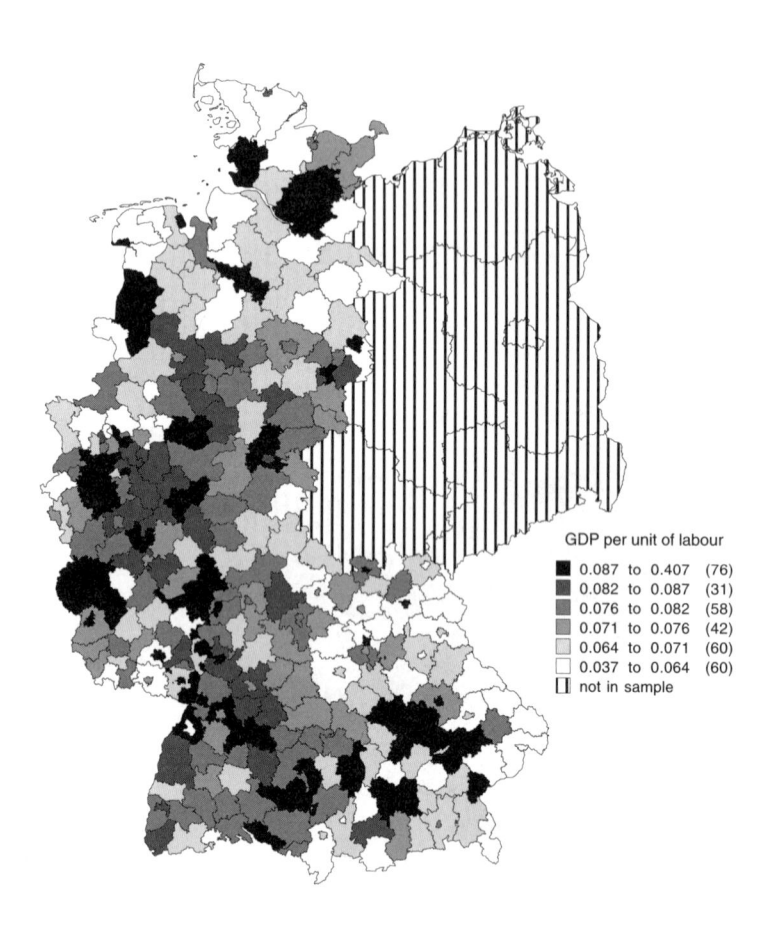

Figure 6.4: Labour Productivity of West-German Kreise (1992)

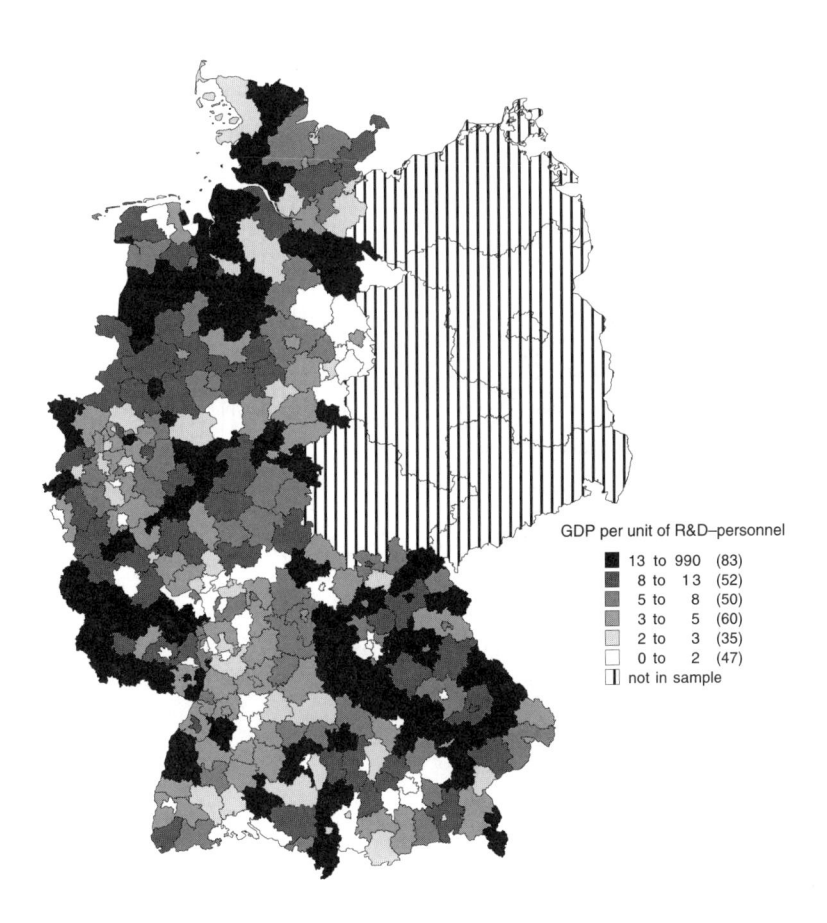

Figure 6.5: Productivity of R&D-personnel of West-German Kreise (1992)

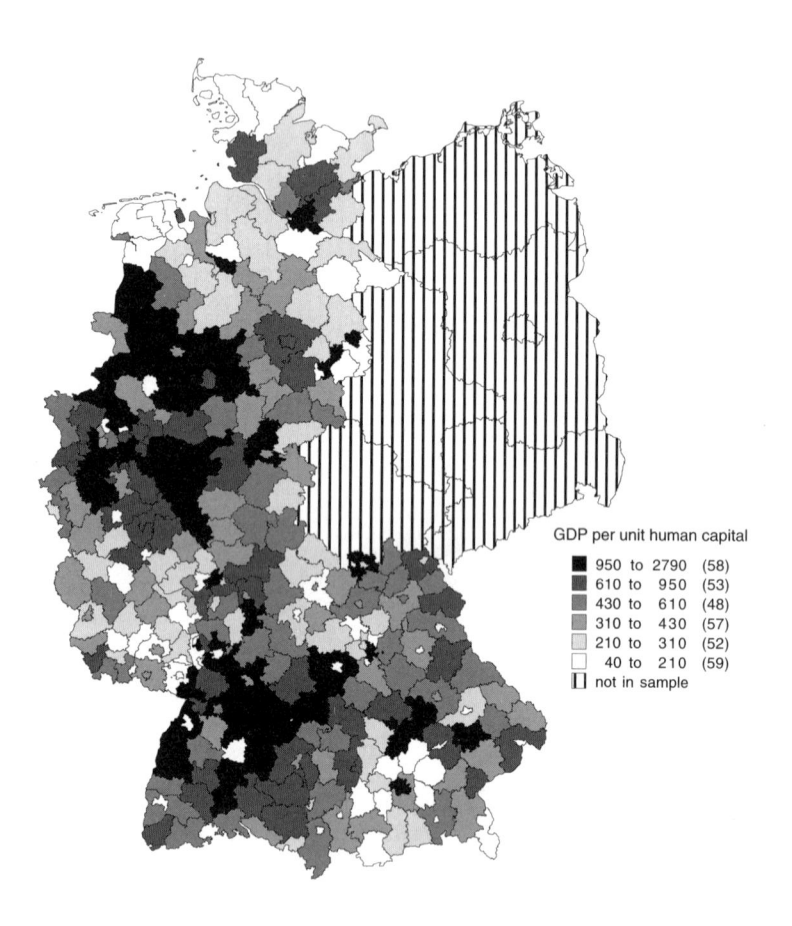

Figure 6.6: Productivity of Human Capital of West-German Kreise (1992)

(from a comparison of Figures 6.4 and 6.1) that labour productivity seems to be higher in densely populated areas, a fact that is reflected in the positive correlation between population density and labour productivity (reproduced in Table 6.3).

Spatial productivity clusters can also be observed for R&D-personnel and human capital.[5] Let me repeat however that Y/R is not an appropriate measure for the productivity of R&D-personnel, though it is consistent with the specification of the production function chosen in section 6.5.1.1. Finally, the productivity of human capital is strongly clustered. Note however that we observe a few outliers which are usually cities dominated by universities (Tübingen, Freiburg, Münster) or other special cases (like Bonn, the seat of the government) where the level of formation is high whereas the part of the productive sector in the local economy is low.

To express these findings statistically: we observe *spatial autocorrelation* in factor productivities. This effect can be expressed in explicit measures of correlation. To do so however I will first present the concept of the spatial weight matrix.

6.3.2 A Useful Matrix – the Spatial Weight Matrix

6.3.2.1 The Simplest Case – the Binary Contiguity Matrix

To describe the concept of *neighbourhood* and the possibilities to implement it in the regression equation let me start with a simple motivating example. Consider a country that is divided in 9 (statistical) regions. Suppose further that these regions are arranged in a 3×3 regional array. That is the spatial distribution of the country's regions can be described by a matrix **B**:

$$\mathbf{B} = \begin{pmatrix} 1 & 2 & 3 \\ 4 & 5 & 6 \\ 7 & 8 & 9 \end{pmatrix}$$

Let me define *neighbourhood* as follows: two regions are neighbours if they have a common border i.e. if it is possible to move from one region to the other

---

[5] I do not present the productivity of infrastructure graphically since it is nearly linearly correlated with population density (as can be seen from Table 6.3) and the map therefore appears very similar to map 6.1. This relationship is easy to understand since infrastructure is more heavily used (and thus more productive) in densely populated regions.

without crossing a third. Formally, we can distinguish three types: a) regions have common edges, b) they have common vertices or c) they have both. Type a) – which is illustrated in Figure 6.7.a – is referred to as "von Neumann"-neighbourhood in the literature on cellular automata[6]. The literature on spatial statistics refers to type a) as "rook"-neighbourhood according to the movements of a rook in the game of chess. Type b) is referred to as "bishop"-neighbourhood. See Figure 6.7.b) for an illustration. Type c) is referred to as "Moore" or "queen"-neighbourhood. From Figure 6.7.c) we see that this type can be seen as a combination of type a) and b). Finally it is possible to define neighbourhoods of higher order but I will not go into detail here, see e.g. Anselin[1988, p.18].

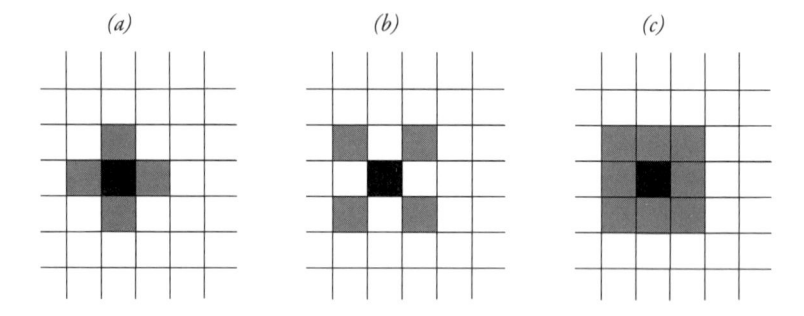

Figure 6.7: Three different types of neighbourhood. a) rook/von Neumann b) bishop and c) queen/Moore neighbourhood

The economically most meaningful type is certainly the third, although the distinction between these three types probably becomes obsolete in most cases if we consider irregularly shaped regions. If we consider a "Moore"/"queen" neighbourhood, the contiguity of regions in country **B** can be described by a *contiguity matrix* **C** that is constructed as follows: let **C** be a $N \times N$-matrix where N is the number of regions in the country under consideration. Hence, each region is represented by both a row and a column (i.e. for country **B** we have $\dim[\mathbf{C}] = 9 \times 9$). The number of entries in the i-th row of **C** equals the number of neighbours of region i. For the binary contiguity matrix, entries of row i are 1 at positions j, where j corresponds to the index numbers of the regions that neighbour i. Thus, for the "Moore"/"queen" neighbourhood the

---

[6]see e.g. Wolfram[1994, p.212] or Gaylord and Wellin[1995]

contiguity matrix for country **B** is

$$\mathbf{C} = \begin{bmatrix} 0 & 1 & 0 & 1 & 1 & 0 & 0 & 0 & 0 \\ 1 & 0 & 1 & 1 & 1 & 1 & 0 & 0 & 0 \\ 0 & 1 & 0 & 0 & 1 & 1 & 0 & 0 & 0 \\ 1 & 1 & 0 & 0 & 1 & 0 & 1 & 1 & 0 \\ 1 & 1 & 1 & 1 & 0 & 1 & 1 & 1 & 1 \\ 0 & 1 & 1 & 0 & 1 & 0 & 0 & 1 & 1 \\ 0 & 0 & 0 & 1 & 1 & 0 & 0 & 1 & 0 \\ 0 & 0 & 0 & 1 & 1 & 1 & 1 & 0 & 1 \\ 0 & 0 & 0 & 0 & 1 & 1 & 0 & 1 & 0 \end{bmatrix}$$

Since of course, a region cannot be contiguous to itself, the diagonal elements of **C** equal zero. Moreover, since neighbourhood is symmetric, **C** = **C'**. Using **C** it is straigthforward to model functional interactions between regions. Let e.g. **y** be a vector of some variable, y_i, say GDP, representing the realization of this variable for region i. Then **Cy** is a vector of the *sum* of the neighbours' GDP. Thus at position i of **Cy** we have $\sum_{j=1}^{n} y_j$, where j are neighbours of i and n is their number. Hence, if there exist spatial effects between regions and their neighbours (as discussed in section 6.4.1) we can expect a regression of the form

$$\mathbf{y} = f(\mathbf{Cy}) \qquad (6.1)$$

to yield a significant result. Very often however, a regression of **y** against the simple sum of the neighbours is difficult to interpret economically. Therefore, a number of generalizations of **C** have been suggested.

6.3.2.2 Generalized Spatial Weight Matrices

Usually it is not mere neighbourhood that leads to spillovers between regions but contacts between regions through local communication and migration. Although two regions might be contiguous, spillovers might be low, due to geographical factors (a mountain or a desert) or cultural factors (language etc.). Moreover, it is clear that *distance* should play a role in some respect. In order to include these phenomena, different approaches have been suggested to generalize the concept of binary contiguity and thus to allow for economically viable interpretations of spatial interaction matrices. Cliff and Ord[1973, 1981][7] suggest a contiguity measure based on distance and the proportion of the border

---
[7] Cited from Anselin[1988].

that is occupied by the respective other region. Other extensions take into account the relative area of the spatial units or logistic features like the accessibility via means of transportation.

There exist of course no objective criteria to choose the appropriate measure of contiguity, hence *which* measure to choose depends on the question under consideration. Obviously, the choice has a direct influence on the realization of the spatial weight matrix and thus on the result of the regression $\mathbf{y} = f(\bar{\mathbf{C}}\mathbf{y})$, $\bar{\mathbf{C}}$ being a *generalized spatial weight matrix*. Hence, the choice of $\bar{\mathbf{C}}$ has a direct influence on the parameter estimates. This is of course a highly undesirable feature of this procedure since it is not intersubjectively comparable and – finally – leaves room for parameter manipulation. A number of authors[8] therefore suggest the use of *neutral* or *general* weight matrices.

One type of generalized spatial weight matrix that is neutral, easy to implement, has some desirable statistical properties and can be economically interpreted is the *row standardized weight matrix*, henceforth referred to as matrix $\mathbf{W}$. The standardization is made such that the entries in each row sum to unity, i.e. if country i has n neighbours, the ith row will contain a $1/n$ at every j (zero otherwise), where j corresponds to the index of each country that neighbours i. The intuition behind $\mathbf{W}$ is as follows. Suppose a vector $\mathbf{y}$ of, say, GDP, i.e. the ith entry of $\mathbf{y}$ is region is GDP. Then $\mathbf{W}\mathbf{y}$ is a vector of the *mean* of the neighbours' GDP, i.e. its ith position will reproduce the mean of the GDP of i's neighbours. In the following statistical and econometric analysis I will use $\mathbf{W}$ and $\mathbf{C}$ where appropriate.

6.3.3 Spatial Correlation of Variables

Spatial weight matrices are a tool that allows to describe spatial interaction statistically. Let me first give some evidence for spatial correlation in the data. Figure 6.8 gives a scatterplot matrix of the variables used in regression against their spatial lags, the definition of spatial lag being

$$\text{lag}[\mathbf{v}] = \mathbf{W}\mathbf{v},$$

where $\mathbf{v}$ represents the variables used in regression and $\mathbf{W}$ is the row standardized spatial weight matrix. Table 6.4 reports the corresponding Bravais-Pearson correlations. We can see from the diagonal of both Table 6.4 and Figure 6.8

---

[8]See the discussion in Anselin[1988, p.21].

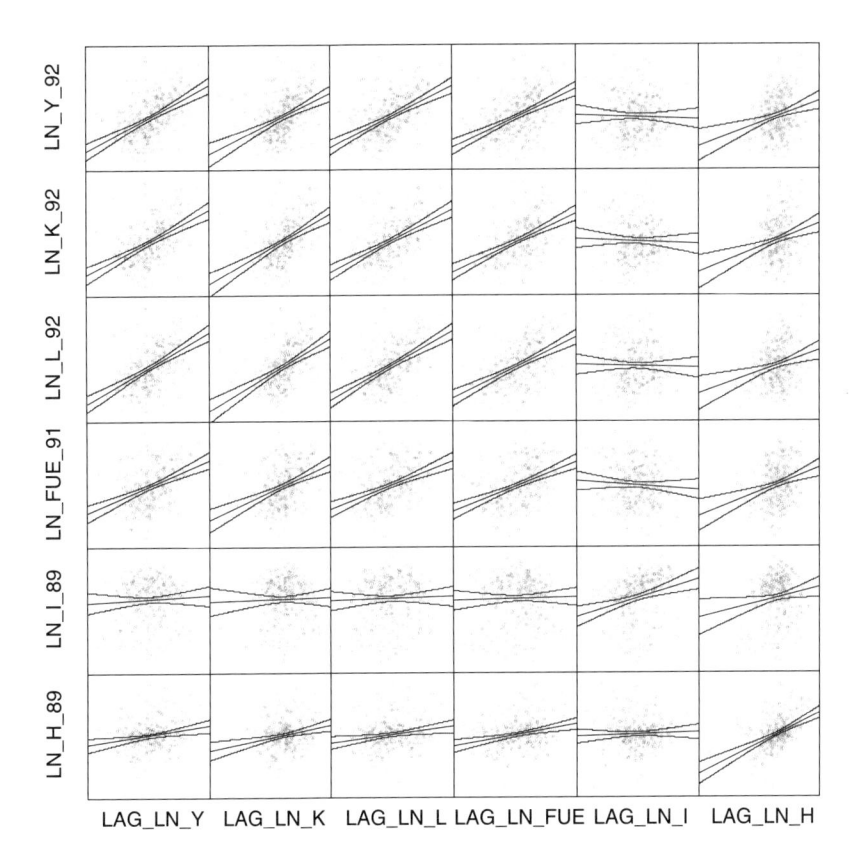

Figure 6.8: Scatterplot matrix of variables used in regresion against their spatial lags. Lines give a descriptive linear fit and a 95% confidence interval of the regression line

that there exists significant positive *spatial autocorrelation* in the data. Moreover, (from the first row of Table 6.4 and Figure 6.8) there exists positive and significant correlation between output and the spatial lags of the input variables with the exception of infrastructure.

Let me now go back to the discussion of section 6.3.1 where I suggested that there exist spatial clusters of factor productivity. If this statement holds we can expect significant positive spatial autocorrelation of factor productivities that is between $\mathbf{y/v}$ and $\mathbf{W(y/v)}$. Table 6.5 gives the Bravais-Pearson cross correlations, i.e. the diagonal reports spatial autocorrelations. Indeed, all autocorrelations are positive and significant. The non-diagonal elements of this table are difficult to interpret and will therefore not be considered further. Of course, from an economic point of view, simple linear correlations are insuffi-

Table 6.4: Pearson correlation matrix of variables against their spatial lags

	lag[ln(Y)]	lag[ln(K)]	lag[ln(L)]	lag[ln(R)]	lag[ln(I)]	lag[ln(H)]
ln(Y)	0.502	0.406	0.498	0.491	-0.030	0.244
	(0.000)	(0.000)	(0.000)	(0.000)	(0.597)	(0.000)
ln(K)	0.477	0.451	0.489	0.475	-0.044	0.254
	(0.000)	(0.000)	(0.000)	(0.000)	(0.483)	(0.000)
ln(L)	0.521	0.460	0.533	0.491	-0.024	0.222
	(0.000)	(0.000)	(0.000)	(0.000)	(0.672)	(0.000)
ln(R)	0.413	0.381	0.401	0.428	-0.064	0.262
	(0.000)	(0.000)	(0.000)	(0.000)	(0.257)	(0.000)
ln(I)	0.047	0.023	0.031	0.028	0.253	0.149
	(0.406)	(0.679)	(0.581)	(0.621)	(0.000)	(0.008)
ln(H)	0.195	0.230	0.176	0.252	0.042	0.451
	(0.000)	(0.000)	(0.002)	(0.000)	(0.457)	(0.000)

Note: p-values of a χ^2-test for $H_0 : \rho = 0$ in brackets

cient to judge the existence of spatial spillovers. The next section will therefore present an approach that allows to test the model of chapter 4 with the data now presented.

6.4 Spatial Econometrics – an Overview

6.4.1 Why *Spatial* Econometrics?

The previous section has shown that the data to be used in the regressions display spatial correlation and even spatial autocorrelation. Anselin[1988, chapter 2] distinguishes two types of *spatial effects* that can occur in an analysis of spatial data: *spatial dependence* and *spatial heterogeneity*.

Spatial dependence can be caused by measurement problems that are mainly caused by spatial externalites or spatial spillovers. The discussion in chapter 3 showed that there is strong evidence that such effects exists. However *if* they exist and they are not included in a regression we can expect the results to be biased. Another cause of spatial dependence can be given by the arbitrary delineation of spatial units of measurement. Very often geographical borders of these statistical units are not identical with "true" spatial limits of economic activity, i.e. economic spaces that can be con-

Table 6.5: Pearson correlation matrix of factor productivities against their spatial lags

	lag $[\ln(\frac{Y}{K})]$	lag $[\ln(\frac{Y}{L})]$	lag $[\ln(\frac{Y}{R})]$	lag $[\ln(\frac{Y}{T})]$	lag $[\ln(\frac{Y}{H})]$
$\ln(\frac{Y}{K})$	0.312 (0.000)	0.074 (0.184)	-0.060 (0.281)	-0.001 (0.979)	-0.027 (0.626)
$\ln(\frac{Y}{L})$	0.068 (0.220)	0.123 (0.027)	-0.257 (0.000)	0.130 (0.019)	0.104 (0.061)
$\ln(\frac{Y}{R})$	-0.035 (0.527)	-0.241 (0.000)	0.244 (0.000)	-0.238 (0.000)	-0.243 (0.000)
$\ln(\frac{Y}{T})$	-0.021 (0.706)	0.082 (0.140)	-0.265 (0.000)	0.391 (0.000)	0.316 (0.000)
$\ln(\frac{Y}{H})$	0.047 (0.396)	0.246 (0.000)	-0.328 (0.000)	0.438 (0.000)	0.499 (0.000)

Note: p-values of a χ^2-test for $H_0 : \rho = 0$ in brackets

sidered as (more or less) closed sub-economies. Think e.g. of an economy with 3 "true" economic spaces whose output is $Y_{(A)}$, $Y_{(B)}$ and $Y_{(C)}$. If statistical measurement aggregates these regions into two units of observation then the output of the latter will be

$$Y_{(1)} = Y_{(A)} + \phi Y_{(B)} \quad \text{and} \quad Y_{(2)} = Y_{(C)} + (1-\phi)Y_{(B)},$$

i.e. the output of region 1 depends on the output of region 2 via ϕ. It is obvious that such a process will yield spatial *autocorrelation*. We see, however, from these equations that this problem is not independent of the actual size of the statistical unit: the larger the statistical units, the more likely the influence of ϕ is simply aggregated away. On the other hand, the smaller the statistical units, the more likely this type of spatial dependence will vanish. This is one reason why I used data for the smallest regional units available.

Very often the notion of *spatial lag* is used in the literature to describe the phenomenon of spatial heterogeneity. Although this sounds familiar to time series econometricians, the methods used there cannot be translated one to one to solve the problem of spatial dependence. This is due to the fact that spatial processes are two-dimensional (not one-dimensional like time-wise dependence) and recursive, i.e. spillovers go in both directions. I will present methods to deal with that problem in section 6.4.2.

Spatial heterogeneity exists if spatial effects are not uniform across regions. Again, the discussion in chapter 3 or in section 6.2 gives evidence that regions differ indeed, think of population density or levels of technological developement. This lack of structural stability can yield spatial *heteroscedasticity* in the regressions. The usual approach to deal with that problem is to refer to standard econometric methods like varying parameters, random coefficients etc. However, spatial heterogeneity is usually not seen as a serious problem in spatial regression[9]. The aim of this work is rather to infer parameters that are constant over space. Then, the best (i.e. the economically most meaningful) strategy is to explain spatial heterogeneity by including new parameters in the regressor matrix. In the analysis of section 6.5 I will run a White-test to see whether heteroscedasticity is present in the error term or to check whether it vanishes with the inclusion of further parameters.

In the context of an *econometric analysis*, both types of spatial effects can be interpreted as a violation of the assumptions of the General Linear Model. OLS regresions can therefore be expected to be biased. Thus, a closer look at the statistical properties of OLS estimation and possibly the use of other regression techniques is required.

6.4.2 OLS–Regression Analysis with Spatial Effects in the Dataset

In this section I will describe the procedure of parameter estimation in the presence of spatially lagged variables. For this purpose, I will specify a regression equation of a spatial economic process in its most general way and derive from this basis its estimation properties. Suppose a model of the form

$$\mathbf{y} = \underbrace{\rho \mathbf{W}_y \mathbf{y}}_{a} + \mathbf{X}_1 \boldsymbol{\beta}_1 + \underbrace{\mathbf{W}_X \mathbf{X}_2 \boldsymbol{\beta}_2}_{b} + \boldsymbol{\varepsilon} \qquad (6.2a)$$

where

$$\boldsymbol{\varepsilon} = \underbrace{\lambda \mathbf{W}_\varepsilon \boldsymbol{\varepsilon}}_{c} + \mathbf{u}, \quad \mathbf{u} \sim N(\mathbf{0}, \sigma_u^2 \mathbf{I}). \qquad (6.2b)$$

$\mathbf{W}_i$ are *spatial weight matrices* for $\mathbf{y}$, $\mathbf{X}$ and $\boldsymbol{\varepsilon}$ respectively. The difference between the general linear model and the model given here is in parts a, b and c. In

---
[9] See e.g. Anselin[1988, p.9] or Klotz[1996, p.4].

principle, a model of form (6.2) can be considered as a *spatial ARMAX*-model, i.e. we have a spatial autoregressive – moving average process with a spatially lagged external variable. Note however – as already mentioned above – that the analogy might be misleading since spatial processes are more complex.[10]

Let me now turn to a description of the statistical properties of an OLS estimation of equations (6.2), including parts a, b and c in turn.

6.4.2.1 OLS–Estimation with Spatially Lagged External Variables

If we consider only part b from model (6.2) then we have

$$\mathbf{y} = \mathbf{W}_X \mathbf{X}_2 \boldsymbol{\beta}_2 + \mathbf{u}, \quad \mathbf{u} \sim N(\mathbf{0}, \sigma_u^2 \mathbf{I}). \tag{6.3}$$

OLS estimation of $\boldsymbol{\beta}_2$ yields

$$\begin{aligned} \hat{\boldsymbol{\beta}}_2 &= (\mathbf{X}_2' \mathbf{W}_X' \mathbf{W}_X \mathbf{X}_2)^{-1} \mathbf{X}_2' \mathbf{W}_X' \mathbf{y} \\ &= \boldsymbol{\beta}_2 + (\mathbf{X}_2' \mathbf{W}_X' \mathbf{W}_X \mathbf{X}_2)^{-1} (\mathbf{W}_X \mathbf{X}_2)' \mathbf{u}. \end{aligned}$$

This estimation is unbiased since if $E[\mathbf{X}_2' \mathbf{u}] = \mathbf{0}$, the spatial lag of $\mathbf{X}_2$ is also uncorrelated with $\mathbf{u}$ i.e. $E[(\mathbf{W}_X \mathbf{X}_2)' \mathbf{u}] = \mathbf{0}$. The covariance matrix of $\hat{\boldsymbol{\beta}}_2$ can be shown to be $\sigma_u^2 (\mathbf{X}_2' \mathbf{W}_X' \mathbf{W}_X \mathbf{X}_2)^{-1}$ which is known to be the most efficient estimate in a model of type (6.3). Thus, in the case of spatially lagged external variables OLS is BLUE, i.e. we can stack

$$\mathbf{X} = \mathbf{X}_1 \vdots \mathbf{X}_2 \quad \text{and} \quad \boldsymbol{\beta} = \begin{pmatrix} \boldsymbol{\beta}_1 \\ \boldsymbol{\beta}_2 \end{pmatrix}$$

and model (6.2a) simplifies correspondingly.

6.4.2.2 OLS–Estimation in the Case of Spatial Autocorrelation in the Dependent Variable

Considering only part a of model (6.2) we obtain

$$\mathbf{y} = \rho \mathbf{W}_y \mathbf{y} + \mathbf{u}, \quad \mathbf{u} \sim N(\mathbf{0}, \sigma_u^2 \mathbf{I}). \tag{6.4}$$

---

[10]Anselin[1988, p.34] considered a more general model where he allowed for heteroscedasticity in the error term, i.e. $\mathbf{u} \sim N(\mathbf{0}, \boldsymbol{\Omega})$, where $\Omega_{ii} = h_i \cdot (\mathbf{z}\boldsymbol{\alpha})$ and $\Omega_{ij} = 0$. As discussed above however, I will not consider the case of heteroscedasticity here.

An OLS-estimate of ρ yields

$$\hat{\rho} = (\mathbf{y}'\mathbf{W}'_y\mathbf{W}_y\mathbf{y})^{-1}\mathbf{y}'\mathbf{W}'_y\mathbf{y}$$
$$= \rho + (\mathbf{y}'\mathbf{W}'_y\mathbf{W}_y\mathbf{y})^{-1}\mathbf{y}'\mathbf{W}'_y\mathbf{u}$$

which is a consistent estimate if

$$\text{plim}(1/N)(\mathbf{y}'\mathbf{W}'_y\mathbf{W}_y\mathbf{y}) = \mathbf{Q},$$

$\mathbf{Q}$ being a finite, nonsingular matrix and

$$\text{plim}(1/N)(\mathbf{y}'\mathbf{W}'_y\mathbf{u}) = 0.$$

From equation (6.4) however we have

$$\mathbf{y} = (\mathbf{I} - \rho\mathbf{W}_y)^{-1}\mathbf{u}$$

Hence, the second condition becomes

$$\text{plim}(1/N)(\mathbf{y}'\mathbf{W}'_y\mathbf{u}) = \text{plim}(1/N)\mathbf{u}'\mathbf{W}(\mathbf{I} - \rho\mathbf{W}_y)^{-1}\mathbf{u}$$

which is a quadratic form in the error terms. Thus, this term is does not equal zero unless ρ degenerates to 0. Hence OLS-estimation of the parameter of spatial autocorrelation is biased. A natural approach to tackle this problem is to refer to ML-estimation, an approach which will be presented in section 6.4.3.

A different question arises in the following situation. Consider a model of the form

$$\mathbf{y} = \rho\mathbf{W}_y\mathbf{y} + \mathbf{X}\boldsymbol{\beta} + \mathbf{u}, \quad \mathbf{u} \sim N(\mathbf{0}, \sigma_u^2\mathbf{I})$$

which corresponds to (6.2a), with the restriction $\lambda = 0$ and with $\mathbf{X}_1$ and $\mathbf{W}_X\mathbf{X}_2$ merged into $\mathbf{X}$ as described in section 6.4.2.1. An OLS estimation of $\boldsymbol{\beta}$ under neglection of $\rho\mathbf{W}\mathbf{y}$ would of course be biased. The bias can be shown to be

$$E[\hat{\boldsymbol{\beta}} - \boldsymbol{\beta}] = E[(\mathbf{X}'\mathbf{X})^{-1}\mathbf{X}'\rho\mathbf{W}\mathbf{y}] = \rho\boldsymbol{\beta}_L,$$

where $\boldsymbol{\beta}_L$ corresponds to the expected value of a regression of $\mathbf{X}$ against $\mathbf{W}\mathbf{y}$, the spatial lag of $\mathbf{y}$. For a detailed proof see appendix B.1 on page 153.

6.4.2.3 OLS–Estimation in the Presence of Spatial Residual Autocorrelation

Consider a model of the form

$$\mathbf{y} = \mathbf{X}\beta + \varepsilon \quad \text{with } \varepsilon = \lambda \mathbf{W}_\varepsilon \varepsilon + \mathbf{u}, \quad \mathbf{u} \sim N(\mathbf{0}, \sigma_u^2 \mathbf{I}) \quad (6.5)$$

which is equation (6.2) with part a omitted and again $\mathbf{X}_1$ and $\mathbf{W}_X \mathbf{X}_2$ merged into $\mathbf{X}$. Solving (6.2b) for ε and inserting yields

$$\mathbf{y} = \mathbf{X}\beta + (\mathbf{I} - \lambda \mathbf{W}_\varepsilon)^{-1} \mathbf{u}. \quad (6.6)$$

Although OLS-estimation would be unbiased as

$$E[\hat{\beta} - \beta] = E[(\mathbf{X}'\mathbf{X})^{-1}\mathbf{X}'\varepsilon] = 0$$

it is inefficient since

$$\begin{aligned}
E[(\hat{\beta} - \beta)(\hat{\beta} - \beta)'] &= E[(\mathbf{X}'\mathbf{X})^{-1}\mathbf{X}'\varepsilon\varepsilon'\mathbf{X}(\mathbf{X}'\mathbf{X})^{-1}] \\
&= \sigma_u^2 (\mathbf{X}'\mathbf{X})^{-1}\mathbf{X}'((\mathbf{I} - \lambda\mathbf{W})'(\mathbf{I} - \lambda\mathbf{W}))^{-1}\mathbf{X}(\mathbf{X}'\mathbf{X})^{-1}.
\end{aligned}$$

Note however that model (6.6) corresponds to the general linear model with a known covariance structure in the error term. Thus, we can refer to common econometric methods, in this case the GLS procedure. It will be described in the next section.

6.4.3 Different Approaches: Regression Analysis Based on ML or EGLS

If OLS can be shown to be biased, a natural approach to tackle this problem is to refer to *maximum likelihood* (ML) estimation which has been shown to yield consistent parameter estimates.[11] Under the assumption of joint standard normal distribution of the error ν, the log-likelihood function for a model of the form (6.2) is (see appendix B.2 on page 154 for a derivation)

$$\ell = -\frac{N}{2}\ln\pi - \frac{N}{2}\ln(\sigma_u^2) + \ln|\mathbf{N}| + \ln|\mathbf{M}| - \frac{1}{2}\nu'\nu, \quad \nu \sim s.n.i.i.d. \quad (6.7a)$$

where

$$\nu'\nu = \frac{1}{\sigma_u^2}(\mathbf{My} - \mathbf{X}\beta)'\mathbf{N}'\mathbf{N}(\mathbf{My} - \mathbf{X}\beta) \quad (6.7b)$$

---

[11] See e.g. Greene[1991] or Griffiths, Hill and Judge[1993].

with

$$\mathbf{M} = (\mathbf{I} - \rho \mathbf{W}_y) \quad \text{and} \quad \mathbf{N} = (\mathbf{I} - \lambda \mathbf{W}_\varepsilon).$$

Deriving ℓ with respect to β, ρ and λ yields three first order conditions that maximize the likelihood with respect to these parameters and thus can be transformed into regression equations (see appendix B.2 on page 154 for a detailed description). However, all three equations are nonlinear in the parameters. Therefore I will consider the cases of spatial autocorrelation in the depending variable and spatial residual autocorrelation seperately.

6.4.3.1 ML-Estimation in the Case of Spatial Autocorrelation in the Dependent Variable

Consider the case where $\rho \neq 0$ and $\lambda = 0$. Now ℓ will simplify to

$$\ell_\rho = -\frac{N}{2} \ln \pi - \frac{N}{2} \ln(\sigma_u^2) + \ln |\mathbf{M}| - \frac{1}{2\sigma_u^2} \mathbf{M}'\mathbf{M}$$

Deriving the first order conditions with respect to β yields the ML-estimator

$$\tilde{\boldsymbol{\beta}} = (\mathbf{X}'\mathbf{X})^{-1}\mathbf{X}'\mathbf{M}\mathbf{y}$$

which can be decomposed into

$$\tilde{\boldsymbol{\beta}} = (\mathbf{X}'\mathbf{X})^{-1}\mathbf{X}'\mathbf{y} - \rho(\mathbf{X}'\mathbf{X})^{-1}\mathbf{X}'\mathbf{W}\mathbf{y} = \hat{\boldsymbol{\beta}} - \rho\hat{\boldsymbol{\beta}}_L$$

where $\hat{\boldsymbol{\beta}}$ corresponds to an OLS-estimate of $\mathbf{y}$ against $\mathbf{X}$ and $\hat{\boldsymbol{\beta}}_L$ corresponds to an OLS-estimate of $\mathbf{y}_L = \mathbf{W}\mathbf{y}$ against $\mathbf{X}$. From the proof in appendix B.1 we know that this estimate is unbiased. Correspondingly, a consistent estimate of σ_u^2 can be shown to be

$$\tilde{\sigma}_u^2 = \frac{1}{N}(\tilde{\mathbf{u}}'\tilde{\mathbf{u}}) = \frac{1}{N}(\hat{\mathbf{u}} - \tilde{\rho}\hat{\mathbf{u}}_L)'(\hat{\mathbf{u}} - \tilde{\rho}\hat{\mathbf{u}}_L)$$

where

$$\hat{\mathbf{u}} = \mathbf{y} - \mathbf{X}\hat{\boldsymbol{\beta}}$$
$$\hat{\mathbf{u}}_L = \mathbf{W}\mathbf{y} - \mathbf{X}\hat{\boldsymbol{\beta}}_L.$$

Inserting this estimate into the log-likelihood function we obtain the *concentrated log-likelihood function* (see e.g. Greene, 1991, p.344):

$$_c\ell_\rho = -\frac{N}{2} \ln \pi - \frac{N}{2} \ln[\frac{1}{N}(\hat{\mathbf{u}} - \rho\hat{\mathbf{u}}_L)'(\hat{\mathbf{u}} - \rho\hat{\mathbf{u}}_L)] + \ln |\mathbf{I} - \rho\mathbf{W}_y|,$$

a function that is highly nonlinear in the variable ρ. Thus, ρ has to be estimated numerically. A procedure to obtain an estimate of ρ is given by the following pseudo-code (Anselin, 1988, p.183):

ML-Estimation of ρ

1. Carry out OLS of $\mathbf{X}$ on $\mathbf{y}$ to obtain $\hat{\boldsymbol{\beta}}$.
2. Carry out OLS of $\mathbf{X}$ on $\mathbf{W}\mathbf{y}$ to obtain $\hat{\boldsymbol{\beta}}_L$.
3. Compute $\hat{\mathbf{u}}$ and $\hat{\mathbf{u}}_L$.
4. Given $\hat{\mathbf{u}}$ and $\hat{\mathbf{u}}_L$, find $\tilde{\rho}$ that maximizes ${}_c\ell_\rho$.
5. Given $\tilde{\rho}$ compute $\tilde{\boldsymbol{\beta}} = \hat{\boldsymbol{\beta}} - \tilde{\rho}\hat{\boldsymbol{\beta}}_L$ and $\tilde{\sigma}_u^2$.

6.4.3.2 ML-Estimation in the Case of Spatial Residual Autocorrelation

According to Anselin [1988], the case of *spatial residual autocorrelation* is the empirically more relevant one. Assuming spatial autocorrelation in the residuals alone implies $\lambda \neq 0$ and $\rho = 0$, i.e. we have a model of the form (6.5). Thus, equations (6.7) simplify to

$$\ell_\lambda = -\frac{N}{2}\ln\pi - \frac{N}{2}\ln(\sigma_u^2) + \ln|\mathbf{N}| - \frac{1}{2\sigma_u^2}(\mathbf{y} - \mathbf{X}\boldsymbol{\beta})'\mathbf{N}'\mathbf{N}(\mathbf{y} - \mathbf{X}\boldsymbol{\beta}).$$

Deriving the first order condition for $\boldsymbol{\beta}$ yields the ML-estimator

$$\tilde{\boldsymbol{\beta}} = (\mathbf{X}'\mathbf{N}'\mathbf{N}\mathbf{X})^{-1}\mathbf{X}'\mathbf{N}'\mathbf{N}\mathbf{y}$$

and the corresponding estimate for σ_u^2 is

$$\tilde{\sigma}_u^2 = \frac{1}{N}(\tilde{\mathbf{u}}'\mathbf{N}'\mathbf{N}\tilde{\mathbf{u}}),$$

where $\tilde{\mathbf{u}} = \mathbf{y} - \mathbf{X}\tilde{\boldsymbol{\beta}}$. Note that these estimators correspond to the GLS estimator with a known covariance structure $\boldsymbol{\Omega} = (\mathbf{N}'\mathbf{N})^{-1}$ in the error term. Again, we derive the concentrated log-likelihood

$${}_c\ell_\lambda = -\frac{N}{2}\ln\pi - \frac{N}{2}\ln[\frac{1}{N}(\tilde{\mathbf{u}}'(\mathbf{I} - \lambda\mathbf{W}_\varepsilon)'(\mathbf{I} - \lambda\mathbf{W}_\varepsilon)\tilde{\mathbf{u}})] + \ln|(\mathbf{I} - \lambda\mathbf{W}_\varepsilon)|$$

which is a highly nonlinear equation in λ. In this case, the estimation procedure is even more complex than in the previous case since both $\boldsymbol{\beta}$ *and* $\mathbf{u}$ are a function of λ. Therefore, λ has to be estimated iteratively.

This estimation procedure can be shown to be identical to the *general least squares* or GLS procedure which is indicated if the assumption of independence of the error term is violated. The procedure allows for a generalized error covariance matrix Ω. In the case of spatial correlation of unitary lag in the error term it can be shown that $\Omega = [(\mathbf{I} - \lambda \mathbf{W}_\varepsilon)'(\mathbf{I} - \lambda \mathbf{W}_\varepsilon)]^{-1}$, i.e. the structure of the covariance matrix is known and can be expressed as a function of λ alone. Thus, the approach is to estimate λ and then to transform the regression model accordingly. Since the estimate of λ is necessary, this method is referred to as *estimated GLS* or EGLS-procedure.[12] Due to the nonlinearity of the matrix $(\mathbf{I} - \lambda \mathbf{W}_\varepsilon)$, λ cannot be estimated by a single step procedure. The pseudo-code of the estimation procedure is as follows (Anselin, 1988, p.183):

Iterative EGLS-Estimation of λ

1. Carry out OLS of $\mathbf{X}$ on $\mathbf{y}$ to obtain $\hat{\beta}$.
2. Compute $\hat{\mathbf{u}} = \mathbf{y} - \mathbf{X}\hat{\beta}$.
3. Given $\hat{\mathbf{u}}$, find λ that maximizes $_c\ell_\lambda$
4. Based on this estimate of λ carry out ML-esimation to obtain $\tilde{\beta}$
5. Compute $\tilde{\mathbf{u}} = \mathbf{y} - \mathbf{X}\tilde{\beta}$.
6. If convergence criterion is met go to 7, else go to 3.
7. Given $\tilde{\mathbf{u}}$ and λ compute $\tilde{\sigma}_u^2$.

Neither this, nor the previous algorithms are implemented in the usual regression packages. The algorithms therefore were programmed in *Mathematica*, a computer algebra system that allows to implement efficient iteration loops.[13] However, since the way in which these two parameters are estimated does not allow for interval-estimation, i.e. checking if the estimates are significant or not, I will present some tests that can be used for this .

6.4.4 Test Procdedures

The procedures presented above provide consistent estimates for ρ and λ. However, they do not allow to determine whether these estimates differ significantly from zero or not. I will now present a set of tests to investigate this.

---

[12] See e.g. Greene [1991, p.388] or Griffiths *et al.* [1993, part V] for a detailed description of the GLS or EGLS pocedures and how it is related to ML estimation.

[13] The package can be made available upon request.

6.4.4.1 Testing for Spatial Autocorrelation in the Dependent Variable

To test for statistical significance of ρ I will use a *likelihood ratio test*[14], a general test procedure to test for restrictions of any kind. The principle is as follows: given the null and alternative hypotheses

$$H_0 : \rho = 0 \quad \text{(the restriction applies)}$$
$$H_1 : \rho \neq 0 \quad \text{(no restriction applies)}$$

we can compute the maximized values of the log-likelihood functions under H_0 and H_1, $L(H_0)$ and $L(H_1)$ respectively. Then the likelihood ratio statistic under H_0 is

$$\mathcal{LR} = 2[L(H_1) - L(H_0)] \overset{asy}{\sim} \chi^2_{(R)}$$

R being the number of restrictions under H_1. H_0 is to be rejected if $\mathcal{LR} > \chi^2_c$, the critical value of the $\chi^2_{(R)}$-distribution. It can be shown that $\mathcal{LR}$ simplifies to

$$\mathcal{LR} = N(\ln SSE_R - \ln SSE_U),$$

SSE_i being the sum of squares of errors in the restricted and unrestricted cases. In our case we have

$$\mathcal{LR} \overset{asy}{\sim} \chi^2_{(1)} \quad \text{or} \quad \sqrt{\mathcal{LR}} \overset{asy}{\sim} N(0,1)$$

6.4.4.2 Testing for Spatial Autocorrelation in the Error Term

Although the same testing principle could be applied for the case of spatial autocorrelation in the error term, in the regressions I will use two different tests that are common in the literature of spatial statistics: a test based on Moran's I and a Lagrange Multiplier test.

A test based on Moran's I. Moran [1948] suggested a statistic to quantify spatial autocorrelation. This so-called Moran's $\mathcal{I}$ statistic is

$$\mathcal{I} = \frac{N}{S} \frac{\mathbf{u'Wu}}{\mathbf{u'u}}$$

---
[14] See e.g. Griffiths *et al.* [1993, p.453] for a description.

where S equals the sum of all elements in $\mathbf{W}$, i.e. $N/S = 1$ if $\mathbf{W}$ is row standardized. $\mathbf{u}$ are residuals obtained from an OLS procedure. Although, according to Anselin[1988, p.101], this test is by far the most widely used approach to test for spatial correlation in the errors, it does not have a precise expression for the alternative hypothesis (the null being absence of spatial autocorrelation). Cliff and Ord[1981] suggest a transformation of $\mathcal{I}$ such that the transformed variable follows a normal distribution

$$\mathcal{I}_n = \frac{\mathcal{I} - \mathrm{E}(\mathcal{I})}{\mathrm{Var}(\mathcal{I})^{(1/2)}}$$

with

$$\mathrm{E}(\mathcal{I}) = \frac{N}{S} \frac{\mathrm{tr}(\mathbf{X}^+\mathbf{W})}{N - K} \quad \text{and}$$

$$\mathrm{Var}(\mathcal{I}) = \left(\frac{N}{S}\right)^2 \frac{\mathrm{tr}(\mathbf{X}^+\mathbf{W}\mathbf{X}^+\mathbf{W}') + \mathrm{tr}(\mathbf{X}^+\mathbf{W})^2 + [\mathrm{tr}(\mathbf{X}^+\mathbf{W})]^2}{(N-K)(N-K+2)} - [\mathrm{E}(\mathcal{I})]^2$$

where $\mathbf{X}^+ = \mathbf{I} - \mathbf{X}(\mathbf{X}'\mathbf{X})^{-1}\mathbf{X}'$. I will report on $\mathcal{I}_n$ with the results of the regression. What we can derive from this test statistic is that there is evidence for "some spatial process" in the data if $\mathcal{I}_n > \mathrm{N}_c$, the critical value taken from the standard normal distribution. Let me however emphasize again that the alternative is unspecified, i.e. rejection of the null does not give us further information about which direction to proceed in. The following test therefore seems more preferrable.

Lagrange Multiplier Test. Just like the Likelihood Ratio test, the Lagrange Multiplier test is a general test principle based on the maximum likelihood approach and that will test for restrictions in general. Both tests can be shown to be asymptotically equivalent. Since the Lagrange Multiplier principle is very similar to the procdure described for the likelihood ratio test it will not be described further (see again Griffiths *et al.*, 1993). In the case of spatial autocorrelation in the residuals we have

$$H_0 : \lambda = 0 \quad \text{and}$$
$$H_1 : \lambda \neq 0$$

The test statistic under H_0 can be shown to be (Anselin, 1988, p.104)

$$\mathcal{LM} = \left(\frac{\mathbf{u}'\mathbf{W}\mathbf{u}}{\sigma_u^2}\right)^2 \cdot \mathrm{tr}[(\mathbf{W} + \mathbf{W}')\mathbf{W}]^{-1} \overset{asy}{\sim} \chi^2_{(1)}.$$

or alternatively $\sqrt{\mathcal{LM}} \overset{asy}{\sim} \mathrm{N}(0,1)$. Realizations of this test statistic will be reported in the regression tables.

6.4.4.3 A General Test for Heteroscedasticity: The White Test

To test finally for heteroscedasticity I will implement a very general test for heteroscedasticity: the White test. This test is not bound to any hypotheses as to the form of heteroscedasticity, i.e. we have

$$H_0 : \sigma^2_{u(i)} = \sigma^2_u \text{ and}$$
$$H_1 : \text{not } H_0$$

The idea of this test is that under H_0, the variance of the estimated β-vector is asymptotically identical under OLS and GLS-estimation if errors are homoscedastic. White derived a complex test statistic but showed as well that the term $N \cdot R^2$ of the regression of the model

$$\hat{u}_i^2 = \alpha_i + \sum_{j=2}^{K} \sum_{k=2}^{K} \alpha_{jk} x_{ij} x_{ik}$$

is asymptotically

$$\mathcal{W} \overset{asy}{\sim} N \cdot R^2 \overset{asy}{\sim} \chi^2_{K(K+1)/2},$$

$\hat{u}_i$ being error terms obtained from an OLS regression. I will report realizations of $\mathcal{W}$ in the regression tables.

6.5 Empirical Implementation of the Model and Results

To test the model developed in chapter 4 I will transform it into an econometrically testable form. Obviously, the rather stylized model has to be modified in several respects.

1. Since no data on firms is available, estimates of spillovers between firms cannot be obtained. It therefore seems reasonable to refer to a regionally disaggregated dataset if we assume that spillovers between firms of a region also imply spillovers between neighbouring regions. I will therefore refer to a dataset of 327 West-German *Kreise* (excluding Berlin) to obtain

Table 6.6: Results of Unrestricted Estimation for German Kreise

Dependent variable is ln Y	OLS–regressions			EGLS–regressions		
	(1)	(2)	(3)	(4)	(5)	(6)
Constant	-3.034	-2.709	-2.691	-2.988	-2.730	-2.719
	(0.215)	(0.227)	(0.226)	(0.231)	(0.239)	(0.237)
ln K	0.225	0.203	0.204	0.253	0.232	0.231
	(0.041)	(0.041)	(0.041)	(0.043)	(0.043)	(0.029)
ln L	0.867	0.830	0.817	0.840	0.813	0.803
	(0.050)	(0.050)	(0.051)	(0.053)	(0.052)	(0.053)
ln R		0.036	0.037		0.030	0.032
		(0.009)	(0.009)		(0.009)	(0.009)
ln $\tilde{R}$			0.013			0.010
			(0.007)			(0.008)
R_c^2	0.941	0.943	0.944	0.941	0.943	0.943
Estimated λ	–	–	–	0.269	0.222	0.205
Implied δ	–	–	0.351	–	–	0.292
W	10.153*	12.635*	14.572	10.445*	12.948*	14.845
$\sqrt{\mathcal{LM}}$	3.728*	2.838*	2.469*	3.943*	3.202*	2.925*
$\mathcal{I}_n$	3.911*	3.018*	2.663*	3.970*	3.146*	2.834*

Note: Estimated standard errors in brackets. An asterix signifies that the H_0 of the respective test was rejected at $\alpha = 0.05$.

an estimate of δ. To investigate whether spillovers exist between more remote regions (i.e. to test for Δ), I will refer to a dataset of 121 national states.

2. Of course, whether we would look at firms or at regions, it is necessary to allow for more than one neighbour (as opposed to the simplifying assumption made in section 4.3). Thus, instead of referring to K_j in equation (4.1) I will refer to the sum of the capital stock of neighbouring regions

$$\tilde{K}_i = \sum_{j=1}^{n} K_j \quad \text{or in matrix notation} \quad \tilde{\mathbf{K}} = \mathbf{C}\mathbf{K}$$

as to the factor that spills over to region i, j being neighbouring regions of i. $\mathbf{C}$ is the *unweighted* spatial weight matrix, (cf. equation 6.1 on page 117).

3. I will now depart from the "broad concept of capital" as used in the

Table 6.7: Results of Unrestricted Estimation for German Kreise

Dependent variable is ln Y	ML–regressions			ML/EGLS–regressions		
	(1)	(2)	(3)	(4)	(5)	(6)
Constant	-3.044 (0.223)	-2.700 (0.237)	-2.513 (0.226)	-2.910 (0.263)	-2.646 (0.266)	-2.500 (0.274)
ln K	0.226 (0.042)	0.203 (0.041)	0.197 (0.041)	0.252 (0.044)	0.231 (0.043)	0.228 (0.042)
ln L	0.866 (0.052)	0.832 (0.051)	0.833 (0.051)	0.845 (0.054)	0.818 (0.053)	0.809 (0.053)
ln R		0.036 (0.009)	0.040 (0.009)		0.030 (0.010)	0.035 (0.010)
ln $\tilde{R}$			0.023 (0.007)			0.018 (0.009)
R_c^2	0.941	0.943	0.944	0.940	0.943	0.944
Estimated ρ	-0.009	-0.016	-0.052	-0.015	-0.017	-0.045
Estimated λ	–	–	–	0.278	0.234	0.217
Implied δ	–	–	0.575	–	–	0.503
$\mathcal{W}$	10.302	13.227	14.877	10.449	13.266	14.863
$\sqrt{\mathcal{LR}}$	0.425	0.736	2.048*	0.625	0.708	1.666
$\sqrt{\mathcal{LM}}$	3.696*	2.872*	2.661*	4.090*	3.375*	3.118*
$\mathcal{I}_n$	3.894*	3.068*	2.873*	3.178*	3.280*	3.202*

Note: Estimated standard errors in brackets. An asterix signifies that the H_0 of the respective test was rejected at $\alpha = 0.05$.

model of chapter 4. This is necessary if real data is used since physical capital – as used in production – cannot spill over to a neighbouring region as opposed to factors that carry a public-good characteristic (see the discussion on page 62). As discussed in sections 4.1 and 6.2, I will use personnel employed in R&D, human capital and infrastructure.

I will present the estimation results for West-German *Kreise* in sections 6.5.1.1 to 6.5.1.3 where I include *R&D - personnel*, *human capital* and *infrastructure* respectively. The estimation results for the dataset of national states are presented in section 6.5.2

Table 6.8: Results of Restricted Estimation for German Kreise

Dependent variable is $\ln(Y/L)$	OLS–regressions			EGLS–regressions		
	(1)	(2)	(3)	(4)	(5)	(6)
Constant	-1.950 (0.026)	-1.865 (0.080)	-2.075 (0.105)	-1.895 (0.086)	-1.831 (0.083)	-2.002 (0.104)
$\ln(K/L)$	0.307 (0.040)	0.251 (0.040)	0.238 (0.040)	0.334 (0.042)	0.283 (0.041)	0.267 (0.041)
$\ln(R/L)$		0.049 (0.009)	0.047 (0.009)		0.042 (0.009)	0.045 (0.009)
$\ln \tilde{R}$			0.022 (0.007)			0.019 (0.007)
R_c^2	0.152	0.219	0.238	0.154	0.219	0.239
Estimated λ	–	–	–	0.292	0.212	0.164
Implied α	0.307	0.251	0.238	0.334	0.283	0.267
Implied β	0.693	0.700	0.715	0.666	0.675	0.688
Implied γ		0.049	0.047		0.042	0.045
Implied δ			0.447			0.425
$\mathcal{W}$	5.937*	9.189*	12.388	6.181*	9.458*	11.020
$\sqrt{\mathcal{LM}}$	4.165*	2.677*	1.953	4.308*	3.055*	2.302*
$\mathcal{I}_n$	4.309*	2.819*	2.121*	4.433*	3.176*	2.448*

Note: Estimated standard errors in brackets. An asterix signifies that the H_0 of the respective test was rejected at $\alpha = 0.05$.

6.5.1 Evidence from a Dataset of West-German Kreise

6.5.1.1 The Case of R&D-Personnel

Let me start with an OLS regression of a model of the form

$$Y = CK^\alpha L^\beta R^\gamma \tilde{R}^{\gamma\delta} e^u$$

estimated in log-log form, where I include local R&D-personnel, R, and the sum of the neighbours R&D-personnel, $\tilde{R}$, stepwise, C being a constant. From columns (1) and (2) of Table 6.6 we see that estimated figures correspond to what could have been expected (e.g. from Cobb and Douglas, 1928), i.e. α is roughly $1/4$ and β is roughly $3/4$. If we include R the elasticity of capital and labour is estimated lower, as could have been expected. Note that the test statistic reports evidence in favour of heteroscedasticity and spatial autocorrelation in the error term. Including $\tilde{R}$ (column 3) yields a significant estimate for $\alpha\delta$ and eliminates heteroscedasticity. In column (6) $\tilde{R}$ is insignificant. Note however that there is still evidence in favour of spatial autocorrelation in the error

Table 6.9: Results of Restricted Estimation for German Kreise

Dependent variable is $\ln(Y/L)$			
	ML–regressions		
	(1)	(2)	(3)
Constant	-1.387	-1.268	-1.673
	(0.079)	(0.235)	(0.316)
$\ln(K/L)$	0.302	0.252	0.242
	(0.039)	(0.040)	(0.040)
$\ln(R/L)$		0.043	0.044
		(0.009)	(0.009)
$\ln \tilde{R}$			0.016
			(0.008)
R_c^2	0.187	0.160	0.241
Estimated ρ	0.223	0.252	0.084
Implied α	0.302	0.252	0.242
Implied β	0.698	0.705	0.714
Implied γ		0.043	0.044
Implied δ			0.365
W	8.022*	11.811	13.562
$\sqrt{\mathcal{LR}}$	3.537*	1.860	1.243
$\sqrt{\mathcal{LM}}$	0.990	0.775	0.146
$\mathcal{I}_n$	-0.861	-0.638	0.313

Note: Estimated standard errors in brackets. An asterix signifies that the respective H_0 was rejected at $\alpha = 0.05$.

term. Note also, that the estimates of $\alpha + \beta(+\gamma) > 1$, i.e. the estimates imply increasing returns to scale in K, L and R. The estimates imply a spillover coefficient δ of approximately 0.3.

Table 6.7 reports similar regressions, however with an ML estimation of ρ included. The regression results do not differ fundamentally from those in Table 6.6 apart from the ML-estimate of $\tilde{R}$ (column 3), which is now considerably higher compared to column (3) of Table 6.6. This is probably due to the fact that $\tilde{R}$ in Table 6.6 also encompassed the influence of lag Y which is (as can be see from the estimate of ρ in Table 6.7, column 3) negative. It is interesting to observe that the inclusion of $\tilde{R}$ leads to significant autocorrelation in the dependend variable ($\sqrt{\mathcal{LR}}$ of column 3) which is removed if we correct for spatial autocorrelation in the error (column 6). Note that the ML/EGLS-estimate of $\tilde{R}$ is now significant at $\alpha = 0.95$. Note also that the correction for the spatial lag of Y leads to a higher estimate of the spillover coefficient δ which is now approximately 0.5 (columns 6 of Tables 6.6 and 6.7).

Table 6.10: Results of Unrestricted Estimation for German Kreise

Dependent variable is ln Y	OLS–regressions			EGLS–regressions		
	(1)	(2)	(3)	(4)	(5)	(6)
Constant	-3.034	-2.970	-2.949	-2.988	-2.956	-2.939
	(0.215)	(0.207)	(0.208)	(0.231)	(0.219)	(0.219)
ln K	0.225	0.172	0.172	0.253	0.204	0.203
	(0.041)	(0.041)	(0.041)	(0.043)	(0.043)	(0.042)
ln L	0.867	0.885	0.876	0.840	0.860	0.854
	(0.050)	(0.049)	(0.049)	(0.053)	(0.051)	(0.051)
ln H		0.139	0.143		0.123	0.130
		(0.028)	(0.028)		(0.029)	(0.030)
ln $\widetilde{H}$			0.019			0.013
			(0.015)			(0.015)
R_c^2	0.941	0.945	0.945	0.941	0.945	0.945
Estimated λ	–	–	–	0.269	0.203	0.191
Implied δ	–	–	0.148	–	–	0.100
$\mathcal{W}$	10.153*	11.167	14.0448	11.337	14.235*	43.290
$\sqrt{\mathcal{LM}}$	3.728*	2.417*	2.181*	2.633*	4.467*	4.441*
$\mathcal{I}_n$	3.911*	2.610*	2.385*	2.977*	2.809*	4.608*

Note: Estimated standard errors in brackets. An asterix signifies that the H_0 of the respective test was rejected at $\alpha = 0.05$.

Table 6.8 reproduces results of a similar regression, but with the restriction of constant returns to scale in K, L and R, i.e. $\alpha + \beta + \gamma = 1$. This approach has been included since these restriction corresponds to the approach chosen by Mankiw, Romer and Weil[1992], to be presented in section 6.5.2. Of course, regression results differ slightly though not fundamentally (compare with Table 6.6). Note that δ has been estimated slightly higher (around 0.43) and that with the exception of column (3) the test statistics correspond to those of Table 6.6, i.e. we have still significant autocorrelation in the error term and autocorrelation in $\ln(Y/L)$. Finally, Table 6.9 reports results of a regression where the influence of the spatial lag of $\ln(Y/L)$ is estimated. Note from $\sqrt{\mathcal{LR}}$, $\sqrt{\mathcal{LM}}$ and $\mathcal{W}$ of column (3) of Table 6.9 that a model of this type displays neither autocorrelation of any kind nor heteroscedasticity. Due to that reason, EGLS-estimates of λ in the presence of ρ did not converge. Thus, since none of the tests in column (3) of table 6.9 rejects the Null, I suggest placing most trust in this specification. Hence, the production elasticity of R&D–personnel is 0.016 i.e.

Table 6.11: Results of Unrestricted Estimation for German Kreise

Dependent variable is ln Y	ML–regressions			ML/EGLS–regressions		
	(1)	(2)	(3)	(4)	(5)	(6)
Constant	-3.044 (0.223)	-2.878 (0.206)	-2.805 (0.205)	-2.910 (0.263)	-2.823 (0.248)	-2.758 (0.274)
ln K	0.226 (0.042)	0.166 (0.041)	0.163 (0.041)	0.252 (0.044)	0.200 (0.043)	0.198 (0.043)
ln L	0.866 (0.052)	0.903 (0.048)	0.898 (0.048)	0.845 (0.054)	0.870 (0.052)	0.865 (0.052)
ln H		0.147 (0.028)	0.157 (0.028)		0.129 (0.030)	0.142 (0.031)
ln $\widetilde{H}$			0.030 (0.015)			0.021 (0.016)
R_c^2	0.941	0.945	0.945	0.940	0.943	0.945
Estimated ρ	-0.031	-0.045	-0.052	-0.015	-0.028	-0.038
Estimated λ	–	–	–	0.278	0.218	0.205
Implied δ	–	–	0.191	–	–	0.147
$\mathcal{W}$	12.718	13.227	14.938	10.449	12.837	15.075
$\sqrt{\mathcal{LR}}$	0.425	1.095	1.098	0.625	1.239	1.573
$\sqrt{\mathcal{LM}}$	3.696*	2.570*	2.367*	3.026*	3.375*	2.818*
$\mathcal{I}_n$	3.894*	2.782*	2.583*	3.178*	3.212*	3.018*

Note: Estimated standard errors in brackets. An asterix signifies that the H_0 of the respective test was rejected at $\alpha = 0.05$.

an increase of this factor by 1% would increase the output of the manufacturing sector by 0.016 %. At the same time, approximately 37% of the contribution of R&D-personnel of a region will spill over to its neighbours, who benefit from this asset as an external effect.

6.5.1.2 The Case of Human Capital

Let me now consider *human capital* as another factor that can spill over to neighbouring regions. I estimate the model

$$Y = CK^\alpha L^\beta H^\gamma \widetilde{H}^{\gamma\delta} e^u$$

with the techniques used in the previous section. Results are reproduced in Tables 6.10 to 6.12. An OLS estimate of the model yields significant (at $\alpha = 0.1$) estimates for $\widetilde{H}$ (see column (3) of Table 6.10). Note however from $\sqrt{\mathcal{LM}}$ that there is evidence for significant autocorrelation in the error term. EGLS

Table 6.12: Results of Restricted Estimation for German Kreise

Dependent variable is $\ln(Y/L)$	OLS–regressions			ML–regressions		
	(1)	(2)	(3)	(4)	(5)	(6)
Constant	-1.950	-2.388	-2.492	-1.895	-2.082	-2.320
	(0.026)	(0.100)	(0.110)	(0.086)	(0.100)	(0.109)
$\ln(K/L)$	0.307	0.201	0.195	0.334	0.205	0.197
	(0.040)	(0.041)	(0.041)	(0.042)	(0.041)	(0.041)
$\ln H$		0.175	0.174		0.164	0.168
		(0.026)	(0.026)		(0.026)	(0.026)
$\ln \widetilde{H}$			0.033			0.029
			(0.014)			(0.014)
R_c^2	0.152	0.254	0.264	0.154	0.264	0.268
Estimated ρ	–	–	–	0.292	0.110	0.057
Implied α	0.307	0.201	0.195	0.334	0.205	0.197
Implied β	0.693	0.799	0.805	0.666	0.795	0.803
Implied γ		0.175	0.174		0.164	0.168
Implied δ			0.189			0.172
W	5.937*	9.534*	11.983	6.181*	8.287	12.702
$\sqrt{\mathcal{LR}}$	–	–	–	4.308*	1.729	0.855
$\sqrt{\mathcal{LM}}$	4.165*	2.078*	1.810	4.308*	2.078*	0.633
$\mathcal{I}_n$	4.309*	2.215*	1.946	4.433*	2.235*	0.781

Note: Estimated standard errors in brackets. An asterix signifies that the H_0 of the respective test was rejected at $\alpha = 0.05$.

estimation of this process (column (6) of the same table) yields a value of $\lambda \approx 0.2$ but the test statistic is still significant. Table 6.11 reports results of a similar approach but with ρ explicitly specified. Estimates of ρ are negative, though not significant. Note that λ is still significant and estimated at 0.2.

Autocorrelation in the error term is insignificant in an estimate where the restriction $\alpha + \beta = 1$ (constant returns in capital an labour)[15] applies (see column (3) of Table 6.12). Therefore (as in the case of R&D–personnel) EGLS–estimates of λ did not converge. Also, ML-estimates of ρ yielded insignificant results (see column (6) of the same Table). I therefore suggest to take column (6) of Table 6.12 as the most reliable specification. Thus, the output of a region will increase by a little less than 0.2% if its human capital increases by 1%. Roughly 20% of a region's human capital will spill over to its neighbours who

---

[15]The restriction $\alpha + \beta + \gamma = 1$ (constant returns in capital, labour and human capital) led to negative parameter estimates for H. I therefore rejected this restriction as being too strong.

Table 6.13: Results of Unrestricted Estimation for German Kreise

	Dependent variable is ln Y		
	OLS–regressions		
	(1)	(2)	(3)
Constant	-3.034 (0.215)	-2.963 (0.210)	-2.753 (0.226)
ln K	0.225 (0.041)	0.186 (0.040)	0.195 (0.040)
ln L	0.867 (0.050)	0.932 (0.049)	0.918 (0.049)
ln I		-0.051 (0.014)	-0.080 (0.019)
ln $\tilde{I}$			0.002 (0.001)
R_c^2	0.941	0.945	0.946

Note: Estimated standard errors in brackets

benefit from this asset as an external effect.

6.5.1.3 The Case of Infrastructure

Finally, I specify a model of the form

$$Y = CK^\alpha L^\beta I^\gamma \tilde{I}^{\gamma\delta} e^u$$

where I is *infrastructure*. Table 6.13 reproduces results of an OLS-regression of the above specification. We see that the estimate of γ is negative (and signifiant at $\alpha = 0.05$). This is result is highly suspect[16]. I therefore take it as evidence that indeed the inclusion of city places and rural field paths does lead to a bias in the measurement of infrastrucutre services. Therefore I do not continue the estimation procedure with this variable. Probably, an estimation of the above equation is not possible at the level of *Kreise*. A possible approach to proceed further could be either to use *Gewerbesteuer* (trade tax) as a proxy for infrastructure services[17] or to limit the investigation to those German Federal States (Nordrhein-Westfalen and Baden-Württemberg) which publish data on streets

---

[16] See again the discussion Seitz [1993], Seitz [1995b], Seitz and Licht [1995] or Mas *et al.* [1996] and the results published there.

[17] Seitz [1998] suggested this approach in a discussion.

alone for *Kreise*. I shall leave this for further research and turn now to evidence from data of national states.

6.5.2 Evidence from a Dataset of National States

Let me finish the empirical investigation with a dataset on the level of national states. Data is taken from Mankiw, Romer and Weil[1992] (MRW), who present data on GDP, its growth rate, the growth rate of labour, the investment-GDP ratio as a proxy for the saving rate and a vector called SCHOOL (the fraction of population aged 12 to 17 enrolled in secondary school) which can be used as a proxy for human capital. The data covers the period from 1960 – 1985 and includes 121 national states, excluding those that were central planning countries at that time.

To use the MRW-data has a twofold advantage. First, it is publicly available and second, the results of MRW can be taken as a benchmark.[18] Based on the experience of the regressions in the previous sections I will now run four regressions where two correspond to regressions of MRW. In the remaining two I will include spatial effects. All estimates will be OLS since the MRW model is restricted to constant returns to scale in K, L, and H.

6.5.2.1 Regressions Without Spatial Effects

Let me start with two regressions MRW present in their section I and II (equations 7 and 11). However, I will not run separate regressions for different types of countries (as MRW did). Instead I use dummy variables for OECD-countries and for oil-producing countries (OIL). Column (1) of Table 6.14 gives the result of the "simplest" regression, i.e. the regression that corresponds to Table I in Mankiw *et al.* The estimated α is – as could be expected – somewhere between those estimated by MRW.[19] Note that $\mathcal{LM}$, the test statistic for spatial autocorrelation in the error term, is highly significant, i.e. the regression exhibits significant spatial relationships in the error term.

---

[18] Details on the MRW-data will not be discussed here, nor will the data be reproduced. The interested reader might want to refer to the original publication. The dataset is however extended to account for spatial relationships. Ciccone[1997] also used the MRW-data to investigate international diffusion of technology, where he used a similar approach.

[19] Please refer to the MRW paper or to my regression equation 6.9 on page 142 for explanation on how to compute the production elasticities.

6.5 Empirical Implementation of the Model and Results

Table 6.14: Estimation Results on the Level of National States

Dependent variable is ln(Y/L)	(1)	(2)	(3)	(4)
Constant	6.841	6.434	5.988	4.207
	(0.255)	(0.171)	(0.219)	(0.583)
OECD	1.003	0.653	0.564	0.438
	(0.296)	(0.197)	(0.191)	(0.186)
OIL	0.945	1.138	1.076	0.817
	(0.275)	(0.191)	(0.184)	(0.193)
$\ln(I/GDP) - \ln(n+g+d)$	0.475	0.244	0.228	0.187
	(0.140)	(0.095)	(0.091)	(0.088)
ln(SCHOOL)		0.700	0.632	0.523
		(0.064)	(0.065)	(0.070)
ln(LAGSCHOOL)			0.223	0.110
			(0.072)	(0.076)
ln(LAGGDP)				0.288
				(0.088)
R_c^2	0.486	0.785	0.804	0.823
$\sqrt{\mathcal{LM}}$	6.854	3.501	2.895	0.687
Implied α	0.322	0.196	0.185	0.157
Implied β		0.563	0.488	0.425
Implied δ			0.353	0.210

Note: Estimated standard errors in brackets

For the regression in column (2) I interpret *SCHOOL* as a proxy for human capital, i.e. I regress equation (12) of MRW, rather than their equation (11). This interpretation is more coherent with the approach chosen in section 6.5.1.2. The regression results and the implied α and β correspond to those in MRW (their Table II). Note from $\sqrt{\mathcal{LM}}$ that there is still significant spatial autocorrelation in the error term.

6.5.2.2 Regression Including Spatial Effects

To introduce spillovers I extend the production function of MRW (their equation 8) as follows (compare my equation (4.1) on page 68)

$$Y_i = K_i^\alpha \left(H_i \cdot \widetilde{H}_i^\delta \right)^\beta (AL_i)^{1-\alpha-\beta} \tag{6.8}$$

where i indicates a region and

$$\widetilde{H}_i = \sum_{j=1}^{n} H_j \quad \text{or in matrix notation} \quad \widetilde{\mathbf{H}} = \mathbf{CH},$$

H_j being the level of human capital of i's neighbour j and n being the number of neighbours of i; $\mathbf{C}$ is the binary contiguity matrix as discussed in section 6.3.2.1. Following the procedure described in MRW, I derive the steady state level of k and h:

$$k^* = \left(\frac{s_k^{1-\beta} s_h^{\beta} \widetilde{H}^{\delta\beta}}{n+g+d} \right)^{\frac{1}{1-\alpha-\beta}}$$

$$h^* = \left(\frac{s_k^{\alpha} s_h^{1-\alpha} \widetilde{H}^{\delta\beta}}{n+g+d} \right)^{\frac{1}{1-\alpha-\beta}}$$

where lower-case letters denote per capita variables (with the exception of the saving rate s). Note, that these levels are higher than those given by MRW (equation 10). This follows from the positive externality of the neighbours' human capital. Inserting these variables in equation (6.8) and taking logs we obtain the following regression equation

$$\ln\left[\frac{Y_i}{L_i}\right] = \ln A + \frac{\alpha}{1-\alpha}\left[\ln(s_i) - \ln(n_i + g + d)\right] \\ + \frac{\beta}{1-\alpha}\ln(h_i) + \frac{\delta\beta}{1-\alpha}\ln(\widetilde{H}_i) \quad (6.9)$$

where i is a national state. The result of this regression is given in column (3) of table 6.14. The regression coefficient is significant and the implied spillover coefficient δ suggests that if a neighbour to i raises its level of human capital by 1% then the per-capita income of region i will increase by $\beta \cdot \delta$%, i.e. by 0.172%. I expect this value to be higher if the same analysis is done in a regionally more disaggregated level, since then distance is smaller.

Returning to column (3) of Table 6.14, note that the effect of h_i (β) has decreased by 15% compared to column (2). That is, if we do not correct for spatially lagged human capital, we tend to overestimate the effect of the domestic human capital. Note finally, that $\mathcal{LM}$ is still significant. Hence, even the inclusion of the spatially lagged log of h did not remove all the spatial autocorrelation. To correct for this effect we specify a spatial lag of $\ln(Y/L)$ which is included in the last column. In this final regression, $\mathcal{LM}$ does not give evidence of spatial autocorrelation anymore. Note that the estimates of *all* parameters are smaller than the results of the previous regression. Thus, due to the omission of the spatial lag of GDP the estimates were biased.

6.6 Summary and Conclusion

The aim of this chapter was to investigate whether evidence can be found for the existence of spatial spillovers of different factors that obey a public good characteristic, like R&D-personnel, human capital or infrastructure. Thi shas been done to give support to the model developed in chapter 4. To do so, I first used a dataset for West-German *Kreise* and investigated if spillovers could be detected by means of simple descriptive statistics. Although this result was positive, it did not allow yet to test the model developed in chapter 4. Therefore newer spatial econometric methods have been used which allowed to implement this model empirically.

Estimates at the level of West-German *Kreise* and on the level of national states (where the data have been taken from Mankiw *et al.*, 1992) give strong evidence in favour of spatial knowledge spillover and thus for the model specified in the previous chapters.

Chapter 7

Summary and Conclusion

The main purpose of this book is to investigate how it is possible to observe convergence of the per-capita income of regions although there might be increasing returns to the accumulation of knowledge. To investigate this puzzle I put forward the hypothesis that since parts of that knowledge are tacit and therefore cannot be communicated via means of telecommunication, the notion of distance is of importance. If, however, distance plays a role, the level of spatial aggregation in convergence analysis can be assumed to be of vital importance.

This hypothesis is investigated on the basis of a formal model, a simulation study and an empirical investigation. These approaches integrate two bodies of literature, new growth theory and new economic geography. To establish a basis of the analysis, the literature on both fields is summarized in chapter 2 and chapter 3 respectively. Chapter 2 made evident that convergence is a property that can be derived from the neoclassical growth model as suggested by Solow[1956] and Ramsey[1928]. Regressions at the level of US federal states or European Regions at NUTS level 1 (which corresponds to German federal states) do not reject this property. A closer look (in section 2.3.2.2) however indicates that convergence property depends on the *level of regional aggregation* – regressions at the level of national states and West-German *Kreise* reject the convergence hypothesis. The conclusion of this chapter (section 2.4) is that a neglect of the spacial dimension might lead to a bias in the analysis.

Chapter 3 gives an overview of some of the literature that deals with spatial aspects of economic activity. There, existing models are classified into two types: models that refer to transportation costs (section 3.2) and those that refer to externalities in production (section 3.3). In the latter section I presented different concepts of externalities and literature that gives evidence in favour of the existence of *spatial knowledge spillovers*. I argue in conclusion of this chapter that if spatial knowledge spillovers exist, they will not only influence the dynamics of agglomeration but also regional growth.

This hypothesis is investigated on the bais of a model that is developed in chapter 4. This model explicitly sets up a formal link between the forces of growth and agglomeration; growth being the accumulation of factors in time and agglomeration being accumulation in space. This two-region, two-firm model gives indeed evidence in favour of the hypothesis. That is, the regional convergence behaviour may indeed depend on the level of spatial aggregation – regional aggregates always display convergence even if their subaggregates display divergence.

In chapter 5 this model is extended to a multi-region agent-based model to explore the self-organizing properties of the model and to be able to perform a simulation study. The tool that underlies this approach – cellular automata – can be used to investigate spatial economic processes where the regions interact on the basis of local recursive rules. The results of the simulations (section 5.5) confirm the findings of chapter 4. Another finding of this chapter is that cellular automata can be a powerful tool to model spatial and recursive economic processes; a tool that is only starting to be explored.

Finally, chapter 6 tests a reduced form of the model proposed in chapter 4 empirically. For this purpose, I collected data for relevant factors for 327 West German counties (*Kreise*), presented in section 6.2. Regressions using this dataset and another one taken from Mankiw *et al.* [1992] strongly confirm the hypothesis that spatial knowledge spillovers exist and thus do not reject the model depicted in chapter 4.

These results suggest that studies of regional growth should take into account the dynamics induced by external effects caused by spatial knowledge spillovers. Otherwise, results can be assumed to be biased. Thus, the approach suggested in this thesis offers an explanation why the empirical evidence on convergence differs depending on the level of spatial aggregation. The concept of convergence is therefore only of limited use in describing the dynamics of regional growth. Ultimately, the findings of this thesis imply that convergence should be considered as a statistical artifact. As a consequence, I would argue that it is not a meaningful statement to project that regional growth rates converge (somewhat *automatically*) by 2% a year. Rather, it is necessary to take a close look at the actual processes that make regional growth rates converge: does labour migrate? Are there transfers of money (as in the case of the German unification)? Do certain regions enjoy a preferred status when it comes to public offers (like the Italian *Mezzogiorno*)? etc. All these questions are averaged away by the convergence approach which therefore does not offer an operational tool for the economic advisor. The work offered here has the potential of being extended in this direction.

Appendix A

Generalization of the Model Developed in Chapter 4

A.1 Illustration of the Allocation Dynamics for a Region with an Arbitrary Number of Firms

Consider an arbitrary number of firms n_A located in area A. Then production function (A.1) becomes

$$Y_i = \left(K_i \cdot \tilde{K}_j^\delta\right)^\alpha L_i^\beta \qquad \text{(A.1)}$$
$$\alpha, \beta, \delta \in [0, 1],$$

where K_i, L_i are factor endowments of firm i, α, β are production elasticities and δ is a spillover-coefficient.

$$\tilde{K}_j = \left(\prod_{j \neq i} K_j\right)^{1/(n_A - 1)}$$

is an index of the capital endowment of all other firms in region A that spills over to the i'th firm, $j = 1, 2, \ldots, n_A - 1$ being the set of firms that are situated together with firm i in region A. Thus, in this simple specification, δ incorporates two effects, 1) the fact that only a part of $\tilde{K}_j$ is human (or public) capital and 2) only a part of that capital actually spills over to firm i. Note, that we assume that these coefficients be identical for all firms. To analyze the dynamics of factor allocation among firms in region A, I express the factor distribution with *share parameters* and suppose during this section, that the aggregates of capital and labour in region A (K_A and L_A) are fixed. then, I can describe the spatial distribution of capital and labour in economy A as follows:

$$K_i = \phi_i K_A; \quad L_i = \theta_i L_A, \qquad \text{(A.2)}$$

where i denotes the i'th firm. Inserting these share equations into production function (A.1) yields

$$Y_i = (\phi_i K_A)^\alpha \left(\prod_{j\neq i} \phi_j K_A\right)^{\alpha\delta/(n_A-1)} (\theta_i L_A)^\beta . \tag{A.3}$$

Rearranging this equation yields

$$Y_i = K_A^{\alpha(1+\delta)} L_A^\beta \cdot \phi_i^\alpha \theta_i^\beta \left(\prod_{j\neq i} \phi_j\right)^{\alpha\delta/(n_A-1)}.$$

Thus, the output of region A can be described as

$$Y_A = \sum_{i=1}^{n_A} Y_i = K_A^{\alpha(1+\delta)} L_A^\beta \cdot \underbrace{\left[\sum_{i=1}^{n_A}\left(\phi_i^\alpha \theta_i^\beta \prod_{j\neq i}\phi_j^{\alpha\delta}\right)\right]}_{\mu}, \tag{A.4}$$

where μ is a constant which depends on the actual distribution of K_A and L_A within the firms of region A. In Appendix A.1 (page 149) I show, that in equilibrium

$$\frac{\phi_i}{\theta_i} = \frac{\phi_j}{\theta_j} \text{ if } \delta = 0$$

i.e. all firms employ identical factor *ratios* or even

$$\phi_i = \theta_i = \phi_j = \theta_j = \frac{1}{n_A} \text{ if } \delta > 0$$

i.e. all firms employ identical factor *shares* (which is of course a stronger condition). This result is known from the literature on agglomeration economies[1] though obtained via a different apporach. If all firms employ identical factor ratios we obtain

$$\mu = \left(\frac{1}{n_A}\right)^{\alpha\delta}.$$

which degenerates to 1 if no spillovers exist (where $\delta = 0$). Appendix A.2 illustrates this findings for a two-firm economy.

A.2 Proof that Firms Employ Identical Factor Ratios or Identical Factor Shares

Suppose that factors can migrate freely to firms that offer higher wage or rent. If wage/rent equals the factor's marginal product, this process will lead to a situation,

---
[1] See e.g. Rivera-Batitz[1988].

A.2 Proof that Firms Employ Identical Factor Ratios or Identical Factor Shares

where firms will produce with identical marginal product and thus offer the same wage. Otherwise higher marginal product (and thus wages) will lead to an immigration of factors into the firm. This will reduce their marginal product and thus lead to an equalization of the marginal product. Hence in equilibrium we have

$$\frac{\partial Y_i}{\partial K_i} = \frac{\partial Y_j}{\partial K_j} \quad \text{and} \quad \frac{\partial Y_i}{\partial L_i} = \frac{\partial Y_j}{\partial L_j}$$

where i, j denote two arbitratry firms of region A. Using share equations (A.2) on page 149 these equations become

$$\frac{\partial Y_i}{\partial \phi_i} = \frac{\partial Y_j}{\partial \phi_j} \quad \text{and} \quad \frac{\partial Y_i}{\partial \theta_i} = \frac{\partial Y_j}{\partial \theta_j}$$

To derive the inter-firm distribution of K_A and L_A (i.e. factor shares) in equilibrium let me distinquish two cases: a) $\delta = 0$ and b) $\delta > 0$.

Case 1: If $\delta = 0$ production function (A.3) becomes

$$Y_i = (\phi_i K_A)^\alpha (\theta_i L_A)^\beta$$

Thus the conditions for inter-firm equilibrium become

$$\phi_i^{\alpha-1} \theta_i^\beta = \phi_j^{\alpha-1} \theta_j^\beta \quad \text{and} \quad \phi_i^\alpha \theta_i^{\beta-1} = \phi_j^\alpha \theta_j^{\beta-1}.$$

If the production function has constant returns to scale, i.e. $\alpha + \beta = 1$, the condition

$$\frac{\phi_i}{\theta_i} = \frac{\phi_j}{\theta_j}$$

yields immediately. This implies that all firms use *identical factor ratios*.

Case 2: If $\delta > 0$ production function (A.3) is

$$Y_i = (\phi_i K_A)^\alpha \left(\prod_{j \neq i} \phi_j K_A \right)^{\alpha\delta} (\theta_i L_A)^\beta$$

and the conditions for inter-firm equilibrium become

$$\phi_i^{\alpha-1} \prod_{k \neq i} \phi_k^{\alpha\delta} \theta_i^\beta = \phi_j^{\alpha-1} \prod_{l \neq j} \phi_l^{\alpha\delta} \theta_j^\beta \quad \text{and} \quad \phi_i^\alpha \prod_{k \neq i} \phi_k^{\alpha\delta} \theta_i^{\beta-1} = \phi_j^\alpha \prod_{k \neq i} \phi_k^{\alpha\delta} \theta_j^{\beta-1}.$$

Dividing by $\prod_{k \neq i} \phi_k^{\alpha\delta}$ and rearranging yields for the first condition

$$\phi_i^{\alpha-1-\alpha\delta} \theta_i^\beta = \phi_j^{\alpha-1-\alpha\delta} \theta_j^\beta$$

and for the second

$$\phi_i^{\alpha-\alpha\delta} \theta_i^{\beta-1} = \phi_j^{\alpha-\alpha\delta} \theta_j^{\beta-1}.$$

Setting again $\alpha + \beta = 1$ and rearranging yields the conditions

$$\phi_i = \phi_j \quad \text{and} \quad \theta_i = \theta_j$$

i.e. in inter-firm equilibrium, firms will employ *identical factor shares*. This will either be the trivial case where all shares equal zero or

$$K_i = \phi_i K_A = \frac{1}{n_A} K_A$$

where n_A is the number of firms located in region A. The next section will illustrate this for a region that hosts two firms.

Appendix B

Mathematical Appendix

B.1 Proof that the Bias of an OLS Estimation in the Presence of Spatial Autocorrelation is Biased

The following proofs are summarized from Anselin [1988]. Consider a model of the form

$$\mathbf{y} = \rho \mathbf{W}_y \mathbf{y} + \mathbf{X}\beta + \mathbf{u}, \quad \mathbf{u} \sim N(0, \sigma^2 \mathbf{I})$$

OLS estimation of β under neglection of $\rho \mathbf{W}_y \mathbf{y}$ yields

$$\hat{\beta} = (\mathbf{X}'\mathbf{X})^{-1}\mathbf{X}'\mathbf{y}$$

which, inserting $\mathbf{y}$, becomes

$$\hat{\beta} = (\mathbf{X}'\mathbf{X})^{-1}\mathbf{X}'\rho \mathbf{W}_y \mathbf{y} + (\mathbf{X}'\mathbf{X})^{-1}\mathbf{X}'\mathbf{X}\beta + (\mathbf{X}'\mathbf{X})^{-1}\mathbf{X}'\mathbf{u}.$$

The expected value is

$$E[\hat{\beta}] = E[(\mathbf{X}'\mathbf{X})^{-1}\mathbf{X}'\rho \mathbf{W}_y \mathbf{y}] + \beta$$

or expressed as bias

$$E[\hat{\beta} - \beta] = E[(\mathbf{X}'\mathbf{X})^{-1}\mathbf{X}'\rho \mathbf{W}_y \mathbf{y}].$$

Since ρ is a scalar we can write

$$E[\hat{\beta} - \beta] = E[\rho(\mathbf{X}'\mathbf{X})^{-1}\mathbf{X}'\mathbf{W}_y \mathbf{y}] = \rho E[(\mathbf{X}'\mathbf{X})^{-1}\mathbf{X}'\mathbf{W}_y \mathbf{y}].$$

The last part corresponds to ρ times an OLS regression of $\mathbf{X}$ against the spatial lag of $\mathbf{y}$ which would yield a BLU estimate of the model

$$\mathbf{y}_L = \mathbf{X}\beta_L + \mathbf{e}$$

with $\mathbf{y}_L = \mathbf{W}_y \mathbf{y}$. Thus the bias can be expressed as

$$E[\hat{\beta} - \beta] = \rho \beta_L$$

B.2 Derivation of the Log-Likelihood Function of Model (6.2)

The following derivation is taken from Anselin[1988, p.61] with some inor modifications. Consider model 6.2

$$\mathbf{y} = \rho \mathbf{W}_y \mathbf{y} + \mathbf{X}\boldsymbol{\beta} + \boldsymbol{\varepsilon}$$

with

$$\boldsymbol{\varepsilon} = \lambda \mathbf{W}_\varepsilon \boldsymbol{\varepsilon} + \mathbf{u}, \quad \mathbf{u} \sim N(\mathbf{0}, \sigma^2 \mathbf{I}).$$

Denote

$$\mathbf{M} = (\mathbf{I} - \rho \mathbf{W}_y) \quad \text{and} \quad \mathbf{N} = (\mathbf{I} - \lambda \mathbf{W}_\varepsilon).$$

Then the above model can be rewritten

$$\mathbf{My} = \mathbf{X}\boldsymbol{\beta} + \boldsymbol{\varepsilon} \quad \text{with} \quad \boldsymbol{\varepsilon} = \mathbf{N}^{-1}\mathbf{u} \quad \text{i.e.} \quad \mathbf{My} = \mathbf{X}\boldsymbol{\beta} + \mathbf{N}^{-1}\mathbf{u}.$$

Rearranging yields

$$\mathbf{u} = \mathbf{N}(\mathbf{My} - \mathbf{X}\boldsymbol{\beta})$$

which is equivalent to

$$\boldsymbol{\nu} = \frac{1}{\sigma_u}\mathbf{N}(\mathbf{My} - \mathbf{X}\boldsymbol{\beta}) \quad \text{with} \quad \boldsymbol{\nu} \sim N(\mathbf{0}, \mathbf{I}). \tag{B.1}$$

Thus, $\boldsymbol{\nu}$ is a function of $\mathbf{y}, \mathbf{X}, \boldsymbol{\beta}, \rho, \lambda$ and σ_u. Since the joint distribution of $\boldsymbol{\nu}$ cannot be observed it is necessary to transform it such that the joint distribution of $\mathbf{y}$ is obtained. To do so we build the determinant of the the Jacobian

$$J = \det(\partial \boldsymbol{\nu}/\partial \mathbf{y})$$

which becomes from equation (B.1)

$$J = \left| \frac{1}{\sigma_u}\mathbf{NM} \right| = \frac{1}{\sigma_u}|\mathbf{N}||\mathbf{M}|.$$

Based on the assumption that $\boldsymbol{\nu} \sim N(\mathbf{0}, \mathbf{I})$ the log-likelihood for the joint distribution of $\mathbf{y}$ becomes

$$\ell = -\frac{N}{2}\ln \pi - \frac{N}{2}\ln(\sigma_u^2) + \ln|\mathbf{N}| + \ln|\mathbf{M}| - \frac{1}{2}\boldsymbol{\nu}'\boldsymbol{\nu},$$

where

$$\boldsymbol{\nu}'\boldsymbol{\nu} = \frac{1}{\sigma_u^2}(\mathbf{My} - \mathbf{X}\boldsymbol{\beta})'\mathbf{N}'\mathbf{N}(\mathbf{My} - \mathbf{X}\boldsymbol{\beta}).$$

Appendix C

Data

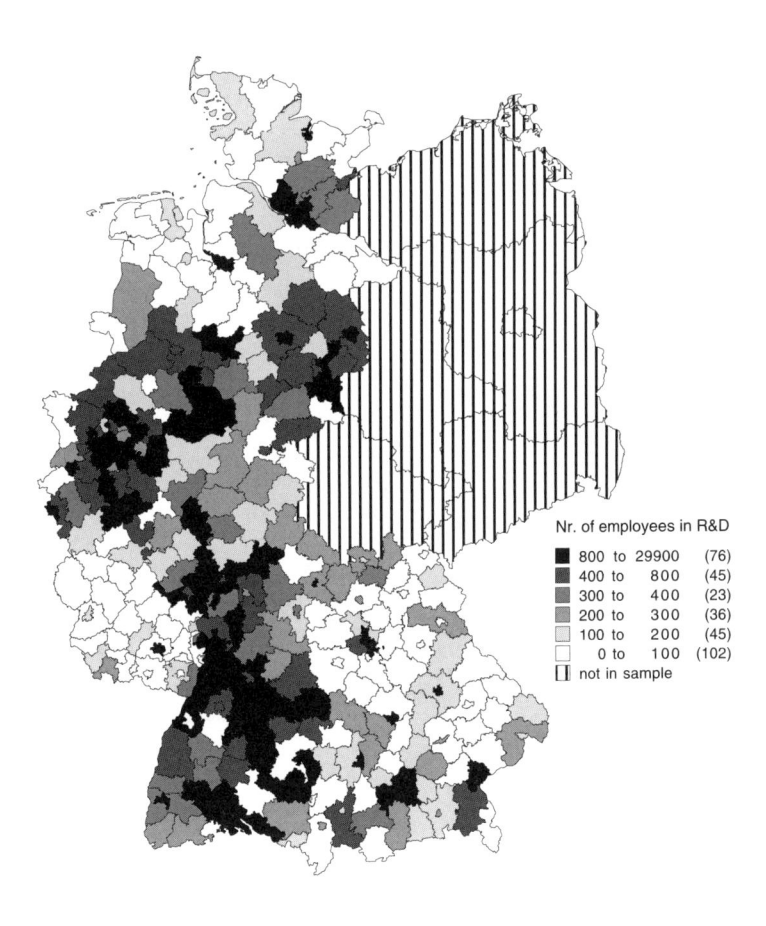

Figure C.1: Spatial distribution of personnel engaged in R&D 1991/92

Index	Code	Region	Surface (km^2)	Inhabitants	Inhabitants per km^2	Gross Value Added 1992	Employees 1992	Capital (Mio DM) 1992	Infrastructure 1989 (hectares)	Uni/FH (%) 1989	Sum of Neighbours' Hcap	Sum of Neighbours' Infrastr.
1	01001	Flensburg, krfr. St.	56.44	87939	1558.097	911	10954	1811.14	663	4.4	2.600	6813
2	01002	Kiel, krfr. St.	116.74	246586	—	2056	26650	3292.59	1587	7.4	6.300	9774
3	01003	Luebeck, krfr. St.	214.16	216854	1012.579	2023	27698	3457.66	1648	4.5	10.699	12059
4	01004	Neumuenster, krfr. St.	71.56	81996	1145.836	757	11564	1564.03	567	3.7	10.000	14763
5	01051	Dithmarschen	1404.87	132963	94.644	2121	11558	2960.23	5521	2.9	11.400	24695
6	01053	Herzogtum Lauenburg	1263.08	168165	133.139	868	13785	1538.31	4421	4.1	22.800	21220
7	01054	Nordfriesland	2049.35	157617	76.911	431	7520	512.64	7451	2.4	5.500	12334
8	01055	Ostholstein	1391.48	196362	141.117	808	10975	1205.09	4339	2.8	14.799	12661
9	01056	Pinneberg	664.29	280937	422.913	2439	27739	3921.04	3421	4.4	13.999	15407
10	01057	Ploen	1082.45	124562	115.074	369	5090	655.10	2725	2.8	21.100	18531
11	01058	Rendsburg-Eckenfoerde	2185.78	255449	116.869	1014	16070	1919.14	7049	3.5	26.000	25584
12	01059	Schleswig-Flensburg	2071.55	186300	89.933	533	9527	1119.79	6813	2.6	13.200	20684
13	01060	Segeberg	1344.32	233938	174.020	2763	26274	3435.97	4989	3.7	31.299	31818
14	01061	Steinburg	1056.26	131914	124.888	826	12791	3642.15	3382	2.9	14.500	20980
15	01062	Stormarn	766.29	206810	269.885	2429	25615	3774.42	3299	3.8	22.500	22433
16	02000	Hamburg	755.33	1705872	2258.446	18622	163325	33750.38	7036	7.4	22.900	25868
17	03101	Braunschweig, krfr. Stadt	192.06	254130	1323.180	2728	35641	5687.19	1693	1.1	16.499	16055
18	03102	Salzgitter, krfr. Stadt	223.91	117842	526.292	3263	36535	7328.37	1414	3.4	16.499	16764
19	03103	Wolfsburg, krfr. Stadt	203.96	126965	622.500	7878	66001	—	1288	4.1	5.800	8893
20	03151	Gifhorn	1561.85	158770	101.655	696	10519	1940.98	6078	2.9	21.799	30265
21	03152	Goettingen	1116.99	266297	238.406	2042	26510	3653.12	6330	7.6	17.500	22500
22	03153	Goslar	965.00	162380	168.269	1334	18555	3391.34	3400	3.9	17.700	19163
23	03154	Helmstedt	673.76	101937	151.296	377	9594	1549.59	2815	2.9	12.299	11950
24	03155	Northeim	1266.63	154200	121.740	1579	20478	2302.62	6268	3.2	26.599	32698
25	03156	Osterode am Harz	636.10	89016	139.940	1231	16797	2515.90	2667	2.7	14.699	15998
26	03157	Peine	534.42	125755	235.311	936	11594	2711.47	2857	3.1	19.600	29037
27	03158	Wolfenbuettel	722.17	121367	168.059	678	8094	1439.43	2891	4.2	18.600	18102
28	03201	Hannover, krfr. St.	204.07	525763	2576.386	6550	82173	14556.22	2672	7.8	3.800	11038
29	03251	Diepholz	1987.26	201514	101.403	992	15890	2368.10	9383	3.3	27.800	39480
30	03252	Hameln-Pyrmont	796.12	163215	205.013	1364	19739	2333.84	3630	3.7	18.100	28430
31	03253	Hannover	2085.61	581831	278.974	3510	48592	6084.04	11038	3.8	33.999	42506
32	03254	Hildesheim	1205.30	291320	241.699	2628	39158	5229.93	5923	4.2	28.600	34302
33	03255	Holzminden	692.51	83263	120.234	1105	12865	2117.55	2804	3.3	19.800	32665
34	03256	Nienburg (Weser)	1398.64	122467	87.561	916	13540	2840.81	6016	2.6	20.400	40731

Table C.1: Data on West German Kreise

C. Data

Index	Code	Region	Surface (km^2)	Inhabitants	Inhabitants per km^2	Gross Value Added 1992	Employees 1992	Capital (Mio DM) 1992	Infrastructure 1989 (hectares)	Uni/FH (%) 1989	Sum of Neighbours' Hcap	Sum of Neighbours' Infrastr.
35	03257	Schaumburg	675.57	161107	238.476	1334	17540	2236.53	3395	3.0	17.799	32754
36	03351	Celle	1544.92	177468	114.872	872	15441	4086.65	5546	3.9	12.399	28533
37	03352	Cuxhaven	2072.26	197337	95.228	571	10711	810.33	8137	2.5	17.600	18754
38	03353	Harburg	1244.47	212416	170.688	546	9074	771.08	5399	2.8	25.600	34511
39	03354	Luechow-Dannenberg	1219.64	51188	41.970	238	4429	1652.97	4722	2.6	7.200	8866
40	03355	Lueneburg	1323.43	153250	115.798	974	13741	1635.30	3838	4.3	15.200	25959
41	03356	Osterholz	650.65	104574	160.722	356	5766	611.06	2728	3.1	19.699	25525
42	03357	Rotenburg (Wuemme)	2069.76	149599	72.278	846	12426	1524.96	8488	2.9	18.899	30718
43	03358	Soltau-Fallingbostel	1873.25	132874	70.932	902	13198	1880.34	6389	2.8	26.800	49079
44	03359	Stade	1265.95	180369	142.477	1153	16244	3925.48	4339	4.1	15.600	29060
45	03360	Uelzen	1453.36	95509	65.716	457	7857	1026.84	5028	2.9	16.499	26573
46	03361	Verden	787.75	126490	160.571	1136	12755	1611.54	3726	3.6	22.000	35767
47	03401	Delmenhorst, krfr. St.	62.35	77899	1249.383	513	7246	806.33	492	2.2	16.300	19837
48	03402	Emden, krfr. St.	112.40	51805	460.899	1537	17607	2721.88	621	2.7	5.000	9631
49	03403	Oldenburg krfr. St.	102.95	149691	1454.017	800	12279	1376.54	1134	5.2	7.900	11021
50	03404	Osnabrueck, krfr. St.	119.79	168050	1402.872	1826	24060	2945.14	1200	5.1	5.800	18634
51	03405	Wilhelmshaven, krfr. St.	103.40	91230	882.302	2602	6405		770	3.3	3.100	2470
52	03451	Ammerland	728.14	102492	140.759	671	9976	977.43	3330	2.2	20.699	24361
53	03452	Aurich	1285.71	178391	138.749	323	7073	608.10	5229	2.6	7.200	7370
54	03453	Cloppenburg	1417.59	136552	96.327	1033	15897	1696.45	6317	2.2	16.000	40350
55	03454	Emsland	2880.29	286282	99.393	3512	34512	6743.14	12935	3.2	13.000	33402
56	03455	Friesland	607.50	97236	160.059	633	9587	1684.07	2470	3.1	13.400	13260
57	03456	Grafschaft Bentheim	980.63	124349	126.805	922	17016	2230.39	4049	2.6	9.400	27828
58	03457	Leer	1085.82	152063	140.044	378	7641	951.40	4402	2.4	18.099	33249
59	03458	Oldenburg (Oldenburg)	1062.81	110914	104.359	580	9018	1060.28	5280	2.3	21.999	27121
60	03459	Osnabrueck	2121.57	335207	158.000	3586	43075	4507.90	10349	2.4	33.799	62094
61	03460	Vechta	812.49	115310	141.922	1135	16634	3381.26	4054	3.5	10.200	31329
62	03461	Wesermarsch	821.89	93072	113.241	1200	14909	2153.39	2411	3.4	32.000	27122
63	03462	Wittmund	656.54	54607	83.174	95	2562	211.20	2347	2.1	10.300	15431
64	04011	Bremen, krfr. St.	326.72	549182	1680.895	8227	79728	15616.63	2763	7.3	15.600	18740
65	04012	Bremerhaven, krfr. St.	77.51	130847	1688.131	1078	15125	978.48	788	4.1	5.900	10548
66	05111	Duesseldorf, krfr. St.	216.99	572638	2639.006	7917	87436	15749.00	2361	8.1	25.600	11945
67	05112	Duisburg, krfr. St.	232.82	536106	2302.663	5497	78523	28018.89	2427	5.1	37.200	18339
68	05113	Essen, krfr. St.	210.35	617955	2937.747	4616	62681	12861.68	2403	8.1	36.100	17207
69	05114	Krefeld, krfr. St.	137.55	249662	1815.064	4307	45636	9866.42	1361	5.5	24.299	17375

Table C.1 continued

158   C. Data

Index	Code	Region	Surface (km^2)	Inhabitants	Inhabitants per km^2	Gross Value Added 1992	Employees 1992	Capital (Mio DM) 1992	Infrastructure 1989 (hectares)	Uni/FH (%) 1989	Sum of Neighbours' Hcap	Sum of Neighbours' Infrastr.
70	05116	Moenchengladbach, krfr. St.	170.43	266073	1561.186	2921	37849	5237.62	1721	4.2	10.500	10353
71	05117	Muelheim a.d. Ruhr, krfr. St.	91.26	176513	1934.177	2166	27099	5873.76	945	5.2	31.499	11520
72	05119	Oberhausen, krfr. St.	77.04	225443	2926.311	1921	23295	6378.58	1106	5.4	24.499	11996
73	05120	Remscheid, krfr. St.	74.60	123069	1649.718	3023	34448	4028.22	593	4.2	18.500	9779
74	05122	Solingen, krfr. St.	89.46	165973	1855.276	1982	29152	3064.67	718	3.2	19.700	7664
75	05124	Wuppertal, krfr. St.	168.37	383776	2279.361	5672	67413	10267.57	1604	4.8	20.899	12119
76	05154	Kleve	1231.29	284448	231.016	1821	25907	3197.40	4884	3.0	8.900	15206
77	05158	Mettmann	407.08	504838	1240.144	7492	79787	10661.14	3223	4.8	65.999	24511
78	05162	Neuss	576.11	432932	751.475	4871	54605	13829.66	3989	5.0	52.500	31119
79	05166	Viersen	562.99	285338	506.826	2751	35759	5014.61	3244	2.9	23.500	20429
80	05170	Wesel	1042.24	462588	443.840	2586	52062	7907.70	5354	3.2	31.599	26138
81	05313	Aachen, krfr. St.	160.82	247113	1536.581	2355	31641	5075.44	1412	10.0	4.200	2938
82	05314	Bonn, krfr. St.	141.23	293072	2075.140	1738	21304	2878.75	1518	11.2	11.399	16737
83	05315	Koeln, krfr. Stadt	405.14	963817	2378.973	13207	120306	27809.43	4607	8.8	33.299	22487
84	05316	Leverkusen, krfr. St.	78.86	161832	2052.143	6542	47500	14389.11	841	7.7	19.500	10074
85	05354	Aachen	546.52	301352	551.402	2304	33654	11394.18	2938	4.2	21.900	15700
86	05358	Dueren	941.18	256310	272.328	2468	33658	6033.92	4723	6.0	19.600	20824
87	05362	Erftkreis	704.89	438760	622.452	5615	49232	14427.70	4332	4.5	28.500	27622
88	05366	Euskirchen	1249.20	180447	144.450	1328	16196	2875.94	6445	3.3	27.100	38107
89	05370	Heinsberg	627.86	235241	374.671	1265	23080	3474.41	3120	2.6	22.299	16615
90	05374	Oberbergischer Kreis	918.15	277444	302.177	4109	47483	5962.70	5213	4.6	32.199	26786
91	05378	Rheinisch-Bergischer Kreis	437.62	268042	612.499	2127	26982	4409.12	2244	5.9	38.699	23053
92	05382	Rhein-Sieg-Kreis	1153.41	538610	466.972	3857	45232	6705.76	7858	5.4	46.599	36744
93	05512	Bottrop, krfr. St.	100.60	119669	1189.553	500	11799	2016.96	867	2.9	24.799	15813
94	05513	Gelsenkirchen, krfr. St.	104.84	293542	2799.905	6169	46524	11094.86	1309	4.1	27.000	11349
95	05515	Muenster (Westf.) krfr. St.	302.62	264887	875.312	1351	21113	2670.48	1871	8.5	10.100	18137
96	05554	Borken	1417.29	338350	238.730	3975	50213	6660.31	6608	2.8	19.199	32990
97	05558	Coesfeld	1110.02	198896	179.182	1120	16315	1601.15	4777	3.0	29.299	32702
98	05562	Recklinghausen	760.18	661915	870.735	4497	75650	17751.84	5641	4.0	45.700	30602
99	05566	Steinfurt	1792.73	410975	229.245	3760	55138	7318.58	8285	3.4	31.299	46864
100	05570	Warendorf	1315.61	270043	205.261	3536	43600	5353.47	5075	3.7	28.100	38288
101	05711	Bielefeld, krfr. St.	257.66	324067	1257.731	4305	54706	5843.97	2068	5.8	9.300	13315
102	05754	Guetersloh	967.16	324333	335.346	6128	72720	8140.28	4813	3.0	28.700	38450
103	05758	Herford	449.92	248334	551.951	3679	46981	4585.54	3232	2.5	18.899	29300
104	05762	Hoexter	1199.63	153379	127.855	1206	17235	1959.08	4749	2.9	24.599	44853

Table C.1 continued

C. Data

Index	Code	Region	Surface (km^2)	Inhabitants	Inhabitants per km^2	Gross Value Added 1992	Employees 1992	Capital (Mio DM) 1992	Infrastructure 1989 (hectares)	Uni/FH (%) 1989	Sum of Neighbours' Hcap	Sum of Neighbours' Infrastr.
105	05766	Lippe	1246.34	356427	285.979	4026	51570	5212.69	5270	3.8	34.500	37232
106	05770	Minden-Luebbecke	1151.99	311963	270.804	4016	48518	5232.51	6800	3.9	17.600	37645
107	05774	Paderborn	1244.97	272571	218.938	3400	39296	6030.21	5741	6.4	16.699	30495
108	05911	Bochum, krfr. St.	145.42	401129	2758.417	5037	57580	15960.19	1744	5.6	33.100	15521
109	05913	Dortmund, krfr. St.	280.24	600918	2144.298	4705	65569	13887.14	3102	6.4	27.299	15413
110	05914	Hagen, krfr. St.	160.36	213747	1332.920	2766	33181	5218.66	1218	4.0	16.899	13862
111	05915	Hamm, krfr. St.	226.38	184020	812.881	1293	22242	3123.96	1478	3.7	13.999	20311
112	05916	Herne, krfr. St.	51.41	180029	3501.823	1194	15641	3486.01	694	6.4	20.100	11796
113	05954	Enepe-Ruhr-Kreis	408.27	352622	863.698	5123	61165	7946.38	2372	4.1	41.500	23151
114	05958	Hochsauerlandkreis	1956.94	281304	143.747	3742	48302	7208.08	8948	2.9	26.399	41044
115	05962	Maerkischer Kreis	1058.92	455310	429.976	8906	104944	12067.75	4644	3.2	25.200	32175
116	05966	Olpe	710.82	136927	192.632	2366	27424	2838.98	3965	2.3	17.500	28544
117	05970	Siegen-Wittgenstein	1131.44	298602	263.913	4928	54077	6809.45	6233	4.5	22.900	46177
118	05974	Soest	1327.45	294829	222.102	3591	41223	7316.64	6715	4.1	26.099	34443
119	05978	Unna	542.50	417899	770.321	2997	52327	8074.27	3744	3.2	28.399	27575
120	06411	Darmstadt, krfr. St.	122.24	139063	1137.623	3374	32840	5243.71	927	13.4	8.400	6866
121	06412	Frankfurt a.M., krfr. St.	248.36	652412	2626.880	12406	113753	21633.03	2940	11.6	46.799	25885
122	06413	Offenbach a. M., krfr. St.	44.84	116482	2597.725	2298	19249	2979.12	549	7.9	21.399	13823
123	06414	Wiesbaden, krfr. St.	203.93	266081	1304.766	2642	26373	5747.09	1838	8.1	36.399	14500
124	06431	Bergstrasse	719.51	258329	359.035	2034	26010	3327.17	3510	3.9	41.899	24259
125	06432	Darmstadt-Dieburg	658.49	276574	420.012	2026	26278	3647.25	4124	3.8	35.900	17908
126	06433	Gross-Gerau	453.08	242832	535.958	5427	48300	11915.45	2906	5.9	62.900	26863
127	06434	Hochtaunuskreis	482.05	219517	455.382	2384	21921	3315.29	2947	8.1	39.100	28886
128	06435	Main-Kinzig-Kreis	1397.35	398288	285.031	4156	52795	7969.28	8141	5.2	41.699	43353
129	06436	Main-Taunus-Kreis	222.41	212326	954.660	1876	18140	2267.35	1841	10.5	39.100	15366
130	06437	Odenwaldkreis	623.96	97755	156.669	1038	15264	1827.70	2591	4.0	18.600	23167
131	06438	Offenbach	356.27	327029	917.925	3585	46165	5604.80	2742	4.6	50.299	22473
132	06439	Rheingau-Taunus-Kreis	811.47	181416	223.565	1197	15844	2133.71	4735	5.4	47.298	21228
133	06440	Wetteraukreis	1100.67	281852	256.073	1560	23192	2592.98	6759	4.6	36.799	35827
134	06531	Giessen	854.62	250006	292.535	2262	28570	4623.18	5968	5.9	16.799	30081
135	06532	Lahn-Dill-Kreis	1066.53	261234	244.938	3851	45094	5453.62	7345	3.8	34.899	40589
136	06533	Limburg-Weilburg	738.32	168796	228.622	1061	15735	1744.59	5266	3.2	22.500	25270
137	06534	Marburg-Biedenkopf	1262.55	250560	198.456	2612	32236	3753.81	7491	6.2	22.799	45700
138	06535	Vogelsbergkreis	1458.98	118540	81.249	973	13813	1485.72	8486	2.2	31.900	51783
139	06611	Kassel, krfr. St.	106.77	201789	1889.941	2531	29346	3810.35	1133	6.8	9.600	13155

Table C.1 continued

160   C. Data

Index	Code	Region	Surface (km^2)	Inhabitants	Inhabitants per km^2	Gross Value Added 1992	Employees 1992	Capital (Mio DM) 1992	Infrastructure 1989 (hectares)	Uni/FH (%) 1989	Sum of Neighbours' Hcap	Sum of Neighbours' Infrastr.
140	06631	Fulda	1380.36	209325	151.645	1858	27038	3778.54	8532	3.1	16.400	32984
141	06632	Hersfeld-Rotenburg	1097.05	133107	121.332	998	18406	2887.86	6221	3.5	11.499	31296
142	06633	Kassel	1292.77	239807	185.499	3227	31120	6124.35	6825	2.0	32.999	44559
143	06634	Schwalm-Eder-Kreis	1538.43	190970	124.133	1476	18484	2429.59	8671	3.4	19.699	43627
144	06635	Waldeck-Frankenberg	1848.58	168711	91.265	1878	24730	2605.33	8997	3.0	21.899	42917
145	06636	Werra-Meissner-Kreis	1024.69	117892	115.051	1035	14052	1879.73	5607	2.8	16.499	28047
146	07111	Koblenz, krfr. Stadt	105.08	109550	1042.539	1019	13935	1777.06	868	5.0	8.100	15207
147	07131	Ahrweiler	786.92	123844	157.378	707	8889	1193.55	5172	2.8	28.099	29989
148	07132	Altenkirchen (WW)	641.95	133879	208.551	1488	17642	1949.87	3506	2.3	22.399	32901
149	07133	Bad Kreuznach	863.74	154705	179.111	1282	18207	2089.40	4666	3.2	17.100	22810
150	07134	Birkenfeld	776.56	90296	116.277	667	9671	711.27	3445	2.4	15.200	28377
151	07135	Cochem-Zell	719.43	64879	90.181	295	4683	530.92	3865	2.0	9.600	22405
152	07137	Mayen-Koblenz	817.06	202380	247.693	1774	20798	3349.77	4964	2.9	22.700	34916
153	07138	Neuwied	626.83	175538	280.041	2099	23711	2948.93	3707	3.2	27.000	28943
154	07140	Rhein-Hunsrueck-Kreis	962.89	102010	105.941	880	11200	1184.48	5564	2.4	20.899	31532
155	07141	Rhein-Lahn-Kreis	782.38	126702	161.944	843	10220	1492.12	4318	2.8	26.699	31216
156	07143	Westerwaldkreis	988.76	193213	195.409	1955	26074	2957.02	5925	2.4	27.700	36207
157	07211	Trier, krfr. Stadt	117.14	99602	850.282	2253	13583	1738.21	819	5.6	2.100	5828
158	07231	Bernkastel-Wittlich	1177.70	112475	95.504	1113	12540	1557.79	6380	2.2	13.100	31786
159	07232	Bitburg-Pruem	1625.93	95108	58.493	764	8004	1382.43	7587	2.1	9.700	24150
160	07233	Daun	910.94	62300	68.391	605	6337	1024.60	5497	2.1	15.299	34413
161	07235	Trier-Saarburg	1090.81	132990	121.919	599	8103	890.05	5828	2.1	18.199	23377
162	07311	Frankenthal (Pf), krfr. Stadt	43.78	47609	1087.460	994	9390	1115.77	433	6.7	23.200	8012
163	07312	Kaiserslautern, krfr. Stadt	139.71	101910	729.440	1719	18471	3511.40	836	4.9	6.600	8845
164	07313	Landau i.d.Pf., krfr. Stadt	82.93	39379	474.846	556	4625	480.10	564	3.7	7.200	9087
165	07314	Ludwigshafen a.R., krfr. Stadt	77.67	167883	2161.491	8462	66909	22455.43	964	8.0	18.000	3971
166	07315	Mainz, krfr. Stadt	97.75	184627	1888.767	2866	26694	5354.29	1124	9.2	24.799	13373
167	07316	Neustadt a.d. Weinstrasse, krfr. S	117.10	53887	460.179	266	3338	410.94	557	3.4	8.700	7256
168	07317	Pirmasens. krfr. Stadt	61.40	48726	793.583	808	10806	1550.18	476	2.1	1.500	3674
169	07318	Speyer, krfr. Stadt	42.59	49496	1162.151	793	7492	1585.29	383	4.8	12.399	12803
170	07319	Worms, krfr. Stadt	108.73	79521	731.362	1247	12640	2574.34	996	3.5	18.100	14469
171	07320	Zweibruecken, krfr. Stadt	70.64	35882	507.956	356	4277	549.61	514	3.9	6.000	5741
172	07331	Alzey-Worms	588.03	115352	196.167	253	6193	423.80	3854	2.3	27.399	21315
173	07332	Bad Duerkheim	594.76	129414	217.590	825	9521	1476.46	2356	3.0	29.599	21183
174	07333	Donnersbergkreis	645.48	75294	116.648	690	8455	1325.48	2987	2.5	12.700	16757

Table C.1 continued

C. Data 161

Index	Code	Region	Surface (km^2)	Inhabitants	Inhabitants per km^2	Gross Value Added 1992	Employees 1992	Capital (Mio DM) 1992	Infrastructure 1989 (hectares)	Uni/FH (%) 1989	Sum of Neighbours' Hcap	Sum of Neighbours' Infrastr.
175	07334	Germersheim	463.27	117576	253.796	4373	23100	3647.08	2041	2.9	23.399	14432
176	07335	Kaiserslautern	639.82	107617	168.199	383	6587	584.71	2815	2.1	18.500	14986
177	07336	Kusel	573.54	79071	137.865	417	5533	691.18	3066	2.1	23.099	24001
178	07337	Suedl. Weinstrasse	639.88	105990	165.640	505	7618	954.57	3057	2.7	17.500	11035
179	07338	Ludwigshafen	304.88	142161	466.285	409	5821	480.41	1843	3.0	56.600	26952
180	07339	Mainz-Bingen	605.88	185844	306.734	1313	14982	2545.78	3894	5.4	39.299	29005
181	07340	Suedwestpfalz	953.74	104863	109.949	593	9490	943.17	3674	1.5	29.000	15751
182	08111	Stuttgart, krfr. St.	207.33	588482	2838.383	15456	128074	27916.45	2543	11.3	23.700	19025
183	08115	Boeblingen	617.82	348244	563.666	11407	95730	19692.39	4346	7.4	40.899	25694
184	08116	Esslingen	641.49	489528	763.111	9206	105493	14462.75	4449	5.6	42.800	29977
185	08117	Goeppingen	642.37	254230	395.769	3576	47010	6409.78	3515	3.6	25.899	30509
186	08118	Ludwigsburg	687.19	483057	702.945	6860	81786	9505.88	4997	5.4	29.300	22498
187	08119	Rems-Murr-Kreis	858.10	396461	462.022	6211	73605	8087.81	5233	5.3	35.600	36756
188	08121	Heilbronn, krfr. St.	99.86	122253	1224.244	1885	25182	3345.29	898	4.7	2.800	7439
189	08125	Heilbronn	1099.60	298448	271.415	3954	47597	6380.64	7439	2.8	35.299	41467
190	08126	Hohenlohekreis	776.69	102043	131.382	1524	20384	2251.71	4689	2.6	11.099	25727
191	08127	Schwaebisch Hall	1483.95	178001	119.951	2091	27922	2699.95	7269	3.0	19.000	39375
192	08128	Main-Tauber-Kreis	1304.58	135041	103.513	1653	22047	2028.04	6535	2.9	18.400	44240
193	08135	Heidenheim	627.18	136572	217.756	2581	32421	4190.59	2903	4.5	17.700	30428
194	08136	Ostalbkreis	1511.47	309205	204.572	4438	58757	7149.61	6544	3.9	20.400	34033
195	08211	Baden-Baden, krfr. St.	140.19	52570	374.991	425	7210	628.51	542	3.7	3.900	2689
196	08212	Karlsruhe, krfr. St.	173.44	277011	1597.158	11926	41417	.	1700	8.8	10.400	10121
197	08215	Karlsruhe	1084.93	401909	370.447	4516	58178	6595.18	5143	5.0	36.200	27990
198	08216	Rastatt	738.79	222313	300.915	4259	45170	6693.27	2689	3.9	20.499	20133
199	08221	Heidelberg, krfr. St.	108.83	138964	1276.891	1916	20348	2508.71	751	12.6	12.700	7512
200	08222	Mannheim, krfr. St.	144.95	316223	2181.601	7204	70117	11731.62	1695	8.3	38.600	13318
201	08225	Neckar-Odenwald-Kreis	1126.32	145787	129.437	1403	19936	2173.80	4484	2.4	18.300	29417
202	08226	Rhein-Neckar-Kreis	1061.76	509668	480.022	5289	63642	9784.98	5817	4.4	46.800	27839
203	08231	Pforzheim krfr. St.	97.84	117960	1205.642	2119	28030	2575.08	714	4.6	5.600	6078
204	08235	Calw	799.54	157200	197.106	1265	16929	1722.78	3141	3.1	35.000	21991
205	08236	Enzkreis	573.91	185485	323.195	2440	23798	3070.90	2937	2.5	37.099	27480
206	08237	Freudenstadt	870.64	120046	137.882	1488	18977	2219.45	3202	3.0	23.600	22615
207	08311	Freiburg im Breisgau, krfr. St.	153.06	198496	1296.851	1641	19636	2958.45	1215	9.7	6.100	7433
208	08315	Breisgau-Hochschwarzwald	1378.40	227989	165.401	1848	23361	2552.42	4958	3.3	24.299	14565
209	08316	Emmendingen	679.87	144842	213.044	1348	19775	1895.20	2475	2.8	20.100	16033

Table C.1 continued

162   C. Data

Index	Code	Region	Surface (km^2)	Inhabitants	Inhabitants per km^2	Gross Value Added 1992	Employees 1992	Capital (Mio DM) 1992	Infrastructure 1989 (hectares)	Uni/FH (%) 1989	Sum of Neighbours' Hcap	Sum of Neighbours' Infrastr.
210	08317	Ortenaukreis	1860.75	395070	212.318	5672	66801	8426.10	6064	2.8	16.899	15631
211	08325	Rottweil	769.45	137999	179.348	2082	27479	3206.10	3469	2.9	14.899	20219
212	08326	Schwarzwald-Baar-Kreis	1025.27	208646	203.503	3728	46118	4860.07	3796	4.3	24.199	27642
213	08327	Tuttlingen	734.36	128237	174.624	2429	31021	3015.85	2865	2.5	18.399	19782
214	08335	Konstanz	817.96	256900	314.074	2903	36920	4558.95	3825	6.5	19.199	13685
215	08336	Loerrach	806.83	210596	261.017	2849	34190	5595.12	3093	4.1	6.700	8944
216	08337	Waldshut	1131.20	162275	143.454	1704	24017	3536.81	3986	3.4	11.699	11847
217	08415	Reutlingen	1094.20	270038	246.790	4190	49530	5690.14	4667	4.4	35.600	36890
218	08416	Tuebingen	519.18	203522	392.007	1568	19328	1881.87	2960	8.6	25.800	24097
219	08417	Zollernalbkreis	917.72	192155	209.383	3133	44657	4584.92	4292	2.3	23.799	21563
220	08421	Ulm, krfr. St.	118.68	115123	970.029	2863	31159	4309.77	999	7.6	5.800	9518
221	08425	Alb-Donau-Kreis	1357.33	179018	131.890	1933	24911	3736.20	6713	2.2	36.200	29262
222	08426	Biberach	1409.86	173664	123.178	2730	30764	3395.85	6215	3.5	22.600	28848
223	08435	Bodenseekreis	664.67	191735	288.466	3453	35481	4736.83	2624	10.0	17.100	14458
224	08436	Ravensburg	1631.67	259951	159.316	3141	38886	4857.73	5280	4.6	27.299	21639
225	08437	Sigmaringen	1204.33	129112	107.206	1689	20947	2392.47	4400	2.4	33.799	29768
226	09161	Ingolstadt, krfr. St.	133.37	110910	831.596	4244	37958	9630.18	900	4.4	9.200	10759
227	09162	Muenchen, krfr. St.	310.47	1244676	4009.006	22258	171938	37295.64	3810	12.1	21.100	7038
228	09163	Rosenheim, krfr. St.	37.02	58601	1582.955	759	9355	986.24	240	4.1	2.800	3784
229	09171	Altoetting	569.57	104404	183.303	3136	22257	5991.63	1873	4.9	8.200	8945
230	09172	Berchtesgadener Land	839.89	98561	117.350	439	7799	889.26	2066	2.8	3.700	3223
231	09173	Bad Toelz-Wolfratshausen	1110.66	110040	99.076	889	12440	1082.75	1604	4.0	30.000	9712
232	09174	Dachau	579.19	120175	207.488	574	9277	1614.00	2029	3.4	44.698	20521
233	09175	Ebersberg	549.35	108895	198.232	666	9533	1311.61	1373	5.1	20.600	11677
234	09176	Eichstaett	1214.68	111242	91.581	2281	8685		5056	2.9	22.000	31827
235	09177	Erding	870.97	102370	117.536	441	7121	884.73	2518	2.3	28.399	14094
236	09178	Freising	799.29	138513	173.295	1131	16964	2174.72	2817	5.8	26.399	19431
237	09179	Fuerstenfeldbruck	434.73	185340	426.334	1000	11177	1218.98	1883	4.7	42.999	15957
238	09180	Garmisch-Patenkirchen	1012.29	85383	84.346	259	5802	446.95	1397	2.9	10.200	7608
239	09181	Landsberg a. Lech	804.41	97952	121.769	518	8237	1009.92	2564	3.5	30.299	17894
240	09182	Miesbach	863.52	88608	102.613	559	8323	946.55	1517	2.4	19.800	8514
241	09183	Muehldorf a. Inn	805.32	105052	130.448	944	14293	1727.10	2249	2.5	22.800	20773
242	09184	Muenchen	667.26	278227	416.969	4885	41549	6264.30	3126	13.0	50.800	22581
243	09185	Neuburg-Schrobenhausen	739.72	84922	114.803	754	10862	1489.45	2932	3.4	18.900	20116
244	09186	Pfaffenhofen a. d. Ilm	760.14	104019	136.842	3575	12292	1668.31	2771	2.9	25.499	21374

Table C.1 continued

C. Data   163

Index	Code	Region	Surface (km^2)	Inhabitants	Inhabitants per km^2	Gross Value Added 1992	Employees 1992	Capital (Mio DM) 1992	Infrastructure 1989 (hectares)	Uni/FH (%) 1989	Sum of Neighbours' Hcap	Sum of Neighbours' Infrastr.
245	09187	Rosenheim	1438.78	222064	154.342	1435	20526	2810.54	3784	2.8	30.800	11728
246	09188	Starnberg	487.92	118764	243.409	1026	10812	1520.44	1246	8.2	28.700	11603
247	09189	Traunstein	1533.96	161304	105.155	1571	22571	3132.66	3223	3.7	13.000	9972
248	09190	Weilheim-Schongau	966.42	119378	123.526	1361	15969	2800.31	2426	3.5	21.299	10389
249	09261	Landshut, krfr. St.	65.74	59351	902.814	706	10532	2353.12	428	3.9	2.000	4529
250	09262	Passau, krfr. St.	69.75	51265	734.982	610	10141	1390.41	507	4.9	2.000	6041
251	09263	Straubing, krfr. St.	67.64	43860	648.433	493	7657	788.76	370	3.2	1.600	3797
252	09271	Deggendorf	861.13	111424	129.393	1335	17229	2815.54	3048	2.9	11.099	22182
253	09272	Freyung-Grafenau	984.23	81290	82.592	579	10632	966.72	3327	1.8	6.600	11445
254	09273	Kelheim	1066.90	102563	96.132	3390	14147		4458	2.8	17.100	27218
255	09274	Landshut	1342.97	131183	97.681	1466	16122	1181.29	4529	2.0	24.500	28502
256	09275	Passau	1530.29	179964	117.601	1449	22971	2118.85	6041	2.0	11.600	10355
257	09276	Regen	975.08	81758	83.847	596	11616	1416.69	2356	1.7	7.900	15143
258	09277	Rottal-Inn	1281.32	114359	89.251	728	13111	940.47	3473	2.0	16.300	20928
259	09278	Straubing-Bogen	1202.23	89787	74.684	407	7369	702.92	3797	1.6	14.999	24036
260	09279	Dingolfing-Landau	877.76	84725	96.524	2336	26098	5820.49	3188	2.0	8.500	14847
261	09361	Amberg, krfr. St.	50.07	44199	882.744	683	11146	1496.84	357	4.0	1.900	4544
262	09362	Regensburg, krfr. St.	80.81	125608	1554.362	2797	29773	5165.93	830	6.7	1.600	5574
263	09363	Weiden i. d. Oberpf., krfr. Stadt	68.49	43138	629.844	534	8071	1026.77	509	2.7	1.900	4807
264	09371	Amberg-Sulzbach	1255.25	104716	83.422	757	11677	2294.75	4544	1.9	15.400	25283
265	09372	Cham	1510.30	128682	85.203	937	17088	1474.53	4971	1.6	6.800	17513
266	09373	Neumarkt i.d. Opf.	1344.21	118925	88.472	869	13883	1319.81	6471	1.9	16.699	32304
267	09374	Neustadt a.d. Waldnaab	1429.99	98711	69.029	897	14960	1638.84	4807	1.9	10.000	19079
268	09375	Regensburg	1395.21	164118	117.630	895	12560	1209.91	5574	1.6	18.500	30842
269	09376	Schwandorf	1472.62	138961	94.363	1406	20674	3802.55	5786	1.9	8.900	26367
270	09377	Tirschenreuth	1083.54	80209	74.025	887	14486	1644.72	3647	1.4	6.600	11424
271	09461	Bamberg, krfr. St.	54.62	70216	1285.536	1471	20587	2677.95	518	4.4	1.500	4300
272	09462	Bayreuth, krfr. St.	66.89	72840	1083.952	2434	10778		533	5.0	2.100	4593
273	09463	Coburg, krfr. St.	48.12	43928	912.884	1044	11371	1374.48	350	3.8	1.700	2727
274	09464	Hof, krfr. St.	57.89	52658	909.622	609	9717	1551.90	328	2.5	2.200	3198
275	09471	Bamberg	1167.92	134906	115.510	721	12132	1323.09	4300	1.5	26.499	36271
276	09472	Bayreuth	1272.97	106520	83.678	857	13494	1287.72	4593	2.1	26.200	33213
277	09473	Coburg	590.50	90105	152.591	1975	24660	2622.35	2727	1.7	11.100	12628
278	09474	Forchheim	643.03	108949	169.431	659	12090	1364.49	2449	2.3	10.900	14830
279	09475	Hof	892.29	110315	123.631	1589	24591	2948.89	3198	2.2	11.599	11265

Table C.1 continued

164 C. Data

Index	Code	Region	Surface (km^2)	Inhabitants	Inhabitants per km^2	Gross Value Added 1992	Employees 1992	Capital (Mio DM) 1992	Infrastructure 1989 (hectares)	Uni/FH (%) 1989	Sum of Neighbours' Hcap	Sum of Neighbours' Infrastr.
280	09476	Kronach	651.52	76865	117.978	1244	20165	2141.57	1753	2.1	7.700	10367
281	09477	Kulmbach	656.52	77783	118.478	1219	15341	2300.35	2567	2.3	9.400	15719
282	09478	Lichtenfels	521.79	70069	134.286	909	13496	1365.61	1875	1.5	9.700	15940
283	09479	Wunsiedel i. Fichtelgebirge	606.71	89340	147.253	1330	21887	2050.57	2024	2.6	5.700	11438
284	09561	Ansbach, krfr. St.	99.94	39448	394.717	569	8588	873.73	602	3.1	1.500	8935
285	09562	Erlangen, krfr. St.	76.97	101450	1318.046	5150	36170	5123.42	774	18.1	17.800	6942
286	09563	Fuerth, krfr. St.	63.34	107799	1701.910	1486	20456	2402.43	677	5.6	30.300	7039
287	09564	Nuernberg, krfr. St.	185.81	495845	2668.559	7971	97994	14224.23	2252	6.2	38.400	12663
288	09565	Schwabach, krfr. St.	40.71	37575	922.992	414	5586	528.97	313	3.1	8.200	5869
289	09571	Ansbach	1972.15	176031	89.258	1595	25241	2477.36	8935	1.5	23.700	42311
290	09572	Erlangen-Hoechstadt	564.58	123107	218.051	701	14558	1507.04	2668	3.7	41.500	20787
291	09573	Fuerth	307.61	108502	352.726	674	8559	981.21	1345	2.3	39.000	24644
292	09574	Nuernberger Land	800.82	165131	206.202	1722	24131	2265.52	3269	3.6	20.099	26594
293	09575	Neustadt a.d. Aisch- Bad Windshr	1267.59	93928	74.100	532	10349	1703.69	5721	1.9	16.400	33128
294	09576	Roth	895.31	117884	131.668	747	10711	1048.97	3617	2.0	23.600	32141
295	09577	Weissenburg-Gunzenhausen	970.88	93594	96.401	1114	16064	1698.85	4500	2.1	8.900	23786
296	09661	Aschaffenburg, krfr. St.	62.76	66028	1052.071	1190	14936	1813.29	428	3.7	4.100	5232
297	09662	Schweinfurt, krfr. St.	35.75	55524	1553.119	2048	27986	4529.87	409	5.5	2.000	4864
298	09663	Wuerzburg, krfr. St.	87.66	127946	1459.571	1339	16536	1977.02	860	6.4	2.100	5406
299	09671	Aschaffenburg	699.11	168912	241.610	1893	25116	3012.92	2886	2.5	26.200	25762
300	09672	Bad Kissingen	1136.60	108360	95.337	581	10249	981.93	5069	1.9	17.199	31994
301	09673	Rhoen-Grabfeld	1021.90	85806	83.967	893	13391	1620.75	5067	3.6	9.200	22815
302	09674	Hassberge	956.59	86448	90.371	932	12560	1463.22	4350	2.2	8.800	16958
303	09675	Kitzingen	684.46	86875	126.925	881	12109	1719.87	3939	2.4	7.500	20291
304	09676	Miltenberg	715.63	126872	177.287	1682	23565	2281.21	2346	1.6	22.600	26438
305	09677	Main-Spessart	1322.66	130563	98.712	1899	22009	2057.85	5390	3.3	18.200	35247
306	09678	Schweinfurt	839.85	112609	134.082	289	5375	456.48	4864	2.0	22.500	33930
307	09679	Wuerzburg	968.28	152208	157.194	607	7607	1049.50	5406	2.1	18.899	27309
308	09761	Augsburg, krfr. St.	147.16	262110	1781.123	4825	52099	8170.21	916	5.9	8.800	10409
309	09762	Kaufbeuren, krfr. St.	40.02	42638	1065.417	377	6357	872.44	277	3.8	2.700	3578
310	09763	Kempten (Allgaeu), krfr. St.	63.29	61421	970.469	609	9464	1171.67	428	4.3	2.400	2464
311	09764	Memmingen, krfr. St.	70.19	40324	574.498	848	9704	1101.71	444	3.2	10.300	16034
312	09771	Aichach-Friedberg	780.85	116664	149.406	812	12389	1174.64	3182	2.8	28.799	23936
313	09772	Augsburg	1071.10	222289	207.533	2123	24211	4100.18	4663	2.5	25.099	28435
314	09773	Dillingen a. d. Donau	791.91	89426	112.924	1080	13395	1819.25	3769	2.1	12.900	17453

Table C.1 continued

Index	Code	Region	Surface (km^2)	Inhabitants	Inhabitants per km^2	Gross Value Added 1992	Employees 1992	Capital (Mio DM) 1992	Infrastructure 1989 (hectares)	Uni/FH (%) 1989	Sum of Neighbours' Hcap	Sum of Neighbours' Infrastr.
315	09774	Guenzburg	762.30	118126	154.960	1214	17495	2105.56	3709	3.4	17.099	25392
316	09775	Neu-Ulm	515.66	156318	303.142	2541	27105	3228.24	2805	3.6	18.899	22175
317	09776	Lindau (Bodensee)	323.35	75459	233.366	984	12703	1449.39	953	3.6	17.000	10368
318	09777	Ostallgaeu	1395.05	126420	90.620	1146	16547	2601.70	3578	2.7	20.799	18330
319	09778	Unterallgaeu	1230.36	128900	104.766	1256	15631	2009.21	4539	2.2	25.899	29158
320	09779	Donau-Ries	1274.92	126697	99.376	1649	22121	2957.85	6178	2.5	25.700	42484
321	09780	Oberallgaeu	1527.45	144017	94.236	1131	17727	2212.71	2464	2.4	17.399	14778
322	10041	Saarbruecken Stadtverband	410.62	359224	874.833	3469	59197	11737.63	2653	6.5	11.499	5766
323	10042	Merzig-Wadern	554.77	105210	189.646	909	12755	2127.20	2273	2.7	8.600	10926
324	10043	Neunkirchen	249.11	150159	602.782	1058	15032	2721.59	1474	3.7	19.599	12884
325	10044	Saarlouis	459.12	215513	469.405	2288	31631	7395.73	2225	3.3	16.099	9273
326	10045	Saarpfalz-Kreis	420.25	158309	376.702	2185	27965	4910.67	2067	4.5	19.800	14196
327	10046	Sankt Wendel	476.13	95786	201.176	612	8042	1082.49	2873	3.2	16.300	18311

Table C.1 continued

Nr.	Country	N	I	O	GDP/adult 1960	GDP/adult 1985	GDP	working age pop.	I/Y	SCHOOL	Lag of 85 GDP/ad.	Lag of SCHOOL
1	Algeria	1	1	0	2485	4371	4.80	2.60	24.10	4.60	4789.71	3.90
2	Angola	1	0	0	1588	1171	0.80	2.10	5.80	1.80	1981.00	3.18
3	Benin	1	0	0	1116	1071	2.20	2.40	10.80	1.80	965.50	1.53
4	Botswana	1	1	0	959	3671	8.60	3.20	28.30	2.90	2889.75	2.90
5	Burkina	1	0	0	529	857	2.90	0.90	12.70	0.40	1005.17	2.20
6	Burundi	1	0	0	755	663	1.20	1.70	5.10	0.40	758.75	1.73
7	Cameroon	1	1	0	889	2190	5.70	2.10	12.80	3.40	2082.20	2.10
8	Central Afr. Rep.	1	0	0	838	789	1.50	1.70	10.50	1.40	1345.20	2.64
9	Chad	1	0	0	908	462	-0.90	1.90	6.90	0.40	1208.80	1.92
10	Congo	1	0	0	1009	2624	6.20	2.40	28.80	3.80	1982.40	2.56
11	Egypt	1	0	0	907	2160	6.00	2.50	16.30	7.00	6745.00	6.66
12	Ethiopia	1	1	0	533	608	2.80	2.30	5.40	1.10	3199.80	1.84
13	Gabon	0	0	0	1307	5350	7.00	1.40	22.10	2.60	2407.00	3.60
14	Gambia, the	0	0	0	799	.	3.60	0.00	18.10	1.50	1450.00	1.70
15	Ghana	1	0	0	1009	727	1.00	2.30	9.10	4.70	1179.67	1.87
16	Guinea	0	0	0	746	869	2.20	1.60	10.90	0.00	1122.60	1.84
17	Ivory Coast	1	1	0	1386	1704	6.10	4.30	12.40	2.30	821.40	1.72
18	Kenya	1	1	0	944	1329	4.80	3.40	17.40	2.40	736.00	1.16
19	Lesotho	0	0	0	431	1483	6.80	1.90	12.60	2.00	7064.00	3.00
20	Liberia	1	0	0	863	944	3.30	3.00	21.50	2.50	1126.00	1.33
21	Madagascar	1	1	0	1194	975	1.40	2.20	7.10	2.60	1571.00	2.83
22	Malawi	1	1	0	455	823	4.80	2.40	13.20	0.60	987.67	1.20
23	Mali	1	1	0	737	710	2.10	2.20	7.30	1.00	1590.00	1.50
24	Mauritania	1	0	0	777	1038	3.30	2.20	25.60	1.00	2177.00	2.43
25	Mauritius	1	0	0	1973	2967	4.20	2.60	17.10	7.30	975.00	2.60
26	Morocco	1	1	0	1030	2348	5.80	2.50	8.30	3.60	6700.33	6.13
27	Mozambique	1	0	0	1420	1036	1.40	2.70	6.10	0.70	1842.29	2.46
28	Niger	1	0	0	539	841	4.40	2.60	10.30	0.50	1442.83	1.75
29	Nigeria	1	1	0	1055	1186	2.80	2.40	12.00	2.30	1141.00	1.53
30	Rwanda	1	0	0	460	696	4.50	2.80	7.90	0.40	613.00	1.40
31	Senegal	1	1	0	1892	1450	2.50	2.30	9.60	1.70	654.25	0.88
32	Sierra	1	0	0	611	805	3.40	1.60	10.90	1.70	906.50	1.25
33	Somalia	1	0	0	901	657	1.80	3.10	13.80	1.10	968.50	1.75
34	S. Africa	1	1	0	4768	7064	3.90	2.30	21.60	3.00	1659.40	2.74
35	Sudan	1	0	0	1254	1038	1.80	2.60	13.20	2.00	2185.50	2.51
36	Swaziland	0	0	0	817	.	7.20	0.00	17.70	3.70	4050.00	1.85
37	Tanzania	1	1	0	383	710	5.30	2.90	18.00	0.50	868.67	1.58
38	Togo	1	0	0	777	978	3.40	2.50	15.50	2.90	885.00	2.30
39	Tunisia	1	1	0	1623	3661	5.60	2.40	13.80	4.30	5151.00	6.27
40	Uganda	1	0	0	601	667	3.50	3.10	4.10	1.10	837.00	1.78
41	Zaire	1	0	0	594	412	0.90	2.40	6.50	3.60	1063.89	1.53
42	Zambia	1	1	0	1410	1217	2.10	2.70	31.70	2.40	1324.13	1.86
43	Zimbabwe	1	1	0	1187	2107	5.10	2.80	21.10	4.40	3247.00	2.25
44	Afghanistan	0	0	0	1224	0	1.60	0.00	69.00	0.90	4787.50	4.75
46	Bahrain	0	0	0	0	0	0.00	0.00	30.00	12.10	15651.25	4.80
46	Bangladesh	1	1	0	846	1221	4.00	2.60	6.80	3.20	1114.67	3.63
47	Burma	1	1	0	517	1031	4.50	1.70	11.40	3.50	1926.67	4.23

Table C.2: Data on a set of national states (taken from Mankiw et al. [1992] and extended by spatial lags)

C. Data   167

Nr.	Country	N	I	O	GDP/adult 1960	GDP/adult 1985	GDP	working age pop.	I/Y	SCHOOL	Lag of 85 GDP/ad.	Lag of SCHOOL
48	Hong Kong	1	1	0	3085	13372	8.90	3.00	19.90	7.20	13331.00	8.90
49	India	1	1	0	978	1339	3.60	2.40	16.80	5.10	1427.00	4.33
50	Iran	0	0	0	3606	7400	6.30	3.40	18.40	6.50	9348.22	4.92
61	Iraq	0	0	0	4916	6626	3.80	3.20	16.20	7.40	9815.00	7.38
62	Israel	1	1	0	4802	10450	5.90	2.80	28.50	9.50	4171.33	8.87
53	Japan	1	1	1	3493	13893	6.80	1.20	36.00	10.90	2387.50	5.10
64	Jordan	1	1	0	2183	4312	5.40	2.70	17.60	10.80	7267.00	7.16
55	KoreaRepof	1	1	0	1285	4775	7.90	2.70	22.30	10.20	6946.50	5.45
56	Kuwait	0	0	0	77881	25635	2.40	6.80	9.50	9.60	6270.75	7.28
57	Malaysia	1	1	0	2154	5788	7.10	3.20	23.20	7.30	5621.75	7.03
58	Nepal	1	0	0	833	974	2.60	2.00	5.90	2.30	1280.00	4.15
69	Oman	0	0	0	0	15684	0.00	3.30	15.60	2.70	9786.25	3.15
60	Pakistan	1	1	0	1077	2175	5.80	3.00	12.20	3.00	7694.67	3.37
61	Philippines	1	1	0	1668	2430	4.50	3.00	14.90	10.60	2649.00	3.80
62	SaudiArabia	0	0	0	6731	11057	6.10	4.10	12.80	3.10	7626.73	5.44
63	Singapore	1	1	0	2793	14678	9.20	2.60	32.20	9.00	3973.50	5.70
64	SriLanka	1	1	0	1794	2482	3.70	2.40	14.80	8.30	1339.00	5.10
65	SyrianArabRep.	1	1	0	2382	6042	6.70	3.00	15.90	8.80	6458.00	8.30
66	Taiwan	0	0	0	.	.	8.00	0.00	20.70	0.00	7032.67	10.57
67	Thailand	1	1	0	1308	3220	6.70	3.10	18.00	4.40	3409.50	5.40
68	U. arab. Emirates	0	0	0	.	18513	0.00	0.00	26.50	0.00	8535.25	6.10
69	Yemen	0	0	0	.	1918	0.00	2.50	17.20	0.60	5832.50	2.10
70	Auatria	1	1	1	5939	13327	3.60	0.40	23.40	8.00	14086.67	6.77
71	Belgium	1	1	1	6789	14290	3.50	0.50	23.40	9.30	11366.40	8.38
72	Cyprus	0	0	0	2948	.	5.20	0.00	31.20	8.20	5656.00	6.70
73	Denmark	1	1	1	8551	16491	3.20	0.60	26.60	10.70	12807.20	9.60
74	Finland	1	1	1	6527	13779	3.70	0.70	36.90	11.50	17150.33	9.53
75	France	1	1	1	7215	15027	3.90	1.00	26.20	8.90	10519.38	7.01
76	GermanyFedRep.	1	1	1	7695	15297	3.30	0.50	28.50	8.40	12928.75	8.16
77	Greece	1	1	1	2257	6868	5.10	0.70	29.30	7.90	4421.50	6.95
78	Iceland	0	0	0	8091	.	3.90	0.00	29.00	10.20	16515.00	9.87
79	Ireland	1	1	1	4411	8675	3.80	1.10	25.90	11.40	13331.00	8.90
80	Italy	1	1	1	4913	11082	3.80	0.60	24.90	7.10	9127.33	6.83
81	Luxembourg	0	0	0	9015	.	2.80	0.00	26.90	5.00	14871.33	8.87
82	Malta	0	0	0	2293	.	6.00	0.00	80.90	7.10	7371.50	5.70
83	Netherlands	1	1	1	7689	13177	3.60	1.40	25.80	10.70	14306.00	8.87
84	Norway	1	1	1	7938	19723	4.30	0.70	29.10	10.00	11767.60	9.84
85	Portugal	1	1	1	2272	5827	4.40	0.60	22.50	5.80	6125.50	5.80
86	Spain	1	1	1	3766	9903	4.90	1.00	17.70	8.00	6893.25	5.73
87	Sweden	1	1	1	7802	15237	3.10	0.40	24.50	7.90	16322.50	10.15
88	Switzerland	1	1	1	10308	15881	2.50	0.80	29.70	4.80	13683.25	8.10
89	Turkey	1	1	1	2274	4444	5.20	2.50	20.20	5.50	5387.20	7.76
90	United Kingdom	1	1	1	7634	13331	2.50	0.30	18.40	8.90	12037.71	9.67
91	Barbados	0	0	0	3165	.	4.80	0.00	19.50	12.10	11285.00	8.80
92	Canada	1	1	1	10286	17935	4.20	2.00	23.30	10.60	18988.00	11.90
93	Costa Rica	1	1	0	3360	4492	4.70	3.50	14.70	7.00	4499.50	8.70
94	Dominican Rep.	1	1	0	1939	3308	5.10	2.90	17.10	5.80	1237.00	1.90

Table C.2 continued

					GDP/adult			working			Lag of 85	Lag of
Nr.	Country	N	I	O	1960	1985	GDP	age pop.	I/Y	SCHOOL	GDP/ad.	SCHOOL
95	El Salvador	1	1	0	2042	1997	3.30	3.30	8.00	3.90	2428.00	3.05
96	Guatemala	1	1	0	2481	3034	3.90	3.10	8.80	2.40	3733.00	4.73
97	Haiti	1	1	0	1096	1237	1.80	1.30	7.10	1.90	3194.00	8.50
98	Honduras	1	1	0	1430	1822	4.00	3.10	13.80	3.70	3003.00	4.03
99	Jamaica	1	1	0	2726	3080	2.10	1.60	20.60	11.20	10112.50	6.90
100	Mexico	1	1	0	4229	7380	5.50	3.30	19.50	6.60	11011.00	7.15
101	Nicaragua	1	1	0	3195	3978	4.10	3.30	14.50	5.80	3157.00	5.35
102	Panama	1	1	0	2423	5021	5.90	3.00	26.10	11.60	9295.00	8.33
103	Trinidad & Tobago	1	1	0	9253	11285	2.70	1.90	20.40	8.80	3168.00	9.55
104	Unit4ed States	1	1	1	12362	18988	3.20	1.50	21.10	11.90	8354.00	10.00
105	Argentina	1	1	0	4852	5533	2.10	1.50	25.30	5.00	4512.00	5.74
106	Bolivia	1	1	0	1618	2055	3.30	2.40	13.30	4.90	4863.60	5.96
107	Brazil	1	1	0	1842	5563	7.30	2.90	23.20	4.70	3501.44	6.91
108	Chile	1	1	0	5189	5533	2.60	2.30	29.70	7.70	3787.67	5.97
109	Colombia	1	1	0	2672	4405	5.00	3.00	18.00	6.10	5039.80	7.70
110	Ecuador	1	1	0	2198	4504	5.70	2.80	24.40	7.20	4090.00	7.05
111	Guyana	0	0	0	2761	.	1.10	0.00	32.40	11.70	3966.33	6.60
112	Paraguay	1	1	0	1951	3914	5.50	2.70	11.70	4.40	4383.67	4.87
113	Peru	1	1	0	3310	3775	3.50	2.90	12.00	8.00	4412.00	6.12
114	Surinam	0	0	0	3226	.	4.50	0.00	19.40	8.10	2781.50	8.20
115	Uruguay	1	1	0	5119	5495	0.90	0.60	11.80	7.00	5548.00	4.85
116	Venezuela	1	1	0	10367	6336	1.90	3.80	11.40	7.00	5313.25	7.83
117	Australia	1	1	1	8440	13409	3.80	2.00	31.50	9.80	5670.33	5.83
118	Fiji	0	0	0	3634	.	4.20	0.00	20.60	8.10	0.00	
119	Indonesia	1	1	0	879	2159	5.50	1.90	13.90	4.10	7769.80	7.64
120	New Zealand	1	1	1	9523	12308	2.70	1.70	22.50	11.90	13409.00	9.80
121	Papua New Guinea	1	0	0	1781	2544	3.50	2.10	16.20	1.50	7784.00	6.95

Table C.2 continued

List of Symbols

A note to the reader: since I present a large variety of models, models that were derived from different theoretical or technical frameworks, it has been unavoidable to use the same variables in different contexts, i.e. to sometimes give the same variable different meanings. This holds especially for models of different chapters. Variables are therefore listed chapter by chapter.

Chapter 2

Greek Variables

α (section 2.2.1) income share of capital in growth accounting equation (2.4)

α production elasticity

β (section 2.3.2) convergence parameter indicating convergence of growth rates of y

β production elasticity

$\boldsymbol{\beta}$ (section 2.3.2, equation 2.13) vector of coefficients

δ_K rate of depreciation of capital

ϵ_{yk} production elasticity of k with respect to y

γ production elasticity

μ_A a constant

μ_k a constant

ϕ_K fraction of capital employed in the goods-producing sector

ϕ_L fraction of labour employed in the goods-producing sector

σ (section 2.3.2) convergence parameter indicating convergence of y

θ production elasticity

ε_i stochastic residual

Other Variables

A total factor productivity (TFP)

F production function

f production function, intensive form
F_K partial derivative of F with respect to K
f_k partial derivative of f with respect to k
F_L partial derivative of F with respect to L
g_A growth rate of total factor productivity
g_K growth rate of capital
g_L growth rate of labour
g_Y growth rate of income
$\overline{g_{y,i}}$ y's average growth rate of region i in period t
$g_\mathbf{x}$ (section 2.2.2.1) growth rates of firm specific factor inputs
$\mathcal{K}$ (section 2.2.2.1) semi-public stock of knowledge
K capital, factor of production
k capital per unit of labour, capital intensity
k_i (section 2.2.2.1) firm specific stock of knowledge
L labour, factor of production
N (section 2.2.2.1) number of firms
n growth rate of labour
r interest rate, remuneration of capital
s saving rate
u_{it} stochastic residual
w wage, remuneration of labour
$\mathbf{X}$ (section 2.3.2) matrix of control variables
$\mathbf{x}_i$ (section 2.2.2.1) firm specific factor inputs
Y output of production
y output per unit of labour
y_{ti} y of region i in period t

Chapter 3

Greek Variables

α, α_i parameter of production function (of sector i)
β, β_i parameter of production function (of sector i)
$\beta_1, \beta_2, \beta_3$ coefficients, elements of $\boldsymbol{\beta}$
$\boldsymbol{\beta}$ vector of coefficients

List of Symbols

δ, δ_i parameter of production function (of sector i)

Δ_t measure of diversity at an industry's location taken at time t

ϵ_i (section 3.3.3) density elasticities, an increas in factor i by 1% implies an increase of output by ϵ_i%

γ parameter of production function

μ share of workers that work in the manufacturing sector

ω_i real wages payed in the manufacturing sector of region i

Π_i index of market potential of region i

π_i profit, locational rent of good i

ρ_i, ρ_t parameter that specifies localization economies (marshallian externalities) within sector i (or at time t)) (of sector i)

σ substitution parameter

τ, τ_i transportation cost (of good i)

Other Variables

A total factor productivity (TFP), external shift factor

a parameter of utility function

$A(\mathbf{S})$ external shift factor subject ot scale and technology measures

b parameter of utility function

c parameter of utility function

$C(\omega, \lambda)$ function to describe the attractiveness of a city as a function of its wage and relative size

ch_{ikt} realization of a measure of geograpical coincidence of university and industry research in region i and patent class k at time t

cit log of total number citations of patents

C_A consumption level of agricultural good

c_i cost of production of good i

C_M consumption level of an aggregate manufacturing good

c_m minimum cost of supply

$\mathbf{D}$ matrix of dummy variables

$D_i(\alpha)$ factor density index for country i

$d, \bar{d}$ distance to market

F level of tariff

f (section 3.2.3) share of workers in region i

$F(\cdot)$ production function

F_K partial derivative of F with respect to K
F_L partial derivative of F with respect to L
g congestion parameter
g vector of goods sorted according to their minimal range
g_i goods (entering the aggregate C_M in section 3.2.3)
HHI Hirschmann-Herfindahl index
h_i human capital measured per capita used by sector i)
im share of imports in GDP
ind_{ikt} R&D by industry in region i and patent class k at time t
I_i Income of region i
k vector of inputs measured per-capita
K, K_i capital, production factor (used by sector i)
L, L_i labour, production factor (used by sector i)
L_{M_i} labour employed in the manufacturing sector of region i
M, M_i land, production factor (used by sector i)
MC marginal cost
n number of potential products c_i
n number of regions that enter the index of market potential
$N(\cdot)$ positive sigmoid function
P population of an urban area
p, p_i price (of good i)
pat_{ikt} number of corporate patents in region i and patent class k at time t
P_i CES price index for manufacturing goods in region i
Q CES aggregate of services
q_i price of output of Y_i
$R^{(d)}, R^{(f)}$ domestic (foreign) sotck of R&D capital
$S(\cdot)$ positive sigmoid function
$selfcit$ log self citations of patents
s_{ij} share of industry j i city i
t_{ij} cost of transportation of a vector of goods from region i to region j
U utility level
uni_{ikt} university research in region i and patent class k at time t
w_i nominal wages payed in the manufacturing sector of region i
X matrix of control variables

List of Symbols

x_i (section 3.2.3) output of manufacturing sector of region i

y (section 3.3.2) income level

Y, Y_i output (of good i)

y_i individual consumption of Y_i

z_i CES aggregate of factors that enters the production function of sector i

Chapter 4

Greek Variables

α parameter of production function

β parameter of production function

Δ parameter that embodies knowledge spillovers between regions

δ parameter that embodies knowledge spillovers between firms of one region

γ parameter of production function

μ a constant

Φ share of capital that enters region A's production function

ϕ share of capital of region A that enters firm 1's production function, factor share

Π, T identity functions (equations 4.7)

π, τ identity functions (equations 4.3)

Θ share of labour that enters region A's production function

θ share of labour of region A that enters firm 1's production function

φ parameter of production function

Other Variables

F production function

F_{K_A} first derivative of F with respect to K_A

F_ϕ first derivative of F with respect to ϕ

g an agent, a firm

g_A growth rate of capital of region A

g_K, g_k growth rate of K (of k)

$g_{A \cup B}$ growth rate of capital of the spatial aggregate of regions A and B

g_ϕ growth rate of ϕ

h an agent, a firm)

i vector of factors internal to agent G's production function

i_k, i_l elements of **i**

k capital per unit of labour, capital intensity

K capital that enters the production function of the spatial aggregate of regions A and B

K_1, K_2 capital used by firm 1 (firm 2) in production

K_A capital used in production in region A, spatial aggregate of K_1 and K_2

K_B capital used in production in region B

L labour that enters the production function of the spatial aggregate of regions A and B

L_1, L_2 labour used by firm 1 (firm 2) in production

L_A labour used in production in region A, spatial aggregate of L_1 and L_2

L_A, L_B labour used by firm 1 (firm 2) in production

x vector of factors external to agent G's production function

x_j element of **x**

Y_1, Y_2 output of production of firm 1 (firm 2)

Y_A, Y_B output of production of region A (region B)

Y_g agent g's output of production

Chapter 5

Greek Variables

α in sections 5.5.1.4 and 5.5.2.2 parameter of convergence regression

α parameter of production function, production elasticity

β in sections 5.5.1.4 and 5.5.2.2 parameter of convergence regression

β parameter of production function, production elasticity

δ parameter that embodies knowledge spillovers between sites of an automaton

η parameter of production function, production elasticity

γ parameter of production function, production elasticity

μ a deterministic function that defines a mapping $S^{(2r+1)} \to S$

$\tilde{\mu}$ a generalized version of μ, a mapping with a higher dimension than μ

ν a function that maps A into Θ

π parameter of production function, production elasticity

θ fraction of labour that actually migrates

$\Theta^{(t)}$ realization of relevant global parameters at time t that enter $\tilde{\mu}$

ε a vector of identically independently distributed random variables

φ_H share of human capital that is employed in the goods producing sector

List of Symbols

φ_K share of capital that is employed in the goods producing sector
φ_L share of labour that is employed in the goods producing sector
ϱ coefficient of elasticity that weighs the difference in neighbours' MPK
ξ binary variable to describe the dynamics of labour migration
ζ binary variable to describe the dynamics of labour migration

Other Variables

A set of all sites of an automaton
$a_{i,j}^{(t)}$ site i, j of an automaton at time t
$\mathbf{a}_{i,j}^{(t)}$ vector of $a_{i,j}$ and its neighbours at time t
d_H rate of depreciation of human capital
d_K rate of depreciation of capital
$\overline{g_{y,i}}$ average growth rate of region's (site's) i income per capita
H human capital, production factor
h number of neighbours of a site of the automaton that offers higher wage
K capital, production factor
k dimension of states of an automaton
L labour, production factor
l number of neighbours of a site of the automaton that offers lower wage
MPK marginal product of capital
n number of neighbours of a site of the automaton
$S^{(k)}$ a k dimensional alphabet of states of an automaton
s_j saving rate of region (site) j
Y production output

Chapter 6

Greek Variables

α parameter of production function, production elasticity
β parameter of production function, production elasticity
$\boldsymbol{\beta}$ vector of coefficients
$\hat{\boldsymbol{\beta}}$ OLS estimate of $\boldsymbol{\beta}$
$\tilde{\boldsymbol{\beta}}$ ML estimate of $\boldsymbol{\beta}$
$\boldsymbol{\beta}_1, \boldsymbol{\beta}_2$ subsets of $\boldsymbol{\beta}$ where $\boldsymbol{\beta}_1 \cup \boldsymbol{\beta}_2 = \boldsymbol{\beta}$ and $\boldsymbol{\beta}_1 \cap \boldsymbol{\beta}_2 = \{\}$

β_L vector of coefficients when dependend variable is spatially lagged
δ parameter that specifies knowledge spillovers
γ parameter of production function, production elasticity
λ parameter specifying spatial autocorrelation in the residual
ν a vector of standard normally identically independently distributed random variables
Ω matrix specifying the autocorrelation structure of the error term
ϕ parameter describing the spatial distribution of $Y_{(B)}$
ρ parameter specifying spatial autocorrelation in the depending variable
σ_u^2 variance of u
$\hat{\sigma}_u^2$ OLS estimate of σ_u^2
$\tilde{\sigma}_u^2$ ML estimate of σ_u^2
ε a vector of random variables subject to spatial autocorrelation

Other Variables

B matrix describing the spatial distribution of a simple stylized country
C binary contiguity matrix, the simplest spatial weight matrix
$\bar{C}$ generalized spatial weight matrix
d (section 6.5.2) rate of depreciation (of capital)
f arbitrary linear function
g (section 6.5.2) advancement of knowledge
H human capital, production factor
H_t human capital input measured at time t
I infrastructure, production factor
$\mathbf{I}$ identity matrix
$\mathcal{I}$ Moran's I statistic
$\mathcal{I}_n$ normalized Moran's I statistic
I_t infrastructure endowment measured at time t
K capital, production factor
K_t capital input measured at time t
ℓ log-likelihood function
ℓ_λ log-likelihood function under the hypothesis that $\rho = 0$
$_c\ell_\lambda$ concentrated log-likelihood function under the hypothesis that $\rho = 0$
ℓ_ρ log-likelihood function under the hypothesis that $\lambda = 0$
$_c\ell_\rho$ concentrated log-likelihood function under the hypothesis that $\lambda = 0$

List of Symbols

L labour, production factor

$\mathcal{LM}$ test statistic of lagrange multiplier test

$\mathcal{LR}$ test statistic of likelihood ratio test

L_t labour input measured at time t

$\mathbf{M}$ transformation matrix

N number of regions entering the regression

n (section 6.5.2) rate of population growth

$\mathbf{N}$ transformation matrix

PD population density

R R&D-personnel, production factor

R_t input of R&D-personnel measured at time t

SSE_R sums of squares of errors of restricted estimation

SSE_U sums of squares of errors of unrestricted estimation

s_h (section 6.5.2) rate of accumulation of human capital

s_k (section 6.5.2) rate of accumulation of capital

$\mathbf{u}$ a vector of identically independently distributed random variables

$\hat{\mathbf{u}}$ OLS estimate of $\mathbf{u}$

$\tilde{\mathbf{u}}$ ML estimate of $\mathbf{u}$

$\hat{\mathbf{u}}_L$ residuals of OLS-regression when dependend variable is spatially lagged

$\mathbf{v}$ vector of explaining variables used in regression

$\mathbf{W}$ row standardized spatial weight matrix

$\mathcal{W}$ test statistic of Wald test

$\mathbf{W}_X$ row standardized spatial weight matrix describing spatial effects in X

$\mathbf{W}_y$ row standardized spatial weight matrix describing spatial effects in y

$\mathbf{W}_\varepsilon$ row standardized spatial weight matrix describing spatial effects in ε

$\mathbf{X}$ matrix of independend, explaining variables

$\mathbf{X}_1, \mathbf{X}_2$ subsets of $\mathbf{X}$ where $\mathbf{X}_1 \cup \mathbf{X}_2 = \mathbf{X}$ and $\mathbf{X}_1 \cap \mathbf{X}_2 = \{\}$

Y production output

$\mathbf{y}$ vector of dependend variables

$Y_{(1)}, Y_{(2)}$ output of region 1 (region 2)

$Y_{(A)}, Y_{(B)}, Y_{(C)}$ output of region A (region B or C)

Y_t output measured at time t

List of Figures

2.1	Graphical representation of the Solow Model.	7
2.2	If $\beta + \theta = 1$ the region converges to a balanced growth path	12
2.3	If $\beta + \theta \neq 1$ the region either shrinks (left) or grows endogenously	13
2.4	Growth rates and steady states for identical (a) and different economies (b)	16
2.5	Average growth rate of per capita income of US states from 1880 to 1988 vs. 1880 initial value (from Barro & Sala-i-Martin, 1992)	19
2.6	Dispersion of per-capita income across US states (from Sala-i-Martin [1996])	20
2.7	Different types of convergence behaviour (from Mankiw, Romer & Weil [1992])	21
2.8	Twin-peaks distribution dynamics (from Quah, 1996)	23
2.9	Plot of the average growth rate in the period 80–94 against Log(GDP80) for 324 West German regional statistical units (Kreise). Data from "Volkswirtschaftliche Gesamtrechnung" 1996.	24
3.1	Emergence of Thünen's Rings for three different crops	32
3.2	System of Central Places according to Christaller (from Schätzl, 1996, p. 74)	34
3.3	System of hexagonal layers of locational hierarchy according to Lösch (from Isard, 1956, p. 270)	35
3.4	Critical threshold of migration as a function of transportation costs (Krugman, 1991, p. 493)	38
3.5	Emergence of spatial concentration in a self-organizing economy (Krugman, 1996, p. 25)	39
3.6	Economic potential of regions in an enlarged Common Market (EC[6] with Scandinavia, UK and Ireland. Clark et al. (1969), p. 205)	40
3.7	Innovation (I), development of new products (P) and increase of diversification according to Jacobs (p. 63 of the German translation)	44
3.8	Circular Causality in Spatial Agglomeration of Firms and Workers (from Fujita, 1993)	49
3.9	Three possible phase diagrams for the model of David & Rosenbloom [1990]	55
4.1	Dynamics of factor migration between two firms if $\delta = 0$ (a: no spillovers between firms) and $\delta > 0$ (b: spillovers between firms)	71
4.2	Dynamics of factor migration between two remote regions if $\delta > 0$ and $\Delta = 0$ (a) or $\Delta > 0$ (b) respectively	73
4.3	Bifurcation diagram: stable attractors of Φ, Θ as a function of Δ	75

4.4	Convergence property of the aggregate of two firms. "−" denotes convergence with increasing ϕ and "+" denotes divergence	78
4.5	Convergence property of the aggregate of two regions where $\Delta = 0$ (a) and $\Delta > 0$ (b)	80
5.1	Metamorphosis from ovum to newt (from Eisenhardt et al, p.132)	84
5.2	Structure of neighbourship in a 1-dimensional (a) and in a 2-dimensional CA (b)	88
5.3	Two ways of connecting a two-dimensionsal quadratic Cellular Automata	92
5.4	Initial factor endowment a two-dimensional economic space	94
5.5	Spatial distribution of capital under decreasing returns ($\gamma + \pi = 0.4$) in a one- and in a two-dimensional country after $t = 50$ iteration steps.	96
5.6	Spatial distribution of capital under constant returns ($\gamma + \pi = 1$) in a one- and in a two-dimensional country after $t = 50$ iteration steps.	96
5.7	Spatial distribution of capital under increasing returns ($\gamma + \pi = 1.4$) in a one- and in a two-dimensional country after $t = 50$ iteration steps.	97
5.8	Spatial distribution of capital in a one-dimensional automaton after $t = 50$ iteration steps	98
5.9	Evolution of spatial concentration of labour and its productivity under decreasing, constant and increasing returns to scale in the R&D-sector	100
5.10	Evolution of spatial correlation of labour and its productivity under decreasing, constant and increasing returns to scale in the R&D-sector	100
5.11	Spatial distribution of L and Y/L after $t = 50$ iteration steps if increasing returns prevail in the R&D-sector	101
6.1	Population density of West-German Kreise	104
6.2	Scatterplot matrix of variables used in regression. Lines give a descriptive linear fit and a 95% confidence interval of the regression line	109
6.3	Capital Productivity of West-German Kreise (1992)	111
6.4	Labour Productivity of West-German Kreise (1992)	112
6.5	Productivity of R&D-personnel of West-German Kreise (1992)	113
6.6	Productivity of Human Capital of West-German Kreise (1992)	114
6.7	Three different types of neighbourhood. a) rook/von Neumann b) bishop and c) queen/Moore neighbourhood	116
6.8	Scatterplot matrix of variables used in regresion against their spatial lags. Lines give a descriptive linear fit and a 95% confidence interval of the regression line	119
C.1	Spatial distribution of personnel engaged in R&D 1991/92	155

List of Tables

2.1 Results of convergence regressions for three different types of West German kreise (from Seitz, 1995, t-values in brackets) 25
4.1 Convergence properties on different levels of spatial aggregates 81
5.1 Results of linear convergence regressions for three different parameter constellations in a regionally disaggregated economy 98
5.2 Results of linear convergence regressions for three different parameter constellations in a regional aggregated economy 99
5.3 Results of linear convergence regressions for a non-aggregated and an aggregated automaton when R&D-sector displays increasing returns to scale 102

6.1 Summarizing statistics of variables used in regression 108
6.2 Pearson correlation matrix of variables used in regression 108
6.3 Pearson correlation matrix of population density and factor productivities . . . 110
6.4 Pearson correlation matrix of variables against their spatial lags 120
6.5 Pearson correlation matrix of factor productivities against their spatial lags . . . 121
6.6 Results of Unrestricted Estimation for German Kreise 132
6.7 Results of Unrestricted Estimation for German Kreise 133
6.8 Results of Restricted Estimation for German Kreise 134
6.9 Results of Restricted Estimation for German Kreise 135
6.10 Results of Unrestricted Estimation for German Kreise 136
6.11 Results of Unrestricted Estimation for German Kreise 137
6.12 Results of Restricted Estimation for German Kreise 138
6.13 Results of Unrestricted Estimation for German Kreise 139
6.14 Estimation Results on the Level of National States 141

C.1 Data on West German Kreise 156
C.2 Data on a set of national states 166

References

Abdel-Rahman, H. M. [1988]. Product Differentiation, Monopolistic Competition and City Size. *Regional Science and Urban Economics, 18*, 69-86.

Aghion, P. and Howitt, P. [1992]. A Model of Growth through Creative Destruction. *Econometrica, 60*, 323-351.

Aghion, P. and Howitt, P. [1998]. *Endogenous Growth Theory.* MIT Press.

Anselin, L. [1988]. *Spatial Econometrics: Methods and Models.* Kluwer.

Anselin, L., Varga, A. and Acs, Z. [1997]. Local Geographic Spillovers between University Research and High-Technoloy Innovations. *Journal of Urban Economics, 42*, 422-448.

Arrow, K. J. [1962]. The Economic Implications of Learning by Doing. *Review of Economic Studies, 29*(June), 155-173.

Arrow, K. J., Chenery, H. B., Minhas, B. S. and Solow, R. M. [1961]. Capital-Labour Substitution and Economic Efficiency. *The Review of Economics and Statistics, 18*, 225-250.

Arthur, W. B. [1994]. Industry Location Patterns and the Importance of History. In *Increasing Returns and Path-Dependence in the Economy.* Addison Wesley.

Audretsch, D. B. and Feldman, M. P. [1996]. R&D Spillovers and the Geography of Innovation and Production. *American Economic Review, 86*(3), 630-640.

Audretsch, D. B. and Stephan, P. E. [1996]. Company-Scientist Locational Links: The Case of Biotechnology. *American Economic Review, 86*(3), 641-652.

Barro, R. J., Mankiw, N. G. and Sala-i-Martin, X. [1995]. Capital Mobility in Neoclassical Models of Growth. *American Economic Review, 85*, 103-115.

Barro, R. J. and Sala-i-Martin, X. [1992]. Convergence. *Journal of Political Economy, 100*, 223-251.

Barro, R. J. and Sala-i-Martin, X. [1995]. *Economic Growth.* McGraw-Hill.

Baumol, W. [1986]. Productivity Growth, Convergence and Welfare. *American Economic Review, 76*, 1072-1085.

Baumol, W. J. and Oates, W. E. [1988]. *The Theory of Environmental Policy* (2nd ed.). Cambridge University Press.

Berck, B. and Sydsæter, K. [1993]. *Economists' Mathematical Manual* (2nd ed.). Springer.

Bernard, A. B. and Jones, J. I. [1996]. Technology and Convergence. *The Economic Journal, 106*, 1037-1044.

Berndt, E. R. and Christensen, L. R. [1973]. The Internal Structure of Functional Relationships: Separability, Substitution and Aggregation. *The Review of Economics and Statistics, 40*, 403-410.

Berry, B. J. and Marble, D. F. [1968]. *Spatial analysis*. Englewood Cliffs (N.J.): Prentice-Hall.

Bode, E. [1996]. *Ursachen regionaler Wachstumsunterschiede: Wachstumstheoretische Erkärungsansätze* (Kieler Arbeitspapiere No. 740). Institut für Weltwirtschaft, Kiel.

Bode, E. [1998]. *Lokale Wissensdiffusion und regionale Konvergenz in Deutschland*. Mohr Siebeck.

Boltho, A., Carlin, W. and Scaramozzino, P. [1995]. *Will East Germany Become a New Mezzogiorno?* (Working Paper No. FS I 95-307). WZB.

Buchanan, J. M. and Stubblebine, W. C. [1962]. Externality. *Economica, Nov.*, 371-384.

Christaller, W. [1933]. *Die zentralen Orte in Süddeutschland*. Jena.

Ciccone, A. [1997, September]. *Externalities and Interdependent Growth: Theory and Evidence*. Can be found at http://elsa.berkeley.edu/users/ciccone/.

Ciccone, A. and Hall, E. [1996]. Productivity and the Density of Economic Activity. *American Economic Review*, 86, 54-70f.

Clark, C., Wilson, F. and Bradley, J. [1969]. Industrial Location and Economic Potential in Western Europe. *Regional Studies*, 3, 197-212.

Cliff, A. D. and Ord, J. K. [1972]. Testing for Spatial Autocorrelation Among Regression Residuals. *Geographical Analysis*, 4, 267–284.

Cliff, A. D. and Ord, J. K. [1973]. *Spatial Autocorrelation*. London: Pion.

Cliff, A. D. and Ord, J. K. [1981]. *Spatial Processes, Models and Applications*. London: Pion.

Cobb, C. W. and Douglas, P. H. [1928]. A Theory of Production. *American Economic Review (Supplement)*, 18, 139-165.

Coe, D. T. and Helpman, E. [1995]. International R&D-spillovers. *European Economic Review*, 39, 859-887.

Crihfield, J. B. and Panggabean, P. H. [1995]. Growth and Convergence in U.S. Cities. *Journal of Urban Economics*, 38, 138-165.

David, P. A. and Rosenbloom, J. L. [1990]. Marshallian Factor Market Externalities and the Dynamics of Industrial Location. *Journal of Urban Economics*, 28, 349-370.

Deitmer, I. [1993]. *Effekte der regionalen Strukturpolitik auf Investitionen, Beschäftigung und Wachstum* (Vol. 153). Universität Münster.

Dosi, G. [1988]. The Nature of the Innovative Process. In *Technological Change and Economic Theory*. Pinter Publishers.

Dowling, E. T. [1992]. *Mathematical Economics*. Schaum's Outline Series.

Durlauf, S. N. [1996]. On the Convergence and Divergence of Growth Rates. *The Economic Journal*, 106, 1016-1018.

Economist, The. [March 29th–April 4th 1997]. A Survey of Silicon Valley.

Eisehardt, P., Kurth, D. and Stiehl, H. [1995]. *Wie neues Entsteht. Die Wissenschaften des Komplexen und Fraktalen*. rororo science.

Endres, A. [1994]. *Umweltökonomie*. Wissenschaftliche Buchgesellschaft.

Engelbrecht, H. J. [1997]. International R&D-spillovers, Human Capital and Productivity in OECD economies. *European Economic Review*, 41, 1479-1488.

Fujita, M. [1988]. A Monopolistic Competition Model of Spatial Agglomeration. *Regional Science and Urban Economics*, 18, 78-124.

Fujita, M. [1993]. Monopolistic Competition and Urban Systems. *European Economic Review, 37*, 308-315.

Galor, O. [1996]. Convergence? Inference from Theoretical Models. *The Economic Journal, 106*, 1056-1069.

Gardner, M. [1983]. The Game of Life, Parts I – III. In *Wheels, Life and other Mathematical Amusements* (pp. 214–257). Freeman.

Garrison, W. L. [1967]. *Quantitative geography.* Evanston, Ill.: Northwestern Univ., Dep. of Geography.

Gaylord, R. J. and D'Andria, L. J. [1998]. *Simulating Society.* Springer.

Gaylord, R. J. and Wellin, P. R. [1995]. *Computer Simulations with Mathematica.* Springer.

Glaeser, E. L., Kallal, H. D., Scheinkman, J. A. and Schleifer, A. [1992]. Growth in Cities. *Journal of Political Economy, 100*(4), 1126-1152.

Gleick, J. [1988]. *Chaos: Making a New Science.* Penguin.

Greene, W. H. [1991]. *Econometric Analysis.* Macmillan.

Griffiths, W. E., Hill, R. C. and Judge, G. G. [1993]. *Learning and Practicing Econometrics.* Wiley.

Griliches, Z. [1979]. Issues in Assessing the Contribution of Research and Developement to Productivity Growth. *The Bell Journal of Economics, 10*, 92-116.

Grossman, G. M. and Helpman, E. [1991]. *Innovation and Growth in the Global Economy.* MIT Press.

Haken, H. [1977]. *Synergetics. An Introduction* (2nd ed.). Springer.

Harris, C. [1954]. The market as a Factor in the Localization of Industry in the United States. *Annals of the Association of American Geographers, 64*, 315-348.

Hayek, F. A. v. [1972]. *Die Theorie komplexer Phänomene* (Vol. 38). J.C.B.Mohr.

Henderson, V. [1974]. The Size and Types of Cities. *American Economic Review, 64*(4), 640-656.

Henderson, V. [1986]. Efficiency of Resource Usage and City Size. *Journal of Urban Economics, 19*, 47-70.

Henderson, V. [1997]. Externalities and Industrial Developement. *Journal of Urban Economics, 42*, 449-470.

Henderson, V., Kuncoro, A. and Turner, M. [1995]. Industrial Developement in Cities. *Journal of Political Economy, 103*(5), 1067-1090.

Herbrich, R., Keilbach, M., Graepel, T., Bollmann, P. and Obermayer, K. [1999]. Neural Networks in Economics: Background, Applications and New Developements. In T. Brenner (Ed.), *Computational Techniques for Modelling Learning in Economics* (in preparation). Kluwer.

Holland, J. H. [1992]. Genetic Algorithms. *Scientific American, July*, 44 - 92.

Horgan, J. [1995]. From Complexity to Perplexity. *Scientific American, June*, 74-79.

Hotelling, H. [1929]. Stability in Competition. *The Economic Journal, 39*, 41-57.

Intriligator, M., Bodkin, R. and Hsiao, C. [1996]. *Econometric Models, Techniques and Applications* (2nd ed.). Prentice Hall.

Isard, W. [1956]. *Location and Space-Economy* (Vol. 1). The M.I.T. Press.

Jacobs, J. [1969]. *The Economy of Cities.* Random House. German Translation by Ullstein (1970).

Jaffe, A. B. [1986]. Technological Opportunity and Spillovers of R&D: Evidence from Firms' Patents, Profits and Market Value. *American Economic Review, 76*(5), 984-1001.

Jaffe, A. B. [1989]. Real Effects of Academic Research. *American Economic Review, 79,* 957-970.

Jaffe, A. B., Trajtenberg, M. and Henderson, R. [1993]. Geographic Localization of Knowledge spillovers as evidenced by Patent Citations. *Quarterly Journal of Economics,* 577-598.

Kauffman, S. A. [1996]. *At Home in the Universe: The Search for Laws of Self-Organization and Complexity.* Oxford Univ. Press.

Keilbach, M. [1993, Mai]. *Schätzung eines Produktionsmodells mit Umweltrelevanten Parametern für die Bundesrepublik Deutschland.* Master Thesis, TU Berlin.

Kelly, M. [1992]. On Endogenous Growth with Productivity Shocks. *Journal of Monetary Economics, 34,* 57-56.

Kirman, A. [1992]. Whom or What Does the Representative Individual Represent? *Journal of Economic Perspectives, 6*(2), 117-136.

Kirman, A. [1997]. The Economy as an Evolving Network. *Journal of Evolutionary Economics,* 339-353.

Klotz, S. [1996]. *Ökonometrische Modelle mit raumstruktureller Autokorrelation: eine kurze Einführung.* (Mimeo: Universität Konstanz. Can be downloaded from www.uni-konstanz.de/FuF/wiwi/pohlmei/www.html)

Kocherlakota, N. R. and Yi, K. M. [1995]. Can Convergence Regressions Distinguish between Exogenous and Endogebous Growth Models? *Economics Letters, 49,* 211-215.

Krieger-Boden, C. [1994]. *Die räumliche Dimension in der Wirtschaftstheorie.* Institut für Weltwirtschaft, Kiel.

Krugman, P. [1991a]. *Geography and Trade.* MIT Press.

Krugman, P. [1991b]. Increasing Returns and Economic Geography. *Journal of Political Economy,* 481-499.

Krugman, P. [1995]. *Development, Geography and Economic Theory.* MIT Press.

Krugman, P. [1996]. *The Self-Organizing Economy.* Blackwell Publishers.

Leung, C. K. Y. and Quah, D. T. [1966]. Convergence, Endogenous Growth and Productivity Disturbances. *Journal of Monetary Economics, 38,* 535-547.

Levy, S. [1993]. *Artificial Life: A Report from the Frontier Where Computers Meet Biology.* Pantheon.

Long, J. B. and Plosser, C. I. [1983]. Real Business Cycles. *Journal of Political Economy, 91,* 39-69.

Lösch, A. [1944]. *Die räumliche Ordnung der Wirtschaft.* Jena.

Lucas, R. E. [1988]. On the Mechanics of Economic Developement. *Journal of Monetary Economics, 22,* 3-42.

Lucas, R. E. [1990]. Why Doesn't Capital Flow from Rich Countries to Poor Countries? *American Economic Review, 80,* 92-96.

Lützel, H. [1971]. Das reproduzierbare Anlagevermögen in Preisen von 1962. *Wirtschaft und Statistik, 10,* 593–604.

Mankiw, N. G., Romer, D. and Weil, D. N. [1992]. A Contribution to the Empirics of Economic Growth. *Quarterly Journal of Economics, 107*, 407-437.

Marshall, A. [1920]. *Principles of Economics* (8 ed.). MacMillan, Reprint 1994.

Mas, M., Maudo, J., Perez, F. and Uriel, E. [1996]. Infrastructure and Productivity in the Spanish Regions. *Regional Studies, 30*, 641-649.

McDonald, J. F. [1997]. *Fundamentals of Urban Economics.* Prentice Hall.

Mills, E. [1967]. An Aggregative Model of Resouce Allocation in a Metropolitan Area. *American Economic Review, 57,* 197-210.

Mishan, E. J. [1971]. The Postwar Literature on Externalities: An Interpretative Essay. *Journal of Economic Literature, IX,* 1-28.

Moran, P. [1948]. The Interpretation of Statistical Maps. *Journal of the Royal Statistical Society B, 10,* 243-251.

Morishima, M. [1984]. The Good and Bad Uses of Mathematics. In P. Wiles and G. North (Eds.), *Economics in Disarray* (p. 51-73). Basil Blackwell.

Musgrave, R. A. and Musgrave, P. B. [1973]. *Public Finance in Theory and Practice.* McGraw-Hill.

Nelson, R. [1995]. Recent Evolutionary Theorizing about Economic Change. *Journal of Economic Literature, 33,* 48-90.

Neumann, J. v. [1966]. *Theory of Self-Replicating Automata.* University of Illinois Press.

Nicolis, P. and Prigogine, I. [1989]. *Exploring Complexity.* Freeman.

Ohlin, B. [1933]. *Interregional and International Trade.* Harvard Unversity Press.

Pigou, A. C. [1932]. *The Economics of Welfare* (3 ed.). MacMillan.

Porter, M. E. [1990]. *The Competitive Advantage of Nations.* Free Press. German Translation by Ueberreuter [1991].

Quah, D. T. [1996]. Twin Peaks: Growth and Convergence in Models of Distribution Dynamics. *The Economic Journal, 106,* 1045-1055.

Ramsey, F. [1928]. A Mathematical Theory of Saving. *The Economic Journal, 38,* 543-559.

Richardson, H. W. [1969]. *Elements of Regional Economics.* Penguin Modern Economics.

Riolo. [1992]. Genetic Algorithms. *Scientific American, July,* 89 - 91.

Rivera-Batitz, F. L. [1988]. Increasing Returns, Monopolistic Competition and Agglomeration Economies in Consumption and Production. *Regional Science and Urban Economics, 18,* 125-153.

Romer, D. [1996]. *Advanced Macroeconomics.* McGraw-Hill.

Romer, P. M. [1986]. Increasing Returns and Long-Run Growth. *Journal of Political Economy, 94*(5), 1002-1037.

Romer, P. M. [1990]. Endogenous Technical Change. *Journal of Political Economy, 98,* S71-S102.

Sala-i-Martin, X. [1996a]. The Classical Approach to Convergence Analysis. *The Economic Journal, 106,* 1019-1036.

Sala-i-Martin, X. [1996b]. Regional Cohesion: Evidence and Theories of Regional Growth and Convergence. *European Economic Review, 40,* 1325-1352.

Samuelson, P. A. [1983]. Thünen at Two Hundred. *Journal of Economic Literature, XXI,* 1468-1488.

Schätzl, L. [1996]. *Wirtschaftsgeographie 1* (6 ed.). UTB (Schöningh).

Schelling, T. [1978]. *Micromotives and Macrobehaviour.* W. W. Norton.

Schulman, L. S. and Seiden, P. E. [1978]. Statistical Mechanics of a Dynamical System based on Conway's Game of Life. *J. Stat Phys., 19,* 293.

Schumpeter, J. A. [1954]. *History of Ecoomic Analysis.* Oxford University Press.

Seitz, H. [1993]. A Dual Econmic Analysis of the Benefits of the Public Road Network. *The Annals of Regional Science, 27,* 223-239.

Seitz, H. [1995a]. Konvergenz: Theoretische Aspekte und empirische Befunde für westdeutsche Regionen. *Konjunkturpolitik, 41,* 168-198.

Seitz, H. [1995b]. The Productivity and Supply of Urban Infrastructure. *The Annals of Regional Science, 29,* 121-141.

Seitz, H. [1996]. Stadtökonomie. *WiSt, Juli.*

Seitz, H. and Licht, G. [1995]. The Impact of Public Infrastructure Capital on Regional Manufacturing Production Cost. *Regional Studies, 29,* 231-240.

Sher, W. and Pinola, R. [1981]. *Microeconomic Theory.* E. Arnold.

Smith, A. [1776]. *An Inquiry into the Nature and Causes of the The Wealth of Nations.* Reprinted by *Liberty Classics* [1981].

Solow, R. M. [1956]. A Contribution to the Theory of Economic Growth. *Quarterly Journal of Economics, 70*(1), 65-94.

Solow, R. M. [1957]. Technical Change and the Aggregate Production Function. *Review of Economics and Statistics, 39,* 312-320.

Stull, W. J. [1986]. The Urban Economics of Adam Smith. *Journal of Urban Economics, 20,* 291-311.

Tesfatsion, L. [1997]. How Economists can get Alife. In W. B. Arthur, S. N. Durlauf and D. A. Lane (Eds.), *The Economy as An Evolving Complex Systen II* (p. 533-564). Addison Wesley.

Thünen, J. H. v. [1826]. *Der Isolirte Staat in Beziehung auf Landwirthschaft und Nationalökonomie.* Hamburg.

Tirole, J. [1988]. *Industrial Organization.* MIT Press.

Tobler, W. [1979]. Cellular Geography. In S. Gale and G. Olsson (Eds.), *Philosophy in Geography* (p. 379-386). Reidel.

Upton, G. and Fingleton, B. [1985]. *Spatial Data Analysis by Example.* Wiley.

Varian, H. [1996]. *Intermediate Microeconomics* (4 ed.). W.W. Norton.

Verspagen, B. [1992]. Endogenous Innovation in Neoclassical Growth Models: A Survey. *Journal of Macroeconomics, 14*(4), 631-662.

Viner, J. [1931]. Cost Curves and Supply Curves. *Zeitschrift für Nationalökonomie, III*(Sept.), 23-46.

Waldrop, M. M. [1993]. *Complexity: The Emerging Science at the Edge of Order and Chaos.* Touchstone Books.

Weber, A. [1909]. *Über den Standort der Industrie, Teil 1.* Tübingen.

Wolfram, S. [1994]. *Cellular Automata and Complexity.* Addison Wesley.

Index

agent based computational economics, 86
agglomeration, 62, 95
agglomeration economies, 30, 46
Arbeitsmarktregion, 24
artificial life, 84, 87

benevolent dictator, 39, 84
blueprints, 10, 11, 62

capital
    broad concept of, 68
capital intensity, 14
catch-up, 76
cellular automata, 4, 87
    extensions, 90
central business district, 48
central place theory, 33, 39
centrifugal forces, 39
centripetal forces, 39
chaos theory, 84
cities
    Detroit, 45
    different types of, 36
    seen as local clusters of production factors, 95
communication, 62
competition, 52
    monopolistic, 37, 48
complexity theory, 84
computational economics, *see* agent based c.e.
computer science, 4
congestion effect, 55
contiguity, 118
contiguity matrix

    binary, 115
contiguity measures, 118
convergence, 2, 16, 62, 75
    β convergence, 17, 76, 97
    σ convergence, 17, 19
    converging behaviour, 76
    absolute, 18
    club –, 23
    conditional, 22
    critics, 20
    economic interpretability, 22
    of firm aggregate, 78
    of firms, 77
    of regional aggregate, 79
    of spatial disaggregates, 23
convergence debate, 3, 16–25, 62
convergence regression, 18, 24, 97, 101
core periphery model, 36
costs
    of transportation, 31
        cif prices, 37
        iceberg metaphor, 37
cumulative causation, 49

data
    capital, 106
    correlations, 108
    human capital, 107
    infrastructure, 107
    labour, 106
    output, 105
    R&D personnel, 106
    sources and construction, 104–108
    spatial autocorrelation, 115, 119
    spatial correlation, 118
    summarizing statistics, 108

distance, 56, 63
divergence, 62
diversity, 52
   in production, 52
   of employment, 44
   optimum, 49
dynamical systems
   complex, 89
   discrete, 88

econometrics, 103
economic potential, 40
   index of, 41
economies of scale, *see* agglomeration economies, *see* returns to scale, increasing
elasticities
   of production, 11, 55
endogenous growth theory, *see* growth theory
equations of motion, 70
estimation procedures
   estimated GLS, 127
   maximum likelihood, 125
   OLS, 122
estimation results
   for German *Kreise*, 134–140
   for national states, 140–143
European Union, 41
   common market, 41
evolutionary economics, 86
external effect, *see* spillovers
   (definition), 64
   formal implementation, 66
   Jacobian, 44–45
   Marshallian, 42–44, 55, 57, 83
   pecuniary, 41
   positive — of knowledge, 43
   properties, 64, 65
   spatial, 41, 46
   technological, 41

factor accumulation
   in space, *see* agglomeration
   in time, *see* growth

factor migration, *see* migration
factor productivities, 109
   correlations, 110
   geographic distribution, 110
   spatial clusters, 110
factor shares, 69
factors used in regression, 105–107
footloose industries, 29

game of life, 89
game theory, 86
general equilibrium model, 86
genetic algorithms, 87
Gini coefficient, 58, 99
   spatial, 95
growth
   endogenous, 12
   regional, 13
   through *diversity*, 45
   through *specialization*, 44
growth accounting equation, 8, 10
growth theory
   endogenous, 8
      implications, 15
   Keynesian, 5
   neoclassical, 5, 13
      fundamental differential equation, 7
      implications, 14
   Schumpeterian, 5
   Solowian, *see* neoclassical g.t.

Harrod neutrality, 11
heteroscedasticity, 131
Hicks neutrality, 6
Hirschmann-Herfindahl index, 53
human capital, 15, 16, 21, 22, 63, 91, 105
   spatial spillovers of, 137, 141

Inada conditions, 6
inductive analysis, 86
industrial districts, 81
information
   vs. knowledge, 62

infrastructure, 55, 105
    spatial spillovers of, 139
invisible hand, 85

Kaldorian stylized facts, 107
knowledge, 9, 10, 62
    tacit, 62
    unformalized, 63
    vs. information, 62
knowledge spillovers, *see* spillovers
Kreise, 23, 24, 104, 131, *see* estimation results
Krugman's core periphery model, 36

labour market pooling, 54
Lagrange multiplier test, *see* test procedures
leapfrogging, 19
learning by doing, 9, 15, 54
life cycle of a technology, 45
likelihood ratio test, *see* test procedures
local rules, 88
local trade secrets, 63
localization economies, 30, 43, 46, 47, 49–51

Mandelbrot set, 89
maximum reach, 33
Mezzogiorno problem, 25
migration, 13, *see* equations of motion
    of capital, 70, 93
    of labour, 70, 93
ML estimation, *see* estimation procedures
monopoly, *see* competition, monopolistic
    degree of, 52
Moran's I, 129

neighbourhood, 115
    bishop, 116
    Moore, 116
    queen, 116
    rook, 116
    von Neumann, 116

neoclassical growth theory, *see* growth theory
net product
    private, 64
    social, 64
neural networks, 87
new trade theory, 68
normative analysis, 29

OECD, 21
OLS, *see* estimation procedures

parallel processing, 89
path dependence, 74
perpetual inventory method, 106
planning regions, *see* Arbeitsmarktregionen
population density, 109
positive analysis, 29
production function, 42
    additive, 67
    CES, 67
    Cobb-Douglas, 11, 55, 56, 67, 68
    concave, 10, 14
    convex, 10
    neoclassical, 6
    of knowledge, 56
public goods, 10, 62

Ramsey model, 7, 17, *see* growth theory
representative agent, 85
returns to scale
    constant, 11, 46, 55, 96
    decreasing, 12, 47, 95
    increasing, 12, 30, 34, 37, 46, 48, 49, 97
Route 128, 71, 74
R&D, 10, 57, 63, 95, 105
    spatial spillovers of, 134

Santa Fe institute, 89
saving rate, 7, 21, 22, 92
self organization
    in space, 39, 83

self organizing system, 39
separability, 65
Silicon Valley, 63, 71, 74
simulation
    results, 94
    setup, 91
Solow residual, 8, 22
space, 29, 103
    hexagonal, 34
spatial autocorrelation, 115, 119
    in the data, 121
    in the depending variable, 123, 126, 129
    in the error term, 125, 127, 129
    to describe agglomeration, 95
spatial correlation, 100
    in the independent variables, 123
spatial density, 50
spatial dependence, 104
spatial econometrics, 120–131
spatial effects, 120
    spatial dependence, 120
    spatial heterogeneity, 122
spatial spillovers
    of human capital, 137, 141
    of infrastructure, 139
    of R&D, 134
spatial weight matrix, *see* contiguity matrix, binary, 115–118
    generalized, 117
    row standardized, 118
specialization
    in production, 52
spillovers
    empirical evidence, 108
    of knowledge, 9, 43
    of R&D, 57
    spatial, 71, 92
statistical artifact, 53, 57
synergetics, 89

tacit knowledge, 62
technological change, 10
telecommunication, 62
test procedures
    Lagrange multiplier test, 130
    likelihood ratio test, 129
    test based on Moran's *I*, 129
    White test, 131
Thünen's rings, 31
total factor productivity, 6, 8, 51, 52, 59

urbanization economies, 30, *see* agglomeration economies, *see* localization economies, 43, 51
utility, 86
utility function, 47
    indirect, 47

variety of employment, *see* diversity

Walrasian auctionator, 85
White test, *see* test procedures

Contributions to Economics

Peter Michaelis/Frank Stähler (Eds.)
Recent Policy Issues in Environmental and Resource Economics
1998. ISBN 3-7908-1137-8

Jessica de Wolff
The Political Economy of Fiscal Decisions
1998. ISBN 3-7908-1130-0

Georg Bol/Gholamreza Nakhaeizadeh/ Karl-Heinz Vollmer (Eds.)
Risk Measurements, Econometrics and Neural Networks
1998. ISBN 3-7908-1152-1

Joachim Winter
Investment and Exit Decisions at the Plant Level
1998. ISBN 3-7908-1154-8

Bernd Meyer
Intertemporal Asset Pricing
1999. ISBN 3-7908-1159-9

Uwe Walz
Dynamics of Regional Integration
1999. ISBN 3-7908-1185-8

Michael Carlberg
European Monetary Union
1999. ISBN 3-7908-1191-2

Giovanni Galizzi/Luciano Venturini (Eds.)
Vertical Relationships and Coordination in the Food System
1999. ISBN 3-7908-1192-0

Gustav A. Horn/Wolfgang Scheremet/ Rudolf Zwiener
Wages and the Euro
1999. ISBN 3-7908-1199-8

Dirk Willer
The Development of Equity Capital Markets in Transition Economies
1999. ISBN 3-7908-1198-X

Karl Matthias Weber
Innovation Diffusion and Political Control of Energy Technologies
1999. ISBN 3-7908-1205-6

Heike Link et al.
The Costs of Road Infrastructure and Congestion in Europe
1999. ISBN 3-7908-1201-3

Simon Duindam
Military Conscription
1999. ISBN 3-7908-1203-X

Bruno Jeitziner
Political Economy of the Swiss National Bank
1999. ISBN 3-7908-1209-9

Irene Ring et al. (Eds.)
Regional Sustainability
1999. ISBN 3-7908-1233-1

Katharina Müller/Andreas Ryll/ Hans-Jürgen Wagener (Eds.)
Transformation of Social Security: Pensions in Central-Eastern Europe
1999. ISBN 3-7908-1210-2

Stefan Traub
Framing Effects in Taxation
1999. ISBN 3-7908-1240-4

Pablo Coto-Millán
Utility and Production
1999. 3-7908-1153-X

Frank Riedel
Imperfect Information and Investor Heterogeneity in the Bond Market
2000. ISBN 3-7908-1247-1

Kirsten Ralf
Business Cycles
2000. ISBN 3-7908-1245-5

Michele Bagella/ Leonardo Becchetti (Eds.)
The Competitive Advantage of Industrial Districts
2000. ISBN 3-7908-1254-4

Stefan Baumgärtner
Ambivalent Joint Production and the Natural Environment
2000. ISBN 3-7908-1290-0

Printing: Weihert-Druck GmbH, Darmstadt
Binding: Buchbinderei Schäffer, Grünstadt